# LAWYERS AND THEIR SOCIETY

A COMPARATIVE STUDY OF
THE LEGAL PROFESSION IN GERMANY
AND IN THE UNITED STATES

# LAWYERS
# AND THEIR SOCIETY

A COMPARATIVE STUDY OF
THE LEGAL PROFESSION IN GERMANY
AND IN THE UNITED STATES

*Dietrich Rueschemeyer*

HARVARD UNIVERSITY PRESS
*Cambridge, Massachusetts*
1973

*To Marilyn*

# PREFACE

This is a study of a profession in two countries: of the bar, primarily in private practice, in Germany and in the United States. A study of lawyers may be of interest from several points of view. First, plain curiosity, once aroused, is rewarded by an intrinsically "interesting" subject matter. In other, more technically sociological ways, an analysis of the legal profession and its role in society touches on central issues in sociological theory, issues involving value consensus and power, social integration and conflict as they affect social order and change. While I am concerned here with these general theoretical issues, they remain subordinate. The sociological analysis of the functioning of legal systems and their relation to societal order and change raises more specific theoretical problems. For such an analysis it is indispensable to understand the character of the legal profession and the conditions shaping it. This book thus emphasizes the sociology of law, focusing on the social organization of law work. At the same time it is of relevance to an emerging body of theory that concerns the professions as a specific type of occupation and the social control of occupational behavior in general.

Comparative analysis is essential for any subject if one is to go beyond mere description. Wherever crucial variations in the problems studied occur between rather than within societies, international comparisons become indispensable for significant theoretical advances. This is patently the case for legal systems and also, though less obviously, for the character of the professions.

International comparative study promises disproportionately high returns in the present state of sociological inquiry. After a long period of neglect, the social sciences witnessed a revival of interest in such comparative research since World War II. Problems of developing areas and the increasing involvement of the United States in international politics resulted in demands for sociological generalizations valid beyond the boundaries of one country or one type of society. This coincided with a renewed theoretical interest in macrosociological problems, which by their nature require intersocietal and intercultural comparison. In many respects, this new development of comparative analysis began where the generation of Max Weber or even the earlier work of the evolutionists had left off. However, the maturing of both theoretical reflection and research methodology in the interim period promised to put comparative analysis on a far more solid basis. Even if limited by unresolved problems of comparative methods and by pragmatic obstacles to coordinated empirical research in different countries, this promise has been partially fulfilled, and it remains one of the brightest prospects of the social sciences.

An intensive comparison of two national bars, rather than a quantitative analysis of selected features of the legal profession in many countries, seemed the most fruitful and congenial strategy for this study. This approach permitted me to explore in many ways the interrelations of legal practice with other features of each society and the conditions underlying similarities and contrasts between the two bars, extending, in effect, the scope of the study to include a comparative analysis of the two societies as a whole. Such research can pursue tentative ideas and interpretations; it can generate hypotheses and try out the utility of sociological theories developed in other contexts; yet, limited to two cases, it cannot test the validity of general propositions. Germany and the United States seemed to be a particularly meaningful pair of countries for such research. Similar in basic features of socioeconomic structure, they vary in crucial respects that presumably affect law and legal practice.

The first chapter stands somewhat apart from the others. Not immediately concerned with the German and the American bars, it sets out a theoretical frame of reference for the study. By casting a wider net of considerations it seeks to clarify basic aspects of the intricate role of private legal counsel, discussing it in different societal contexts and contrasting it with other professional roles. I consider the social conditions under which the role of the modern attorney first emerged and examine the factors which shape the character of the bar in traditional and modern societies. The relation between bureaucratization of government and the development of commercial and entrepreneurial activities is shown to be of crucial importance for the social position and the functions of lawyers; and

Prussia/Germany and nineteenth-century America constitute two contrasting cases in this respect. From this perspective, I examine the current theory of the professions, complementing it with considerations which grow out of the review of "legal evolution" as well as with propositions about the peculiar character of the profession of law in contrast to, say, medicine.

The second chapter begins the analysis proper by describing the two bars in general outline. Major overall contrasts are related to differences between the two legal systems and to certain features of the two societies. The analysis focuses on the bar in private practice. It examines firm structure, patterns of specialization, and the internal stratification of the two professions, and briefly discusses the organization and functions of bar associations.

Subsequently, the subcultures of the two bars are related to their positions in the two societies. The place of lawyers in the national hierarchies of income, prestige, and power as well as contrasting value orientations prevalent in the two societies and the patterns of recruitment and legal education are related to attitudes and value orientations characteristic of each professional group. Reference group theory is used as a major tool of analysis. This examination of modal attitudes and value orientations of German and American lawyers is followed up and further confirmed by an analysis of the formal codes of ethics and their interpretation by authoritative sources in the two bars.

A good part of the contrasts discussed can be understood in terms of the development of the two professions during the crucial phases of industrialization. With differences in professional organization and public control firmly established at the beginning of the nineteenth century, industrialization and modernization of the two societies first widened the contrast but then induced trends toward convergence. In both societies, however, these developments stopped short of engendering the same conditions in the two professions.

I began the research for this book in 1960-1961, when I held a postdoctoral fellowship of the Rockefeller Foundation which allowed me to spend one year of study free of any specific obligation in the United States. This support is gratefully acknowledged. During that year I had the opportunity to explore my ideas and plans with many colleagues. I am especially indebted to Jerome E. Carlin and Erwin O. Smigel for the many hours we spent discussing our mutual research interests in the American bar. I owe particular thanks also to Wolfgang Kaupen of the University of Cologne. He carried out a research project in Germany, which we had planned together in the initial stages, and was generous enough to let me make use of his data as they became available. He also read the manuscript, and I benefited from his comments. The first chapter was read by Albert K. Cohen, and I wish to thank him, too, for his criticisms and suggestions. The generous help I received from Brown University and its Department of Sociology in preparing the manuscript is also gratefully acknowledged.

This book could not have been written without the cooperation of lawyers both in the United States and Germany, with whom I explored problems of their profession in a series of intensive interviews. Of special importance for the understanding of similarities and differences between the bars of the two countries were those German-born lawyers who had emigrated from Germany in the 1930's after they had practiced in the German bar. Robert O. Held of the New York bar and formerly a leader of the German *Anwaltschaft* became a friend in the process of discussing these problems.

The book is dedicated to my wife Marilyn. I would scarcely have completed the work without her help in matters of substance, language, and morale.

Unless otherwise noted, all translations are mine.

Dietrich Rueschemeyer

Brown University
Spring 1972

# Contents

# LAWYERS
# AND THEIR SOCIETY

A COMPARATIVE STUDY OF
THE LEGAL PROFESSION IN GERMANY
AND IN THE UNITED STATES

# 1
# LAWYERS, LAW, AND SOCIETY

## THE NATURAL HISTORY OF LEGAL COUNSEL

Under which conditions did the institution of legal counsel first emerge and what are the circumstances under which its presence becomes indispensable? These questions may appear to be an odd and circuitous way to open an analysis of the legal profession in modern societies; however, a brief discussion of these problems of legal evolution may clarify some of the intricacies of the complex role of attorney and give clues to the factors which shape the development and the variations of the institution of legal counsel. Each of these two problems is then taken up in greater detail. Thus, a broader comparative picture and theoretical framework are developed which give sharper contours to the descriptive accounts of the bar in America and in Germany, establish the relevance of this particular comparison, and aid in the theoretical interpretation of contrasts and similarities between the two professions.

### SOCIETAL COMPLEXITY AND THE ADMINISTRATION OF JUSTICE

As a preliminary definition, three core characteristics of the role of attorney are suggested: (1) specialized knowledge of legal rules, (2) partisan advice to clients not related by kinship, and (3) representation of clients in relation both to other parties and to legal authorities. As will become evident, the early forms of the attorney's role exhibit these characteristics in an uneven and often ambiguous way only. Any specialized occupational role may be looked at in analogy to economic investments. Societies or the

1

groups that exercise major control over their resources must be able to "afford" the investment, and they must expect an increased return in—material or immaterial—benefits from it. Occupational specialization in hunting and gathering societies and in simple agricultural societies is therefore very limited. In the latter some full-time specialization occurs, but it is characteristically under the control and in the service of the ruler. It is only in agricultural societies with some development of urbanism that, on the basis of these considerations, we would expect greater occupational differentiation and a greater diversity of social units served by specialists.

Legal counsel is indeed found only in societies of this latter type, but not all of them have the institution. The same is true for another aspect of general sociocultural development, writing. The use of writing appears to be a precondition for the development of a legal system sufficiently complicated to give rise to specialized counsel, but there are literate societies, even great civilizations, without this institution. A study of 51 societies, most of which were labeled in less polite times "primitive," has generally shown a close relation between sociocultural complexity and legal evolution, without specifying the precise social constellations for the emergence of the role of attorney.[1] The study does suggest, however, that several specific legal institutions generally precede the development of legal counsel, namely, (1) the use of "property payments in lieu of other sanctions," (2) the "regular use of non-kin third party intervention in dispute settlement," and (3) the existence of a "specialized armed force used partially or wholly for norm enforcement."[2] But again, while these institutions may be considered necessary conditions, they are by no means sufficient for the development of the role of attorney.

Even a developed court system, tending to monopolize the adjudication of specific types of disputes, works in many societies without anything resembling the role of counsel.[3] A frequent first approximation is a speaker assigned to the parties to insure proper legal wording, a need characteristically based on magical literalism and formalism of procedure. Although at a later point this role often developed into, or merged with, the institution of advocate at court, it is not itself an early form of counsel. The only element of the advocate's role that can be found here is the function of relating the arguments of the party, its grievances and defenses, to the stylized procedure at court, a job of articulation and translation.[4] Neither the elaboration of specialized roles in urban settings, then, nor the development of literate subcultures nor the more or less complete control over the settlement of serious disputes by specialized authorities and the concomitant shift from voluntary mediation to authoritative adjudication of disputes is a sufficient condition for the emergence of the institution of legal counsel.

2

### BUREAUCRACIES AND MARKET EXCHANGE

Two further developments in social and cultural evolution, however, are closely related to the emergence of occupations based on specialized knowledge in the law as well as non-kin representation and the partisan use of legal expertise: the rise of bureaucratic empires and the development of groups involved in extensive market exchange. In combination, they approximately mark the point where the prototype of modern legal counsel enters history.

The development of bureaucratic rule in traditional agrarian societies had without exception a profound impact on the legal order.[5] The main impetus of early bureaucratization was to develop and elaborate legal norms and legal roles that served the centralization of political power as well as the unification of rules and procedures regulating group relations and conflict resolution. Continuous legal innovation and the systematization of increasingly complex legal norms set a premium on specialized legal expertise. The legal roles most favored by these developments were legal specialists within the administration, judges, counselors to judges, and law teachers. Private legal counseling was stimulated by these developments, too. However, the degree to which it expanded seems dependent on two other conditions: the extent to which groups and institutions independent of the central bureaucracy had an interest in using the machinery of coercion that the law provides and the extent to which various agencies of the bureaucracy were involved in the affairs of such groups and institutions and in some sense took care of their needs. In relatively rare cases, these factors may combine to preclude the development of private legal counsel. Ancient China is an example of a country where the role of attorney was virtually lacking while the involvement of the bureaucracy in the legal sphere was particularly strong.[6] Yet, although not the focus of the development of legal roles in pre-modern bureaucratic empires, private legal counseling typically also found a favorable environment in these societies. On the other hand, a differentiated legal profession including private attorneys is also found in some societies without bureaucratic rule, although it may be only weakly developed. Examples are ancient Athens at the time of Pericles, feudal Europe, and the obvious and famous case of republican Rome.

For some such cases, for instance for feudal Europe, it may be argued that the early development of the institution of counsel was the result less of internal social conditions and necessities than of the legacy of a previous, more differentiated social structure and of diffusion from more developed institutional centers and neighboring societies. The Roman law and its complex legal roles grew out of archaic conditions, developed in the Roman city state and matured under bureaucratic rule in the Roman Em-

3

pire. It was imposed on the provinces and later conserved mainly in the institutions of canon law, in the contractual forms used by notaries in Italy and France, and in schools of law and rhetorics. It was revived under changed conditions in the great reception of the Roman law in continental Europe.[7] Cultural retention and diffusion of this kind are likely to introduce additional complexities into the relations between traditional indigenous norms and the more cosmopolitan legal system. It thus adds to the requirement of specialized expertise.

The examples of pre-imperial Rome and Athens, however, are indicative of the second major constellation conducive to the development of legal specialists, the growth of market exchange. In fact, expansion of trade was also characteristic of the periods when a more differentiated system of legal norms and legal roles developed in feudal Europe. It is the expansion of market exchange, rather than bureaucratization, that encourages most the growth of legal expertise available to private parties.

Why does market exchange favor such a differentiation of the legal profession? In the language of the legal historian Sir Henry Sumner Maine, trade relations are the prototype of social relations based on contract rather than on "status." Contractual relations, of the kind most relevant here, are established by agreement between equals who are not related by kinship or similar social ties and who do not rely on direct political protection and sponsorship. Social relations of this sort are vulnerable and fraught with problems of deviance and social control for three distinct reasons: first, in contrast to enduring social ties made "natural" by tradition, they are established and relinquished as economic considerations require; second, impersonal in character, they may bring total strangers together; third, they focus on highly specific transactions in contrast to kinship and similar social relations which cover a broad spectrum of mutual concerns and derive a measure of stability from this "multifunctional" character.[8]

Guarantees for reciprocity and the fulfillment of promises in contractual relations can be secured by more or less traditional means: by invoking the direct protection and involvement of traditional authority, by resorting—as in the use of the oath—to magical sanctions or by fictitiously extending kinship relations. The parties may even simply rely on mutual self-interest. However, where such contractual relationships become differentiated from the political authorities and where increased continuity and greater stakes require predictability and stability, legal guarantees are likely to be sought if the coercive power of the state can be made available for such purposes.

The contractual agreements will then be "consciously and rationally adapted to the expected reaction of the judiciary," and for such adaptation legal counsel is crucial. In turn, the needs of the marketplace articulated by independent legal experts will create strong pressures for legal development and rationalization.[9] Since these legal specialists are not immediately associated with religious, political, and judicial authorities and since control of their work is difficult to implement except indirectly, it is in the context of expanding market relations that partisanship of legal counsel develops most easily.

Development of a market economy and bureaucratization of political rule, then, both contribute to the growth of the legal profession and create, in different manner and degree, conditions favorable for the particular figure of private counsel. However, the interaction between these two complexes of factors is highly intricate and does not amount to a simple accumulation of favorable conditions. Hierarchical bureaucratic organization and contractual relations between peers are similar in many respects when compared with traditional social relations in complex agrarian societies. They share an impersonal character, relative freedom from traditional social bonds, a strong emphasis on achievement, and a high degree of specialization.

A limited emancipation of significant elements of the population from traditional orientations and patterns of association seems to be a precondition for the development of bureaucratic rule out of traditional forms of political authority. Such an emancipation makes personal and material resources free for rational use; it looses them from the restraints of traditional prescription and parochial social bonds. At the same time, it creates problems of social integration, of regulating new interdependencies, and of accommodating social conflicts, which surpass the capabilities of existing social controls and allow bureaucratic regulation to step in. Whether these bureaucratic controls are based on immediate administrative involvement, on command and direct authority, or whether they transform existing regulatory mechanisms by lending the increased coercive power of the state to more or less autonomous associations and relationship patterns, including market exchange, depends largely on the relative timing of the two broad developments.

The less differentiated the sphere of commerce and similar activities at the time bureaucratic rule is established, the greater the likelihood that direct bureaucratic measures and semitraditional controls will predominate. Where, on the other hand, contractual relationships are more developed, they profit from the rationalization of law and its enforcement machinery characteristic of bureaucratic systems. Further complications derive from an inherent contradiction in the policies of early bureaucratic regimes. On the one hand, they need to encourage the development of flexible resources and to support the groups associated with these develop-

5

ments, while curbing the power of more traditional groups like the aristocracy. On the other hand, the strong bent toward centralization as well as the traditional bases of support for the bureaucratic rulers encourage a more or less tight reign over the more modernized groups and their institutions. Flourishing merchants, related professional specialists, and other urban groups were both a resource and a threat to early bureaucratic rulers.

This dilemma is reflected in the typical policies of bureaucratic systems. As Eisenstadt says: "Broadly speaking, the rulers' general objectives in the legal field were to minimize the legal autonomy of traditional groups and strata (e.g., the aristocracy and the urban patriciate) and to advance the development of more complex and differentiated legal institutions and activities. At the same time, however, the rulers wished to maintain control over these institutions and to keep them, as far as possible, from autonomous growth."[10] Thus, while early bureaucratization increased generally the needs for legal expertise, there were also strong tendencies to curb the free development of law in conjunction with the marketplace and the attendant growth of groups of legal practitioners devoted to partisan services.

The extent to which such tendencies stifled the growth of a private bar again seemed to depend on the relative timing of commercialization and bureaucratization and on other factors affecting the strength of relatively modern institutions and groups independent of political authority. The case of Imperial China, where private commerce and nonagricultural production were of low formal standing and subject to both supervision and competition by government agencies and where a private bar was virtually absent, may be compared to seventeenth-century England, where similar policy orientations on the part of the crown met with far greater resistance from vested interests, including those of an autonomously organized legal profession.[11]

Of the three characteristics of the role of the modern attorney listed above, the development of legal expertise is most favored by bureaucratic rule. The growth of commercial trade and its reliance on the law as a mechanism of social control is the single most important basis for the development of counsel's partisan loyalty to private clients. Partisan counsel is found under other conditions, too, in the employment of sublords and corporate associations like cities, for instance, but these conditions do not rival commercial trade as a base for development of a numerous and well-differentiated private bar that offers partisan advice to clients.

The third characteristic, representation of and action for parties both in relation to other parties and to legal authorities, encounters particular obstacles in traditional societies. Representation and action for others tend to be limited here to heads of kin groups and similar roles to which others

6

stand in analogous relations of dependency and solidarity. For representation by attorney and other authorized agents to become objectively reliable and subjectively acceptable to authorities and private parties, both a firm institutionalization of contractual relations and powerful needs for more flexible forms of representation are required.

Both conditions were developed by early bureaucratic rule and commercial trade. Expanding transportation and communication facilities make more far-flung operations possible for rulers and merchants alike. With these arises the necessity of making binding commitments and acquiring rights in many places at the same time where traditionally acceptable representatives are not available. Centralization of adjudication appears to be an important factor in the development of the right of representation in court if it is combined with a growing number of people interested in legal action. Still, in most legal systems the development of the institution of agency was a very complicated and halting one, often preceded by de facto circumvention of explicit prohibitions.[12]

### THE LEGAL PROFESSION IN MODERN SOCIETY

Bureaucratization and expansion of commercial relations are principal elements of modernization. Their forms and interrelations in highly modernized societies shape the positions and functions of modern lawyers in ways analogous to the effects of early trade and bureaucratic government. Generally, law has in modern societies a much wider scope of application than it has in traditional societies. A vast increase in differentiation of social structure has multiplied problems of integration for which traditional and informal means of social control are ineffective. Constant social change in many areas further reduces the viability of regulations that rely on tradition. The role of both contractual relations and bureaucratic organization is thus in all modern societies far greater than in any traditional society. Yet there are substantial differences between modern societies.

One important dimension of such variation—analogous to differences between pre-modern bureaucratic empires discussed above—is the relative importance for societal integration of central bureaucratic administration and of decentralized mechanisms, for which market exchange is the prototype. One does not have to compare the United States in 1890 with the U.S.S.R. in 1940 to obtain significant variations of this kind. Much more subtle differences in the relative role of these two institutional complexes as well as in their interaction and interpenetration are of great importance for the legal profession and the situation it finds itself in. These differences are compounded and modified by several other factors: the persistence of traditional forms of integration and social control, the degree to which the integrative functions of routine administration are linked to or shielded against the political process, and the ways in which dominant social values relate to different types of social conflict and to the various integrative mechanisms.

Private attorneys flourish in those modern societies where an indirect regulative role of government is emphasized, where routine administration, including the administration of justice, is differentiated from the political process, and where social integration is achieved in large measure through market exchange, autonomous vóluntary associations, and contractual relations in general. Freedom of contract within wide limits and the institutionalization of formal, impersonal modes of conflict resolution for a great variety of disputes generate high levels of demand for partisan legal expertise. Partisan loyalty to clients is the more acceptable, the more conflict between autonomous parties is seen as a routine and legitimate phase of social life.

With the greater role of public bureaucracies in all modern societies, an important determinant of the scope and the legitimacy of the attorney's activity is the degree to which government decision-making is subject to legal restraints and legal review.

Bureaucratization, in modern societies as in the historical bureaucratic empires, absorbs lawyers into bureaucratic roles. Bureaucratization of government in both cases is associated with stricter controls imposed on the private legal profession; it limits the role of private law-making arising out of the day-to-day work of lawyers in counseling, contract drafting, and arguing in courts.

Of special importance for the bar is the rise of private bureaucracies, especially business corporations and trade associations, since these bureaucracies depend for their very structure on legal guarantees much as the relations between parties to a contract. They, therefore, require legal expertise loyal to their particular interests. On the other hand, the internal relations of nongovernmental bureaucracies approach in various degrees a pattern of "private government," an authoritative coordination of specialized units which is based on mandatory and prohibitory rules and orders and which frequently is less subject to legal review than comparable government operations. In this respect, private bureaucracies have restrictive effects on the status and functions of counsel that are analogous to the consequences of bureaucratization of government administration. These effects are extended in scope by another aspect of the growth of private bureaucracies. Where the emergence of very large enterprises or the formation of cartels leads to market control in the hands of a few organizations, coordination and control of activities related to whole markets tend to be achieved increasingly through authoritative "political" means, either by actual government intervention or because "private government" deci-sion-making substitutes for the interplay of a multitude of autonomous units.

In all of these respects modern societies differ in subtle and, occasionally, in quite drastic ways, and so does the nature and scope of the legal profession's work. These variations affect the overall demand for legal services as well for different kinds of legal work. They thus influence the size and differentiation of the legal profession. They shape the opportunities for nonlegal work lawyers may engage in. They determine who are the immediate role partners of lawyers, which groups and institutions take an interest in the administration of justice and in the attendant activities of the legal profession, and which groups and institutions are likely to wield control over the work of lawyers, be it institutionalized or not. The specific constellation of these factors, in conjunction with value orientations and historic traditions which may be common to the whole society or peculiar to the legal profession and its more immediate environment, also influences the attitudes lawyers hold toward various social groups and categories. Finally, these factors encourage certain patterns of recruitment into the profession and inhibit others. All of these consequences in various degrees impinge on one another and, in addition, have some "feedback" effects on the social organization of the polity and the economy as well as on the societal value system as it articulates with the institutional structure of legal, political, and economic life. With the exception of rather rare historic constellations, however, these feedback effects tend to reinforce a sociocultural situation which is basically rather independent of the legal profession.

I have argued above that the consequences of early bureaucratization as well as those of the rise of commerce were modified by the institutional structure that preceded any particular development. Similarly, the relative phasing of the modern extension of contractual relations, of the expansion of government bureaucracies, and of the growth of private bureaucratic organizations appears to have modified greatly the effects of any one of these changes. One of the most important differences between Prussia and the United States during the eighteenth and nineteenth centuries is found in the fact that in the latter, private entrepreneurs, and in the former, government bureaucracies were the spearheads of modernization. In spite of later developments, which may be interpreted as convergent trends, these different paths toward modernization set patterns both of institutional structure and of value orientations that proved relatively persistent.

#### LAWYERS IN TRADITIONAL AND TRANSITIONAL SOCIETIES

A differentiated legal profession and the interests it serves can be understood historically as precursors of patterns of social life that have become dominant in modern societies. A few comments on the role of lawyers in societies where modern orientations are not generally accepted may round out this sketch of a "natural history" of legal counsel. Wherever, in relatively nonmodernized societies, the legal system has been rationalized to some degree there tend to be serious discontinuities between the official legal order and the operating institutional orders of many social subsystems.[13] Traditional social values typically tie rights and obligations to birth and membership in given, "ascriptive" collectivities. They emphasize solidarity within narrow communities based on kinship, ethnic affiliation, religion, language, and locally differentiated custom. Relative trust and strong, diffusely defined obligations *within* these communities contrast with suspicion and minimal obligations toward the outsider. For large parts of the population in traditional and transitional societies, contractual, legal relations either are embedded in traditional relations or constitute occasions for extreme mistrust and opportunities for exploitation.[14]

The society-wide unitary law is typically seen by such groups as an alien system imposed by distant authorities and at best tenuously related to the expectations and morals of the community. The imagery of Kafka's *Trial* has as strong a grounding in such pre-modern experiences with the law as it relates to visions of the future. In such a context, use of the legal machinery changes its meaning. Litigation becomes a weapon against one's enemies and serves anything but a resolution of the conflict.[15] Where possible it is often supplemented by threats and the actual use of coercion, and every attempt is made to absorb the administration of justice into prevailing patterns of power and the dominant particularistic moral order.

Such divergence of underlying social and moral principles makes the role of legal counsel highly precarious. The attorney frequently becomes a mediator between disparate subcultures, subject to sharply contradictory expectations from his various role partners. His superior knowledge of arcane though critically important matter, frequently supplemented by a fairly high social status and special privileges, exempts him from the full impact of these conflicting demands. At the same time, such exemption opens opportunities for cheating, fraud, and exploitation.

It is in this perspective that the widespread complaints about lawyers in such societies, for instance in late medieval and postmedieval Europe,[16] find a plausible interpretation. Attorneys did have special opportunities to take undue advantage, but they also were under strong pressures from their clients to deviate from official norms. They were put at a disadvantage by a cumbersome and authoritarian administration of justice, shot through with particularistic favoritism, and at the same time they were blamed for the consequences such adjudication engendered—delays, high costs, and unacceptable decisions that either did not settle the dispute or left a deep sense of injustice done. Finally, many of the suspicions and complaints are likely to have been projections of a public that neither was committed to nor understood a legal system removed from the parochial contexts of traditional social life.

Another aspect of the pre-modern bar that can be understood better when the peculiar cultural heterogeneity of traditional and transitional societies is realized is the great diversity of formal and informal divisions of the legal profession. From the point of view of officials and clients, such divisions allow greater control over at least a part of the bar; from the point of view of the profession, a chain of interlocking roles reduces the "moral distance" between subcultures to be traversed by any one practitioner.

The most famous surviving example of these divisions is the English distinction between solicitor and barrister. Primarily concerned with court work, the barrister is retained by the parties; but he remains largely in the legal realm and is insulated from the outside world by the intermediary role of the solicitor. Such a differentiation between advocate at court and counsel in legal matters outside of court was only the most common type of division. In pre-modern Europe, it frequently coalesced with and was crossed by other lines of division: alignments with different traditions of law where divergent legal systems existed side by side; differences in training, such as apprenticeship in contrast to literary school education; type of clientele, and divergences of social background, including the division between those for whom the role of lawyer was one of several pursuits open by virtue of birth and high status and those who attained a place in legal practice against the odds of low birth by acquiring and successfully using the necessary skills.[17] Such diversification of the profession tends to be reduced greatly with increasing modernization of a society and to be replaced by a functional division of labor based on different legal problems. This displacement is not complete, though, and specialization in terms of clients and their subcultures continues in modern legal professions. Such patterns seem to be related to certain fundamental characteristics of the attorney's role which will concern us later.

The last problem to be discussed here concerns the partisan loyalties of counsel. A partisan orientation involves a delicate balance of commitments to a succession of diverse causes as well as to the institutions of the administration of law and to the values of order and justice underlying the legal system. It is only when obligations are sharply delimited and specified in terms of general principles which govern the various relations of counsel coherently and irrespective of the particular persons and groups involved that such a web of multiple loyalties becomes viable. These requirements run, however, straight against the modal tendencies of traditional morality. And this morality not only is widely held but typically governs the orientations of religious and other authorities in most partially modernized societies.

Furthermore, where magical formalism has been abandoned, traditional morality tends to define justice in substantive rather than procedural and formal terms and to conceive of what is right and good in stark contrast to evil and base things. Thus, there is little support for the suspension of final judgment and the insistence on the safeguards of "due process" associated with the institution of partisan counsel. It is no accident that during the Reformation, which in many respects was an attempt to reestablish and implement medieval value orientations, the question was raised whether a good Christian could be an attorney.[18]

The institutionalization of the partisan role of counsel as well as other crucial aspects of modern legal systems are in jeopardy wherever strongly held substantive ideas about justice and the common good intrude without mediation into the process of adjudication. The modern legal system comes into its own only where, although ultimately grounded in and legitimated by substantive value orientations, it is granted some autonomy, in its norms and in its operations, from these values and from the institutions immediately concerned with them. Such autonomy may be lacking because traditional restraints prevent a sufficient differentiation between the religious realm and the institutions of societal integration. It may also be severely restricted when revolutionary movements with secular ideologies bring about a shift in power arrangements and insist on unmediated implementation of their value orientations. Modern revolutions have typically been hostile to the legal profession and tried to do away with professionally trained and autonomously organized partisan counsel.[19]

In the traditional community partisan loyalty of counsel is more easily accepted in terms of outgroup relations than in terms of ingroup relations. Only when the ingroup solidarities become extended and differentiated enough to absorb conflicts as a routine affair, to be resolved according to well-established universal principles, is the institution of partisan counsel fully acceptable. Here again, the different paths along which modernization develops are likely to be of great significance. It appears that bureaucratic regimes, while in many ways transforming their societies into more modern structures, have typically espoused a conception of the common good and of justice along rather concrete substantive lines. By contrast, where, as in the case of England, commercial and entrepreneurial patterns dominated the thrust toward what we call by hindsight modernization, while with the exception of the law the role of public administration was rather limited, we find a conception of justice that emphasizes ordered dispute solution and compromise, that is, formal and procedural values more than concrete substantive ideals. Tolerance of conflict was relatively high in this latter case, in part because—a self-reinforcing circle—conflicts were less disruptive of the pattern of integration, while bureaucratic regimes typically have shown much less tolerance for conflict. This contrasting picture is, of course, a highly stylized one, but it opens crucial perspectives on some societal determinants of the lawyer's position which will be explored further in the dual case study of the German and the American bar.

## TRUST AND CONTROL

### INSTITUTIONAL PATTERNS FOR EXPERT SERVICES

All occupations which apply a complex body of knowledge to problems that are of great concern to significant groups and categories of people in a society pose difficult problems of trust and suspicion, deviance, and social control. The very expertise of people in these occupations makes it difficult to judge their performance, particularly when not even the final result of their efforts is a safe guide to the quality of work done. At the same time, control as well as trust are particularly important in these fields of work. Assurance of devotion and competence is critical for the client because of the high stakes involved. It is also crucial for the moral fabric of the community at large because the performance of such tasks is of great relevance for central social values. Finally, trust in the expert's skill and commitment may be required for the very success of his efforts. The disclosure of private affairs and intentions, for instance, is often necessary for the services of lawyer, doctor, and priest alike; it would be severely impeded by lack of confidence and trust.

Social control of occupational performance, then, is in these cases at the same time more difficult and more urgently needed than in most other trades. This, of course, is the classical problem of the professions. In contemporary professional ideology as well as in sociological analyses of occupational institutions one finds a solution to this dilemma based on the following elements: Professions "strike a bargain" with society in which trust, autonomy from lay control, protection from lay competition, substantial remuneration, and high status are exchanged for individual and collective self-control, designed to protect the interests of both clients and the public at large. This self-control is grounded in a strong individual commitment to the norms and values guiding professional work and in a cohesive organization of the profession as a group. A "code of ethics"

13

spells out the particular obligations of the professional. Intensive professional education establishes technical competence, provides a basis for the distinction between layman and expert, and induces acceptance and internalization of professional service ideals. The contingencies of the professional career, formal and informal association with immediate colleagues, and the supports and sanctions of professional societies, reinforce the standards of skill and ethics.[20]

This model of a profession and its relations to clients, other role partners, and society at large is quite stylized. It tends to give an exaggerated picture of the professional "service orientation" resulting from socialization and autonomous controls. It pays too little attention to other forms of control, especially governmental and legal ones. It fails to specify sufficiently the consequences that arise when the terms of the "bargain" are not fulfilled and how, if at all, these consequences restore the original pattern. It tends to neglect divisions and conflicts within the profession, and, finally, it underemphasizes the extent to which the patterns of professional orientation are an outgrowth of the class position of professionals and their clients as well as of their membership in particular subcultures.

Nevertheless, the model does indicate the core characteristics of one institutional arrangement in which expert services of great significance to clients and the community at large are dispensed and controlled. It is not the only arrangement known, however, and before we enter a discussion of some special problems of the legal profession, a sketch of several alternatives may broaden our perspective.

One alternative solution to the problem of controlling professional services can be seen in the establishment of "public" bureaucracies, staffed with experts, which either supply the services themselves or intercede as third parties in a variety of ways in the professional-client relationship. Comprehensive legal or medical insurance plans as well as various forms of government supervision illustrate such third-party intervention. These bureaucracies may or may not be governmental agencies; but in either case they would be controlled by goals and orientations independent of both the particular profession and its clients—goals and orientations informed by a "disinterested" conception of the common good.[21]

Because of the technical intricacies of professional work no variant of this alternative can dispense with a strong reliance on personal motivation and with a large degree of autonomy in the details of work. They can, however, substitute closer indirect controls for the very high degree of collective freedom from outside "interference" that is essential to the classical model of professionalism. In similar fashion it may be argued that in all modern societies some professions are to a considerable degree controlled by legal regulations and supervised by governmental agencies; but where professional groups have considerable power and where ideals of professionalism are widely accepted, these agencies tend to be staffed with experts basically loyal to the professional community and the regulations are likely to be shaped according to opinions and values prevalent within the profession.

Although the two patterns of public bureaucratic control and professional autonomy virtually never exist in pure form and completely independent of each other, one often is subordinate to the other and strongly influenced by it. Among modern societies, England and the United States developed the most clear-cut forms of professional autonomy,[22] and it is no accident that the corresponding theoretical model was developed by English and American social scientists. To generalize the model to professional work in all modern societies would be an act of intellectual parochialism.

In spite of their lack of expert competence clients may have the resources—material as well as moral and organizational—to induce sufficient loyalty from the professional. Often this would involve exclusive employment and the absence of equivalent work opportunities for the expert, or at least great obstacles to changing employment. The most clear-cut examples are institutional patterns in certain pre-modern societies where lawyers, physicians, or priests were employed by a lordly patron, a city corporation, or a church institution. Personal loyalty of these retainers toward their powerful employers, embedded in the general ethos of diffuse traditional obligations and sealed by religious prescriptions and sanctions, substituted here for the safe-guards of professional and public bureaucratic controls.

If the major clients in a society—the most powerful as well as those whose interests receive strong legitimation from the dominant value orientations—are in a position to command largely satisfactory professional services in such a way, this pattern may not only fail to generate strains toward more universal institutionalized controls but may constitute a positive obstacle to professional association, self-advancement, and self-control—"men who are in that condition of personal subservience do not easily associate with their fellows"[23]—as well as to central bureaucratic controls which would infringe not only on the autonomy of the professionals but on that of the clients as well.

The employment of professionals by high-status patrons in the context of a traditional stratification system and a traditional ethos maximizes client control over professional work. Client control is important, however, under modern conditions, too. While in the classical pattern of professional autonomy norms concerning advertising, professional referral, and professional solidarity shelter the practitioner to some extent from the client's judgment and sanctions, free choice of the professional, which is considered fundamental for minimal trust between client and expert in many modern societies, gives clients a considerable influence. Public bureaucratic controls also tend to reflect to some degree preferences and dissatisfactions of the clientele, even in totalitarian societies.

Finally, where the client is a bureaucratic organization employing experts on a permanent basis we may speak of the modern equivalent to the pattern of the client as patron. However, the professional's range of alternatives of employment varies much more under modern conditions, and his relationship to the employer is differentiated from his general social status and is freed from the traditional ethos of personal loyalty. Instead, client bureaucracies tend to rely on supplementary controls through the professional community and on public regulation. Such mixed patterns of control seem workable, although they do generate characteristic tensions between professional and bureaucratic orientations.[24]

Another arrangement for the dispensation of expert services found in pre-modern societies is the reverse of the patronage pattern considered before. Here it is the professional who holds high status in a traditional stratification system and acts as a patron toward a clientele of lower rank. This pattern has been of particular importance for lawyers. While the professional is subject to few direct controls, his clientele has little choice but to accept the services as offered. At best the client can turn to another, similarly uncontrolled patron or to practitioners of inferior status who wield less influence and often are less competent. The interests of low-status clients typically are not seen as significant enough to warrant elaborate control mechanisms to protect them, and as a group these clients do not have enough power and influence to effect a change in the overall pattern. Their dissatisfaction has occasionally provided some leverage for bureaucratic governmental reforms, although the power of resistance of professional patrons must not be underestimated.

Ideally, and often in fact, the *nobile officium* of the patron carries obligations, frequently conceived of as religious duties, but these do not deal in detail with the specifics of professional work. They typically form a more diffuse body of norms insisting on gentlemanly behavior toward dependents, the weak, and those in trouble. They do not entail close inspection and tight controls. Needless to say, the image of this professional-client relationship is one of the main sources of the more modern and more specific professional standards; its stylized memory, retained in symbols of language and ritual, supports the collective pride of the more ancient among modern professions.

There is no significant modern equivalent to the professional patron and his traditional clientele. Bureaucratic organizations run and staffed by professionals are gaining in importance, but they do not, in any systematic way, put clients into a position of dependency. They rather constitute a variant of the professional autonomy pattern, modified by internal bureaucratic arrangements and in different degrees subject to public regulation and client controls.

The last pattern to be discussed is one in which neither the professional group nor public or private bureaucracies enforce standards and in which neither the client nor the professional occupies a traditional authority position that is directly integrated with the overall status system and—at least ideally—with the shared moral order of the society. Client and expert meet more or less on an equal footing, and neither is specially protected or insulated against the demands and pressures of the other. The lower ranks of lawyers, scribes, physicians, and, occasionally, priests in pre-modern Europe have often dealt with their clients and patients on such an anomic basis. In spite of its pitfalls the pattern did serve some of the needs of the lower and even the middle strata, if in a haphazard and often treacherous way that generated mistrust and ambivalence.

There are several reasons why this last pattern deserves special attention. First, it may prevent us from making the naive assumption that, because certain social controls are "required" for the smooth functioning of a relationship, they therefore will be present in most cases. This assumption is reasonable only when the interests protected by these controls are associated with sufficient power or are of great moral significance in terms of values shared by those in important power positions. Even then the assumption should be treated as tentative. Second, if the professional patron is one of the positive reference points in the past for contemporary professions, the relatively uncontrolled specialist, not or only loosely integrated in traditional status systems and their moral patterns of mutual obligation, has made for a heritage of remembrance that underlies much of the negative imagination concerning the professions; and here again language preserves obstinate memories of the "pettifogger," the "shyster," the tricky and incompetent *Winkeladvokat*. Third, while in modern societies different combinations of public bureaucratic and professional controls have considerably reduced the scope of operation for charlatans as well as for practitioners of uncertain skills and ambiguous morals, the ranks of modern professions are by no means free of such practitioners. It is not the existence of individual deviance that is asserted here; it is the ineffectiveness of bureaucratic and professional safeguards to uphold the norms governing the work of experts when in one or another segment of a profession public pressure, client demands, professional solidarity—or its absence—and the self-interest of individual practitioners combine to undermine professional ideals.

17

The different institutional patterns for the application of expert knowledge to significant problems of a society which were discussed above do not constitute an exhaustive typology. What has been said appears sufficient, however, to provide a broader framework for a comparative discussion of the legal profession than is found in the model of professional autonomy and self-control which is prevalent in contemporary sociology. One special conclusion which may be drawn from the preceding discussion warrants more detailed attention before we turn to certain particular problems of the bar as a profession.

### PROFESSIONAL IDEALS AND THE SYSTEM OF PRIVILEGE AND PRESTIGE

The three pre-modern patterns discussed are closely intertwined with the stratification system of the society at large. Both the professional patron and the client as patron are figures grounded in a traditional status system where ascription rather than achievement are decisive for one's station in life and where expert functions are embedded in diffuse obligations between people of superior and inferior status. The largely anomic relations between practitioners and clients of low status develop in the interstices of a fragmented system of parochial units characteristic of traditional agrarian societies. By contrast, the bureaucratic and the professional patterns of control are relatively differentiated from the constraints and the privileges established by the system of social stratification. In fact, modern professional and bureaucratic arrangements can develop only to the degree that the pervasive traditional status system breaks down and gives way to a more specific and flexible system of differential wealth, prestige, and power.

However, while social stratification in modern societies is less pervasive, the differentiation of institutional arrangements for expert services from the values, norms, sanctions, and opportunities entailed by the practitioner's position in the stratification system is far from complete. There exist a number of important interlinkages—mutual supports as well as impediments—between modern stratification systems and the bureaucratic and professional modes of control of expert services.

The terms of the "bargain" said to be characteristic of the relations between the professional community and the larger society are in most modern societies not so alien from major tenets and aspirations of the middle and upper middle strata in general. Autonomy from close supervision and the gratifications of meaningful and responsible work are ideals which permeate middle- and upper middle-class cultures, as are, of course, high prestige standing, substantial income, and influence. The relative rank of these life goals varies from society to society as well as between different subcultures within the middle and upper middle strata of one society. But

18

generally, there appears to be a strong correlation between socioeconomic status and a tendency to take economic benefits for granted and to treat them as secondary to intangible satisfactions in work such as personal interest, autonomy, intellectual challenge, and responsibility.[25] Since basic orientations of the professional ethos, then, seem to be grounded in less specific, but similar ideals widespread in the middle and the upper middle strata, it is unlikely that these orientations will be unaffected by variations in the middle- and upper-class cultures in different countries. Similarly, the particular relations a given profession has to these subcultures through service to clients, recruitment, education, competition, and institutionalized control will warrant special attention when the specific shape of the professional orientations of an occupation is to be considered.

When a profession fails to live up to the "bargain" on which its privileges are supposed to depend, its prestige and power may be sufficient to forestall any serious repercussions. The professional privileges of the bar, the medical profession, or certified accountants rest in no small measure on widespread notions of what is "due" to members of the upper middle class, whose work requires a high degree of knowledge and responsibility, as well as on the power of these professions to avert unwanted interference and regulation and to persuade various relevant sectors of the public of their view of the situation. That professional-client relations are greatly influenced by the respective positions in the stratification system and that professional norms about these relations will be affected—modified or undermined—by these influences is a further, more specific hypothesis that follows from the above considerations.

If the foregoing suggests that professional ideals are to some extent a "rhetoric" modified in content and implementation by the interplay of class interests and class subcultures, it is not to imply that professional ideals merely conceal self-serving interests and, beyond that, are of no consequence to the larger community. At a minimum, professions become captives of their own rhetoric; the professed ideals make the open pursuit of self-interest illegitimate, if not impossible, where it clashes with acknowledged interests of clients and the moral concerns of the community. Furthermore, the major professions frequently exert a crucial influence in shaping the values of the public toward which their services are oriented. Medicine as a profession does typically more to determine the ideal standards of health than any other single group. The orientations of lawyers as a group are extremely important for what is concretely conceived of as justice and order in a society.

### SOME SPECIAL PROBLEMS OF THE BAR

Although in all professions there are some conflicts between different responsibilities, these are stronger in the case of the legal profession. For attorneys and advocates the mesh of role obligations is complicated by a number of factors that derive from the distinctive characteristics of the law and the legal profession. First, the relation of legal counsel to his client is fiduciary in a specially marked degree. In addition to legal advice and the drafting of documents, he acts for his clients and is able to make binding commitments. Furthermore, he often acquires confidential information to an extent that is rare in other professions. These circumstances encourage a very strong emphasis on counsel's loyalty to his client. Second and most distinguishing, the work of counsel is always done in a context of actual or potential conflict: his client is a *party* whose interests stand against those of others. True, much of the modern lawyer's work is directly concerned not with disputes but with the drafting of agreements designed to insure cooperation. Yet here, too, anticipation of future conflicts is crucial and strengthening the hand of his client in such future disputes is always an important consideration.

Loyalty of the fiduciary and partisanship in conflict reinforce each other and are in conflict with obligations of counsel that transcend the lawyer-client relationship. This tension is greater and more pervasive in the lawyer's work than in that of the doctor, the priest, or the engineer, and the institutional arrangements protected by the wider responsibilites of counsel are more vulnerable.

The behavior of counsel is crucial for the institutions of adjudication. His responsibilities as an "officer of the court" limit the loyalty toward his client. A delicate blance of commitments and duties is the result. To some extent a balance between these opposing interests and considerations is achieved not through the multiple obligations of counsel but by pitting opposing parties and their legal advisors against each other, ideally reaping the advantages of technical representation of both sides and avoiding the disadvantages of partisan competence. But still, this adversary system, which in various forms is the basic pattern at least of civil proceedings in most modern systems of adjudication, has to rely on a minimum of loyalty and commitment to the institutions of the administration of justice on the part of counsel, commitments which have to be balanced against partisan client loyalty.

Neither is the attorney free from multiple loyalties in his work out of court. The very functioning of those social relations and associations that are grounded in law and contract would be endangered if counsel devoted his expertness exclusively to the short-run interests of his client. Here again the edifice is not simply built on counsel's moral commitments as an officer of the law. If the bulk of the bar's clients did not see their long-run interests best served by a fair use of the forms provided by the law, the ethics of the legal profession would not be sufficient to maintain this system of relationships. However, the bar's integrity and loyalty to the basic premises of the system are important in preventing mistrust and abuse from spreading in a vicious circle.

Finally, innovations in contracts as well as cumulative shifts in the interpretation of the law of which the courts can be persuaded change the system of legal norms in subtle, and occasionally not so subtle, ways. Theodore Roosevelt complained that American lawyers made it "their special task to work out bold and ingenious schemes by which their wealthy clients, individual and corporate, can evade the laws which were made to regulate, in the interests of the public, the uses of wealth."[26] Such "internal" development of the law competes in effect with governmental agencies and the political process as a whole in the setting of public policy. This fact alone would make it unlikely that the legal profession, the judiciary as well as the bar, will approximate closely the model of full professional autonomy. It is rather conducive to measures of governmental regulation and to an interpenetration of the legal and the political realm. Such pressures are counteracted by the needs for predictability within the legal order. In addition, the very fact that clients' interests can and do clash with public policy and the requirements of order make a relationship of trust between counsel and client—and therefore independence of the bar vis-à-vis political agencies—imperative if solution of disputes is to be achieved.

Which of these tendencies predominates in shaping the social framework in which legal work is done will vary with the nature of the political process in a society, the distribution of power, and the dominant values concerning government and the administration of justice. Where solution of disputes outweighs substantive goals of public policy as the primary function assigned to law and the administration of justice, public controls of the legal profession will be relatively weak. Even where the pressures for public controls are very strong, they are limited by the requirements of preventing disputes from arising and by the exigencies of dispute resolution. We will later examine in greater detail some of the complex factors that enter the relationship between the law and political structure and process in the German and American cases.

The fiduciary role of counsel, partisanship in social conflicts, and the peculiar institutional framework of law, designed for conflict resolution and related to the implementation of public policy, give a distinctive character to the legal profession which sets it apart from other professions. Two closely related aspects peculiar to the law as a profession touch on the very core of the theoretical model of professional autonomy. They concern the value orientations—held by different subgroups or shared throughout

21

the society—which give a moral grounding to the system of law and the work of lawyers, and the nature of counsel's particular competence.[27]

In all societies there is some degree of dissension about the values that legitimate law and legal practice. The ideal of justice may be universal and hold in most societies a high rank in the hierarchy of values. The idea that order as such is to be prized has perhaps a less elevated rank, but will typically find widespread consent. There is disagreement, however, on what justice substantively entails, how much order is desired, and what is required for a given ideal of order. While long-standing legal patterns carry the presumption of being just for most people in modern societies, the notion of unjust law is by no means uncommon.

Such different conceptions of justice and order are not identical with divergent interests. Societal integration as well as the situation of the legal profession will be most precarious where divergent interests coalesce with contrasting conceptions of justice and where both are crystallized in such a way that subgroup consensus is combined with deep cleavages in the overall pattern. Max Weber has pointed out that such subcultural differentiation of ultimate ideals and meanings tends to be mediated by a unique feature of modernization: the development of formal, "rational-legal" modes of legitimation. While shared substantive value orientations become more abstract and are, so to speak, removed to the background of the cultural scene, a consensus on formal rules establishing the ways in which more specific norms become binding as well as regulating legal authority can be combined with a diversity of substantive value orientations which are held with varying intensity in different subgroups.[28]

It must be understood that such a formal mode of legitimation has nevertheless substantive implications in any given society. It sanctions indirectly the established arrangements of power and privilege, and in all societies parts of the population will look at the established formal patterns simply as an expression of given power constellations. In more subtle ways, substantive conceptions of what justice entails and how order is to be achieved may compete with formal conceptions that are accepted also. They will thus cast a shadow of doubt and ambivalence on the formalism and reliance on authority by position that is most visibly embodied in the system of law and the work of the legal profession.[29]

If there is any validity to the basic reasoning behind the theoretical model of professional autonomy, disagreement and tension about the "reference values" of a profession should have profound consequences for the relations between practitioner and client, the professional group, and the public at large and for the institutional character and the orientations of the profession. A similar argument can be made about the other central component of that model, technical expertise based on a body of systematic knowledge.

The body of knowledge lawyers have a special competence in is not—as in the case of medicine, physics, or engineering—concerned with laws and regularities independent of human actions or intentions. Rather than natural laws, its subject matter are social norms and rules for their application—norms and rules subject to deliberate change as well as to interpretation and estimates of the likelihood that they will be enforced. Compared with scientific knowledge as well as religious doctrine, "secular law is considerably looser in its points of reference." It does not provide as firm an anchorage of action in the face of cross-pressures as a body of scientific knowledge or religious dogma, believed to be absolute and unchangeable, do.[30]

Furthermore, much of counsel's valued skills is not at all based on his technical legal knowledge or is only tenuously linked to it. This is particularly true of his work out of court. In negotiation and mediation, in the drafting of wills and contracts a great variety of "worldly knowledge" comes into play that is not specifically legal. Organizational "know-how," economic experience, wisdom about personal relations, connections, and "inside" knowledge are often as important for the lawyer's work as knowledge of the law. Modern lawyers often pride themselves on their general ability to grasp the essentials of a situation and to anticipate the relevant future possibilities, and another typical claim is that they can "get things done"—discreetly or deftly, as the case requires. The theoretical model of professionalism does not fully apply to these skills: they are not based on systematic knowledge, the customer may very well be in a position to judge the performance, and society does not imbue these skills with the same moral significance as those of medicine or law in the strict sense.

Thus the problems of social control are even more complex for legal practice than for other professions. These complications revolve around two complementary themes, a greater involvement of legal practitioners with different clienteles representing conflicting interests and value orientations and a weaker solidarity and identification with the professional group and its ideals.

The fiduciary character of counsel's role, his partisan involvement in conflict, and the resulting emphasis on client loyalty are likely to cause a responsiveness to the interests and value orientations of clients, and while the bar as a whole serves a narrower range of interests than some other professions a number of conditions contribute at the same time to a more or less clear-cut specialization within the bar in terms of the socioeconomic status of clients, separating different segments of the bar

23

from each other. There is, first, a rough connection between the class position of clients and the legal character of their problems which aligns various legal specialties with clients in different socioeconomic categories. Furthermore, not all lawyers are trusted with problems the adequate solution of which, in the eyes of the client, not only requires legal competence but a certain set of attitudes and value orientations. Finally, the nonlegal competence of the lawyer, notably his interpersonal skill, is highly class specific. For example, skill in negotiating with executives is quite different from competence in handling minor officials in local administration.

The consequences of this differential association with diverse clienteles seem to be particularly consequential when assessed in the light of the balance of our discussion of special features of law and legal practice. Dissension and ambiguities about central values underlying the profession's work as well as the changeable and interpretable character of law as a system of social norms weaken the authority of the bar and its capacity to resist client pressures while they increase the interest of clients in generalized partisan loyalty of counsel.

Furthermore, clients, when compared with patients, not only have a greater interest in influencing a lawyer's actions, they are also typically in a better position to do so. Their health is not impaired; their education, to a high degree associated with class position, is better than average, and their own occupational competence is often related to the issues at hand. Organizational clients, such as business firms and trade associations, which may have their own staff of experts able to check counsel's performance, exert an even more powerful control and influence over the practitioner than individual clients do.

The various segments of the bar are, then, exposed to more or less powerful influences from different client groups and are in various degrees drawn into diverse client subcultures with their characteristic value orientations and interests. Such divisions of the bar in terms of different client *milieux* tend to be aligned with differences in income and professional esteem. It is this combination of an internal stratification of the bar with a divergence of professional orientations that considerably strains the solidarity of the bar. It reduces identification with the profession as a group and severely limits the efficiency of that self-control which the profession is supposed to exercise according to the theoretical model of professional autonomy. It particularly impedes the moral commitment of the profession to obligations that transcend the lawyer-client relationship.

Such centrifugal tendencies could be counteracted by a pervasive commitment to the "reference values" of a profession, grounded in the culture of society at large, internalized in professional education, supported and controlled by a cohesive professional community. However, such commitments are, in the case of the legal profession, likely to be attenuated by dissension about the concrete meaning of the relevant values; as a consequence, professional norms may even be taken as merely conventional rules the breach of which is of little consequence if one can "get away with it."

We should thus expect that the ideal typical pattern of professional autonomy and self-control will not easily be approximated by the bar in its pure form. Under certain conditions client controls may surpass in importance the individual and collective self-control exercised by the profession. Where government is strong and political concerns have high priority in the hierarchy of dominant values bureaucratic state controls are likely to play a prominent role. Where these diverse controls are weak or work at cross-purposes segments of the bar may approach the state of influence brokers under no more controls than are usual in the business world. In the typical case, though, we would expect the aspirations and ideals of professionalism to persist and form various amalgams with the other types of influence and control.

It should be emphasized finally, that the main factors discussed—social conflict, value dissensus, the stability of the legal order and the nature of the bar's competence—are subject to cultural variation. Societies differ in the incidence and intensity of conflicting interests and in subcultural differentiation of value orientations, and as a society shows less patterned conflict and value dissensus, the hypotheses derived from dissension about justice and order should apply less. Radical social change upsets legitimate arrangements and requires complex innovations in the legal system. The area of substantive consensus is reduced and the system of legal norms is probably more subject to the impact of contending notions of justice and of conflicting interests than an established legal order of long standing that meets more or less standardized legal problems. The profession or significant parts of it are more subject to divergent pressures, while the cultural reference points are at the same time most fluid and ambiguous. Cultural and political traditions differ in dealing with social conflict and value dissensus. If we compare the dominant cultural definitions in nineteenth-century Prussia and nineteenth-century America, we see on the one side a conception of justice and the common good as determined by a priori solutions to be found and formulated by experts and a rather low level of tolerance of conflict and dissension, and on the other a conception of justice and the common good as determined by ordered dispute and compromise and a rather high level of tolerance of conflict and dissension. These different traditions rest, of course, on structural conditions, contemporary and antecedent, among which are the position and structure of the legal profession. At any given time, however, they are relatively independent of the legal profession and determine the sociocultural situation in which the legal profession has to operate. These differences pervade the whole legal system: the system of legal norms, the administration of justice, the political and legal position of government bureaucracy, and the role of law professors, as well as the dominant attitudes in major client groups and in major sources of public opinion. To the degree that the dominant cultural definitions and social institutions shelter the legal profession from the impact of conflict and value dissensus, and create the fiction of law as being derived by scholars, the hypotheses about the consequences of value dissensus and the nonscientific character of legal knowledge have to be modified considerably.

The gap in competence between layman and lawman, finally, depends on the relative legal competence of lawyers and their various role partners as well as on the importance of nonlegal skills in the lawyer's role performance and the relative skill in these respects of lawyers and their role partners. All the factors involved, such as complexity of the system of legal norms, most prevalent types of client, their legal and nonlegal competence and extension of the lawyer's activities into nonlegal areas, are subject to conditions that vary greatly from society to society.

# 2

# THE AMERICAN
# AND THE GERMAN BAR COMPARED

## THE STRUCTURE OF THE TWO SOCIETIES COMPARED

Although the United States and Germany are rather similar in basic socioeconomic features, there are a number of contrasts important for the place and role of the legal profession in the two countries.[1] In both countries, goods and services are produced and exchanged in a market economy. Private property and, in principle, freedom of contract are the central legal institutions of economic life. In both countries, freedom of contract and autonomy of economic decision-making have been restricted by three interrelated developments, which in both cases can be traced to the last decades of the nineteenth century. The first of these is the rise of large enterprises and the organization of cartels and trusts, which established in many industries market control in the hands of a few economic units. Coexisting with these large economic organizations are great numbers of medium-sized and small firms, often subject to indirect controls by dominant large enterprises. The second development is the rise of the labor movement which, in conjunction with the growth of large firms and combines and the development of employers' associations, created monopolistic conditions on the labor market even more pronounced than the similar conditions in product markets. The third factor is increasing intervention of government in economic and professional life through legal regulation of various spheres previously left to private parties, through supervisory control of certain industries, through subsidies and differential taxation, and through government-operated economic activities.

Together with these developments went a host of other changes, two of which may be specifically noted. First, in the large economic organizations decision-making was increasingly separated from ownership and shifted to positions qualified by occupational performance rather than by property title, although the dissociation of decision-making from ownership of productive property is by no means complete. The crucial legal institution in this context is the private corporation. Second, taxation—both a means of indirect economic planning and the source of funds for vastly increased government activities—is of crucial importance for many business decisions and has created a highly complex system of legal norms. The increasing importance of negligence law and the increase in divorce rates may indicate other changes, common to both countries, which are only very indirectly related to the changes in economic structure sketched above.

These and other developments in both countries greatly complicated the system of legal norms and increased, at least potentially, the volume of lawyers' business. They emphasized certain phases of their work like negotiation and counseling. They changed the character of the business clientele, increasing the number of organizational clients with relatively great power and with a leading personnel of professional inclinations and pretensions. Finally, they brought new strata into the potential clientele of the bar.

In addition to the socioeconomic structure, the system of government and the political process are of great importance for the legal profession. Here, too, significant general similarities can be noted in the contemporary patterns of the two societies. Both countries have a pluralistic political system with institutionalized rights to political opposition. Media of mass communication are not subject to central control. A multitude of autonomous interest groups compete with each other for political influence, and in both countries two large parties, based on broad and overlapping sections of the population, articulate variegated interests and integrate them with the operation of the legislative and executive branches of government. Independence of the judiciary from the other two branches of government is in both countries a firmly institutionalized norm, as is the right to counsel. The operations of the administrative and the legislative branches of government, as they affect the rights of individuals and private groups, are subject to judicial and quasijudicial review in both countries. These similarities in the patterns of government and politics create favorable conditions for the bar's work in general, and it seems probable that in both cases lawyers are drawn into areas of work, such as lobbying, that make intense participation and even careers in politics especially likely.

Among the differences in the sociocultural structure of the two societies that are important for the place and function of the legal profession, one is

28

immediately related to the work of lawyers—the contrast between common law and civil law in regard both to the character of the normative system and to the institutions of the administration of justice. It is well, however, to warn against an exaggeration of the differences. The substance of the law seems more similar than popular notions would suggest, and even the important formal difference between codification and reliance on precedent can be overestimated. The older a comprehensive code gets, the more its application has to rely on interpretation and frequently hasty legislative supplements, which in turn often require interpretive integration into the system of living law. That German courts play a lesser role in such interpretation, sharing it with writers of commentaries and law professors and lacking binding authority for their decisions as precedents,[2] is only in part related to this contrast between the legal systems and is otherwise founded in historical developments to be discussed later. Still, the role of legal practitioners, the judiciary and the bar, in shaping the legal order is less significant in Germany. No name of an eminent judge or advocate is a household word in the German educated classes as is the case in the United States, and neither the German judiciary nor the German bar has a tradition of professional pride based on famous lawyers of the past comparable to the American or the English professions.[3] The relative importance of judge and counsel in court proceedings is another difference between the two systems. The Anglo-American adversary pattern of trial tends to move the judge into the position of umpire, leaving the burden of factual and legal investigation largely with counsel. Particularly in criminal, but also in civil cases the German attorney plays a lesser role. Finally, the German legal system is without doubt easier to handle for the legal practitioner. Systematic codification is supplemented by a literature of commentaries that take into account previous decisions and scholarly work. As E. J. Cohn has said: "A question which would require a common law practitioner to search in books of reference for one or several quarters of an hour could be solved by his continental colleague completely satisfactorily in as many minutes."[4]

Also significant is the far greater degree of decentralization of government in the United States. The Federal Republic consists of *Länder*, which in some respects are comparable to American states, but both their autonomy and the factual variation in law and public policy between them are not as great as in the United States.[5]

The two countries exhibit a complex pattern of similarity and contrast in regard to social class. One especially relevant difference concerns the role of higher education. Access to university education, necessary for qualification as a lawyer, is much more restricted in Germany. It is, furthermore, more closely bound up with a favorable position of one's father in society.[6] Predictably, having an academic degree implies better economic opportunity and a greater social distance from other people in Germany than in the United States. Class structure and mobility will occupy us at length later.

Differences in value orientations prevalent in the middle and upper classes of the two societies, such as attitudes toward social conflict, the world of business, and the place of "the state," are especially important. On theoretical grounds it is unlikely that such value orientations are a particularly volatile part of sociocultural structures. On the contrary, they seem to be rather resistant to change except under special circumstances. Thus differences in the histories of the two countries become relevant. Much of today's value orientation was shaped by historical processes and conflicts almost forgotten. Government bureaucracies, the character of their personnel, and their relations to various groups as well as to the particular institutions of the administration of justice and to the norms and traditions of the bar itself can also best be understood through a study of the past.

## THE TWO LEGAL PROFESSIONS: SOME OVERALL CONTRASTS

Although similar in many respects, the two bars differ in a number of remarkable ways. These differences and how they relate to the structure of the two societies, both contemporary and historical, will constitute the subject matter of the remainder of the book. The first contrasts concern the major occupational roles that make up the legal profession.

### THE BRANCHES OF THE LEGAL PROFESSION

In both countries it is customary to distinguish four major subgroups of lawyers: the judiciary, lawyers in private practice, lawyers in government service, and lawyers in private employment. In Germany these four groups are—in type of career, membership in professional associations, and self-image—much more distinct than in the United States; in fact, they are differentiated to such an extent that it is questionable to speak of one profession.

In the standard case, the young German *Jurist* chooses one of these branches of law work after completion of his professional education and stays in it throughout his occupational life. The major exception to this generalization are frequent exchanges between the career lines of the judiciary, prosecuting attorneys, and, to a lesser extent, administrators in the state departments of justice. The careers of prosecuting attorneys and judges are so closely intertwined that they are referred to by one name, the *Justizdienst* ("court service").[7] Judiciary, prosecuting attorneys, and the majority of lawyers in government are *Beamte*, members of the civil service with life tenure and with a long tradition of attitudes and orientations that has been diluted but has not vanished in the twentieth century.

Their civil service character separates these branches of the legal profession from lawyers in private practice and in private employment. A few lawyers will serve as judges or government lawyers for a number of years and then turn to private practice, but a return from the bar to the judiciary or government service is rare. There are some exchanges and a fairly large number of intermediary positions between the bar admitted to the courts and lawyers in private employment, but the self-images differentiate in a fairly clear-cut way between the self-employed *Rechtsanwalt*, who is an "officer of court," and the lawyer employed in business.[8]

Neither American judges nor lawyers in government service are typically involved in careers of a civil service type. American judges reach their positions through appointment by political authorities or popular election. Their tenure in a given position is either for life during good behavior or for a limited period, though generally good chances for reelection tend to lengthen limited periods of tenure. A very large proportion of the American judiciary has worked in private practice before and is likely to return to it if attempted reelection fails.[9]

Government administration in the United States—excepting some newer agencies and top political appointments—tends to hire young lawyers just out of law school, but many of these leave government service after a number of years for private practice. The salary scale is limited, and the legal positions in the federal government are not part of the civil service system.[10] Lawyers in legal departments of business firms, the largest proportion of those in private employment, do not tend to move to other branches of legal work after a number of years. Although many have previously been in private practice or government service, there is an increasing tendency to hire recent law school graduates. While this group seems thus to become relatively distinct from other subgroups of the profession and especially from the main body of lawyers in private practice, it is comparatively small and the self-images of private practitioners and house counsel appear less different from each other than they are in the German legal profession.[11]

Generally, lawyers in private practice constitute—in terms of career patterns, self-image, and, as we will see, in numbers—the central group of the American legal profession from which the other types of practice are branching out. By contrast, in Germany there are for all practical purposes

31

several more or less distinct professions, bound together by a common education, but not by the predominance of experience in private practice or future career possibilities in it.

## SIZE OF THE PROFESSION AND OF MAJOR SUBGROUPS

Seemingly, one of the simplest facts to determine about an occupational group should be its size. However, to ascertain the number of lawyers in the two countries as well as the size of the major subgroups of the two professions is a taxing undertaking. For the United States, the survey of the legal profession made in the 1950's relatively precise and meaningful figures available which have been brought up to date since.[12] In Germany, the size of the judiciary as well as the number of prosecuting attorneys and of lawyers admitted to practice at court have been recorded with great precision for many decades; but for lawyers in private employment, lawyers in public administration, and the size of the total lawyer population there were until recently only vague and divergent estimates available, all of which were proved to be far off—and below—the mark by recent

TABLE 1. *Size of the Legal Profession and Its Major Subgroups in Germany and the United States.*

| Group | United States, 1960[a] | | Germany, 1961[b] | |
|---|---|---|---|---|
| Graduates of law schools | 330-340,000* | | 93,600 | |
| Members of the bar (lawyers reporting to major law directory in the U.S. and those qualified by 2nd state examination in Germany) | 252,385 | | 57-59,000* | |
| | | Percent of whole bar | | Percent of whole bar |
| Lawyers in private practice (excluding syndic-attorneys) | 192,353 | 76 | 13,000 | 22-23 |
| Lawyers in judicial office | 8,180 | 3 | 12,000 | 20-21 |
| Lawyers in government service (including prosecuting attorneys) | 25,621 | 10 | 18-19,000* | 30-33 |
| Lawyers in private employment | 25,198 | 10 | 13-18,000 | 22-30 |

calculations.[13] Even now we have to rely for many important categories on estimates with a wide margin of error.

There is no exact equivalence between any two definitions, meaningful in the respective country, of what a lawyer, a judge, an attorney in private practice, a house counsel or a government lawyer is. If we cut this Gordian knot by using categories that are roughly similar, even those precise figures that are available turn into crude estimates for comparative purposes. Nevertheless, such estimates, given in Table 1, are sufficient to permit several revealing comparisons.

In both countries a fairly large, though in its precise proportions unknown, number of people study law without entering legal practice in any meaningful sense. A more useful definition of the legal profession as a whole, still including many people who do not practice law in a narrow sense, would be all persons who are formally qualified for legal work and care to make themselves known as lawyers. For the United States the register of the leading law directory[14] comes closest to this definition. For Germany I chose the estimated number of lawyers who passed the second state examination, which is a prerequisite for judicial office and admission to practice at court, as roughly equivalent.

The American legal profession, while several times larger in absolute numbers, has a much more moderate edge over the German *Juristen* when the size of both professions is seen in relation to the total population. Both

---

NOTES FOR TABLE 1

*Note*: Starred figures are estimates. All figures are given for an indication of rough proportions only.

[a]*Sources for American data.* Dael Wolfle, *America's Resources of Specialized Talent* (New York, Harper, 1954), p. 295, was used as a base for the extrapolated estimate of the number of law school graduates. For all other figures see U.S. Bureau of the Census, *Statistical Abstract of the United States: 1964* (Washington, D.C., 1964), p. 158. These figures are based on Glen Greenwood, *The 1961 Lawyer Statistical Report* (Chicago, American Bar Foundation, 1961). They include a few duplications. The figure for lawyers in government service includes also incumbents of political office.

[b]*Sources for German data.* Law school graduates: preliminary information of the statistiscal office; see W. Kaupen, *Die Hüter von Recht und Ordnung* (Neuwied and Berlin, Luchterhand, 1969), p. 37, note 49.—Members of the bar: Estimate based on the same information of the statistical office and on examination statistics in *Die Ausbildung der deutschen Juristen*, publication no. 2 of the Arbeitskreis für Fragen der Juristenausbildung (Tübingen, 1960), p. 83.—Lawyers in private practice: *Anwaltsblatt*, 16:55 (1966). This figure excludes 6,000 syndic-attorneys, admitted to court practice but receiving their income predominantly from private employment.—Lawyers in government service: The estimate of a commission for the Ständige Konferenz der Innenminister (permanent conference of state ministers of the interior) approximated 16,000 lawyers in public administration; see *Gutachten über die juristische Ausbildung unter besonderer Berücksichtigung der Verwaltung.* To these I added an estimated number of 2,500 prosecuting attorneys; see *Statistisches Jahrbuch für die Bundesrepublik Deutschland 1959* (Stuttgart and Mainz, Kohlhammer, 1959), p. 107, for data on 1957.—Lawyers in private employment: This figure was estimated by subtracting the three other subgroups from the estimate for the number of all lawyers with a second state examination.

countries have more than one lawyer for every 1,000 persons.[15] It is only when we look at various subgroups that significant differences are revealed. The bulk of American lawyers, in 1960 more than three-quarters, are in private practice. Judges constitute a small minority of 3 percent, and government service and private employment claim about 10 percent each.[16]

In striking contrast, the German legal profession is made up of four subgroups of roughly equal size. Lawyers in private practice constitute a quarter or less of the German profession—an exact reversal of the ratio between the number of private practitioners and all other lawyers in the United States. Estimates of one-third and one-quarter, respectively, seem reasonable for the two groups of lawyers in government service and lawyers in private employment, that is, the share of these groups in the total number of lawyers is two or three times as high as that of the equivalent groups in the American profession.[17]

Possibly the most conspicuous feature of the German profession is, however, the very large judiciary, accounting for about 20 percent of all lawyers. When population size is taken into account, Germany has four to five times as many professionally trained judges as the United States. There is nearly one judge for every lawyer in private practice in Germany.

FUNCTIONS OF THE PROFESSION

These contrasting patterns suggest significant differences in the work done by the profession as a whole and in the division of labor among its branches. We have seen that the common law system is more complex, a fact which is compounded by the political and legal decentralization of the United States. American lawyers thus by and large appear to face more complicated problems than their German colleagues. One might, therefore, expect to find a smaller number of lawyers in Germany. While this expectation is to some extent confirmed, the difference is not very large when the population is taken into account. In addition, one might also guess that German lawyers are often involved in work that is done in the United States by members of other occupations and professions, and there is some evidence that points in this direction. For example, although no inclusive data are available, it is clear that lawyers constitute but a relatively small minority among American higher civil servants.[18] Characteristically, they work as legal specialists, although the pervasive importance of legal considerations in administrative affairs as well as political connections, which seem to be more frequent among lawyer-administrators than among higher civil servants in general, open special chances for advancement into general administrative positions.[19]

By contrast, general administrative positions in German government are typically filled by lawyers, and most German government lawyers act in such an administrative capacity rather than as legal specialists. The monopoly of lawyers over administrative positions in the higher civil service used to be proverbial. Although such positions are now open in principle to other professions as well, it is a reasonable estimate that between two-thirds and three-quarters of all administrative civil servants in federal and state bureaucracies are still lawyers.[20] The rationale advanced for this use of legal training as a preparation for administrative government service is similar to that for the traditional recruitment of the "administrative class" of the British civil service from upper-class educational institutions: the details of administration and of the various fields to which it applies can be learned "on the job" if only the recruit gets the right general formation, sharpening his reasoning and training his "judgment."[21]

The most likely explanation for these different patterns is found in the fact that American public administration developed relatively late, at a time when professionalization and specialization among professions had already reached a fairly high level and government operations required a wide variety of specialized expertise. By contrast, German government bureaucracies developed their basic patterns much earlier, when legal education provided a generalized training in public affairs. The entrenched dominance of lawyers in public administration led only to a gradual cooptation of other professions in technical fields. In part for reasons found in these different development patterns, the relative rewards for American lawyers—income, honor, and professional achievement—in government service and in private practice have been much more weighted in favor of independent work in the bar than they have been in Germany.[22]

Similar differences in the type of work done by lawyers in business employment may be inferred from fragmentary evidence. While it appears that most of the American lawyers employed in business work in legal departments which are often very similar to law firms except that they work only for one client, a large proportion of their German counterparts seem to work in a much broader range of positions. Many of those who are engaged in law work exclusively will be in the group of 6,000 syndic-attorneys who are formally admitted to practice at court and who account only for 30 to 50 percent of all fully qualified lawyers in private employment. One study showed that in the early 1960's more than one-third of the directors of personnel departments in 200 large German corporations had a legal education.[23]

If we consider the wider category of all law school graduates, there is probably not a great difference in patterns of work between German and American lawyers in private employment. In both countries, law-trained people are likely to be involved in a wide variety of positions, including top executive positions. Studies of German and American business leaders found that similar proportions of the top executives have training in law.[24]

In the work of the German judiciary, too, it is possible to point to some elements that lie outside the field not only of American judges but to some extent of the American profession as a whole. German law students after graduation have to enter a formal "preparatory service" of three and a half years if they want to qualify for judicial office or admission to practice at court. The larger part of this training period is spent in the courts. Although one may be skeptical of lawyers' assertions that one population is more "litigious" than another, there are some features of the law and the administration of justice that make it virutally certain that more cases, particularly more cases involving small amounts, are brought to court in Germany than in the United States. The major reasons are that court expenses and lawyers' fees are relatively low, that the loser must pay all fees, including the fees of opponent's counsel, and that legal aid relieving indigent parties of all costs is easily available.[25] While it is doubtful whether other peculiar obligations of the German judiciary are not compensated for by an increased workload of the American bar,[26] it is clear that the introduction of more than 10,000 neophytes into legal work per year and the larger amount of predominantly small-scale litigation constitute demands that are reduced or absent in the American legal profession. The larger share of this additional work is carried by the German judiciary; the rest involves the bar in private practice and public administration.

The bar in private practice is the only branch of the profession which is proportionally smaller in Germany. The major explanation for the fact that only one-quarter of all German lawyers, in contrast to three-quarters of the American legal profession, is in private practice is found—aside from the greater complexity of the American legal system—in three interrelated conditions: (1) German judges play a larger role in court than counsel; (2) the work of German attorneys centers more on litigation than does that of their American colleagues; and (3) corporation and business law is in Germany to a larger extent than in the United States dealt with by house counsel. These conditions will be discussed in turn.

Litigation in civil matters shows in both countries a basic pattern that may be called an adversary system of trial. The initiation of a case, the definition of its scope, offers of proof, and the decision about settlement or continuation to judgment are in principle up to the parties in both countries. A closer look reveals, however, that German judges play a much more active part and that the role of German *Anwälte* is far less significant than the part of their American counterparts.[27]

36

Under German procedure, to begin with, German counsel is much less involved than his American colleague in a search for all the relevant facts before trial; contact with potential witnesses, in particular, is severely limited by standards of good conduct and the prevailing attitudes of judges. During trial the court is charged with a "duty of clarification" pertaining to both the factual and the legal aspects of the case. This obligation is reinforced by "an overriding principle of German law, *jura novit curia*, the court knows—and is bound to apply—general law without prompting from the parties."[28] The presiding judge does a good deal of questioning, gives leads to the parties, and advises them how to strengthen their case.

Procedure is generally more flexible and nontechnical than in American courts. Oral argument is likened by Kaplan, von Mehren, and Schaefer more to "collaborative discussion than . . . adversary argument." ". . . the court seeks to see the controversy raw, as the party sees it, free of any polish put on it by counsel." Thus, in run-of-the-mill cases the role of advocate in a German court is not particularly significant. The questioning of witnesses likewise is mainly done by the court. "A seasoned German lawyer says he is wary of putting 'more than three' questions to a witness. That number is very often exceeded, but in this catch phrase we have an indication of the lawyer's narrow role in proof-taking. For the lawyer to examine at length after the court seemingly has exhausted the witness is to imply that the court has not done a satisfactory job—a risky stratagem."[29]

The role of German counsel appears greater and of better quality in courts of review, but here, too, the basic pattern of judicial dominance obtains. Review in the first instance, which is—in contrast to the American pattern—essentially a retrial at a higher level, allowing new allegations and new lines of legal argument, is comparatively common in Germany. Kaplan, von Mehren, and Schaefer suggest that "perhaps the German system thus compensates in some degree for the lawyer's hobbled role in searching out the facts."[30] On the whole, then the German attorney's role in litigation is considerably less demanding than what is expected of the American trial lawyer. At the same time, the German bar in private practice has less branched out from this traditional center of a lawyer's activity.

Changed economic conditions and attendant shifts in demand for legal services have increased the role of the lawyer as counselor, draftsman, negotiator and general go-between in contrast to his role as advocate. Though this is generally true for both countries, the development is much less clear cut and not as far advanced among German lawyers in private practice as among their American colleagues.

Of the German bar one can say with some confidence that its work still centers around litigation. After World War II counseling gained in importance. However, there are only a few big firms whose work consists mainly in counseling unrelated to litigation. This is frequently linked to developments of international economic integration and cooperation. Aside from these exceptions, even successful lawyers do considerably more than half of their work in litigation and related matters.[31]

The shift in emphasis from court work to counseling began in the United States after the Civil War and has continued up to the present. Today ". . . most lawyers no longer think of themselves primarily as advocates nor are they so considered by their clients."[32] In New York City, one out of every seven lawyers in private practice does not appear in court at all, and 40 percent spend less than two hours per week in court. Legal work unrelated to litigation is, of course, concentrated in the larger firms. In the largest firms its proportion may go up to 90 percent.[33] Of law practice in smaller towns little is known, but there is reason to assume for the "local lawyer" a far less strong, but basically similar shift in emphasis.[34]

Counseling work is roughly indicative of involvement in business law and in the affairs of business clients. We would then expect the German lawyer in private practice to be less concerned with business matters. How is this compatible with an essentially similar economic structure in the two countries? An important part of the explanation is that German business firms have more lawyers in permanent employment. It appears also that in Germany tax specialists and certified public accountants have taken over a larger share of consulting work in business law than is the case in the United States, although complaints about such competition are frequent in the United States, too.[35]

Even if syndic-attorneys are included in the ranks of the German *Rechtsanwaltschaft*, as they formally are, the differences between the two professions are signifcant, though not dramatic.[36] A large proportion of those German lawyers who spend most of their time in business-related law work are, however, de facto house counsel. Those who are employed full-time are not admitted to practice at court—the formal criterion for membership in the German *Rechtsanwaltschaft*; but between a quarter and a third of all *Rechtsanwälte* devote most of their time to an employer, a business firm, or an association, and conduct private practice in their spare time—they are "syndic-attorneys." Often their work in private practice is related to their work as *Syndikus*, such as service for individual clients who are members of the employing association. Thus, in comparison with the American bar, considerably fewer German lawyers who devote full time to private practice do most of their work in business-related fields of law. It appears that in Germany it is the middle-sized business firm which provides most of the counseling and corporate-commercial work for the attorney in private practice. Smaller firms consult a lawyer rarely, and larger firms have most of their work done by house counsel.[37]

Increasingly, young lawyers use an employed position as a springboard for setting themselves up in private practice. The number of house counsel remains high, however, preempting much of the more lucrative corporate and commercial business. On the other hand, corporate and business law appears attractive to a broad segment of the bar; it provides a higher income and brings the prestige that goes with well-to-do clients and technically demanding work.[38]

The number of house counsel is increasing in the United States, but relative to the profession as a whole it is much smaller than in Germany. It is still small enough to allow private law firms to take care of the legal problems of even the largest business concerns. The share of American lawyers in private practice in corporate-commercial legal work is likely to exceed that of house counsel considerably.[39]

The stronger involvement in legal affairs of business frequently spills over into a concern with business administration and decision-making. Already in the 1940's it could be said that "few successful lawyers can today escape having to make managerial decisions that involve a fusion of legal and extra-legal considerations." This statement of a Harvard Law School committee focuses on the involvement in economic matters required of a lawyer to do good law work. The actual involvement goes much further. Jerome E. Carlin found in New York City: "60 per cent of the lawyers in our sample assist their business clients in obtaining financing; an equal proportion are on the lookout for investment opportunities for these clients; close to half are either officers or board members of client corporations (generally taking an active part in corporate affairs); approximately a third hold stock or have other financial interests in such corporations."[40]

Though these findings cannot be generalized throughout the United States, it seems safe to say that such involvement in the nonlegal business concerns of clients has no parallel in the German bar. E. J. Cohn, looking at the German *Rechtsanwaltschaft* from the perspective of the English barrister, contends that the German attorney has a rather "intimate connection with economic life." True, in English terms the *Rechtsanwalt* resembles in many respects more the solicitor than the barrister; he does give business advice; he will handle the client's affairs if he is asked to do so; and he does assume executive positions in corporations. But all these activities appear much more limited in scope than in the United States and a sizeable share of them is likely to be carried out by syndic-attorneys.[41]

Compared to the American bar in private practice, then, the German *Rechtsanwaltschaft* has a more narrowly defined set of functions. While more centered in traditional fashion on litigation and related matters, its role at court is limited by the dominant part of the judiciary. In business matters its involvement is less extensive, partly because of the more widespread employment of house counsel. Finally, it should be mentioned that German law professors play a more prominent part in the legal system outside the confines of legal education than do faculty members of American law schools. Even if legal "theory" is often set apart from "practice," German law professors have long enjoyed great authority in matters of the administration of justice. Aside from the influence of their publications, they have the right to appear as advocates in many courts. Furthermore, their opinions are often requested by parties for submission in crucial lawsuits; as Cohn says, "there can be little doubt that in this field the attorney has been beaten by the academician."[42]

The different patterns of work of the various branches of the profession are likely to affect firm structure and specialization as well as the internal stratification of the two bars. The division of labor in the profession as a whole is also relevant for problems of cohesion and professional identity of the bar in private practice as well as for its characteristic value orientations and reference groups.

## THE ORGANIZATION AND DIFFERENTIATION OF PRIVATE LEGAL PRACTICE

A formal division of the bar, as in the English profession, into barristers pleading at court and solicitors working as counsel out of court does not exist in either the United States or Germany. There are, however, a number of distinctions in the German case which are of some importance. We have already seen that house counsel cannot be admitted to work at court—the criterion for membership in the *Rechtsanwaltschaft*—if they do not maintain a minimum of private practice. Those who do form the somewhat distinct group of syndic-attorneys. A second formal category of lawyers relevant here has an American parallel in name, but in name only. The German *Notar* is a fully trained lawyer and thus a member of the legal profession, while the American notary public is neither. The *Notar*'s function is the certification of legal actions which is required in a large number of legal matters.[43] It frequently involves, in addition, advice pertaining to these transactions. In some German states the office is strictly separated from the role of attorney, in others it is given by appointment to attorneys with long experience at the bar. About 25 percent of all *Rechtsanwälte* are at the same time *Notare*.[44]

Admission to the bar in the United States means admission to the bar of a particular state or admission to federal courts or specialized administrative agencies, but almost all states permit an attorney from another jurisdiction to appear in a specific case. Some, however, require that the attorney become associated with local counsel and in practice many lawyers hesitate to appear in other jurisdictions.[45] Many states have reciprocal agreements with other states to admit lawyers who move without much complication. The German lawyer is, in civil and commercial cases, formally more bound to a specific locality and to a given level in the structure of appeals than his American colleague. Aside from local courts with a jurisdiction over small claims, the German attorney in principle is admitted to one court only, as far as civil and commercial law are concerned, although change of admission is a fairly simple matter. Appealing a decision or pursuing a case in a different locality involves, then, as a rule retaining another attorney. An official rationale for this regulation is that the court should know the attorneys appearing before it. An additional argument about the consequences of this arrangement may be as significant. Limiting the attorney to essentially one court in civil and commercial litigation is deemed to impede the concentration of business in the hands of a few very successful lawyers.[46] No such limitations exist for criminal cases, and practice before administrative and revenue courts is also open to any attorney. Still, both the principle of "localization" and exclusive admission to either a court of the first instance or a court of appeal, as far as substantial civil litigation is concerned, introduce differentiations into the German *Rechtsanwaltschaft* which do not exist in this formal manner in the American bar in private practice.

### FIRM STRUCTURE

Among the most important differences between the American and the German bar in private practice are differences in the size and the character of law firms. Table 2 shows that American firms are larger than German *Sozietäten*. The proportion of firms with four or more partners increased in the United States from 11.6 percent in 1947 to 17 percent in 1967, while in Germany their proportion was 6.4 percent in 1967. This corresponds to the fact that proportionately more American lawyers are members of partnerships, although in both countries individual practitioners constitute the majority of lawyers in private practice.[47] Table 2 does not tell the whole story, however. The most important contrast between the two bars concerns the leading firms of the metropolitan bar—a statistically small group which is nevertheless of great importance for private legal practice as a whole. In Germany, a firm with more than five partners is exceptionally large; including associates, the biggest German *Sozietäten* have virtually never more than fifteen or twenty lawyers. By contrast, the

TABLE 2. *Distribution of Partnerships by Firm Size, Percent.*

| Size of firm (No. of partners) | Germany, 1967 [a] | U.S., 1947 [b] | U.S., 1954 [b] | Size of firm (No. of partners) | U.S., 1967 [c] |
|---|---|---|---|---|---|
| 2 | 76.8 | 72.7 | 67.6 | 2 | 59.7 |
| 3 | 16.8 | 15.7 | 20.0 | 3 | 23.3 |
| 4 | 4.1 | 5.0 | 5.9 | | |
| | | | | 4-10 | 15.1 |
| 5-8 | 2.2 | 5.8 | 5.3 | | |
| 9 or more | 0.04 | 0.8 | 1.2 | 11 or more | 1.9 |

[a] Calculated from "Anwaltssozietäten," *Anwaltsblatt*, 18:109 (1968).
[b] Recalculated from Maurice Liebenberg, "Income of Lawyers in the Postwar Period," *Survey of Current Business*, December 1956, p. 33, table 10.
[c] Calculated from "Why Law Is a Growth Industry," *Business Week*, January 13, 1968, p. 78.

largest American firms have as many as twenty-five to thirty-five partners, and there are twenty-odd firms with a total of more than 100 lawyers. The national pattern in Germany, including conditions in the largest cities, resembles that of nonmetropolitan America. In a typical middle-sized Midwestern community, the largest firm consisted of eight lawyers. Larger firms are rare in American cities of less than 200,000 population.[48] This similarity of the situation in smaller American cities to the overall picture in Germany we will encounter in several other features of private legal practice, too.

The rationale of large law firms is to provide well-rounded service for business clients with complex legal problems, resulting in complementary specialization of lawyers within a firm. This is true for top law firms in both countries. It appears, however, that such complementary specialization is far more common and much more differentiated in the United States. The major factors accounting for this difference are, it seems, the greater complexity of legal problems in common law countries and the greater part played by house counsel in Germany; in addition, the fact that Germany does not have any one economic and financial center as dominant as New York or even Chicago contributes to the same effect. A relatively large German firm is more likely than its American counterpart either to serve mainly medium-sized business clients or to specialize in certain fields like antitrust and brand names, with parallel work done by all or most lawyers in the firms, or to combine these two patterns.[49]

Some considerations underlying the formation and continuation of partnerships are common in both countries, although in the United States they appear to be more important only for the smaller firms: partnership eases the burden of overhead costs; is conducive to consultation; provides for sickness and vacations; is often, and this is characteristic for the majority even of German firms with more than two partners, a consequence of success of the senior principal; provides a training ground and a way of getting business for the young, and .may ease the financial problems of retirement. The last rationale is of particular importance in Germany, where inflations decimated life insurances and savings twice in the last fifty years;[50] the very large proportion of two-man firms in the German bar appears to be in part a consequence of these special problems.

One may see the same situation as the major factor underlying what seems to be a high incidence of partnerships between lawyers related by kinship, between father and son or father-in-law and son-in-law.[51] These family firms appear, however, indicative of more significant matters. Together with the much lower incidence of complementary specialization, with the large proportion of two-man partnerships, and with the frequency of "old age pension and life insurance" arrangements, the family firm is symptomatic for the more traditional character of the organizational patterns in the larger part of private practice in Germany. Differentiation of functions and reintegration in more or less bureaucratic patterns is not highly advanced in either bar when compared with business firms or the newer professions applying scientific knowledge, such as engineers; but this lack of differentiation is far more pronounced in the German bar.

The size and character of German firms is not only similar to that of American firms in smaller cities; it is also comparable to the American pattern around 1900. Hurst says that "no firms of large membership appeared, even in the great cities, until the end of the century. The typical partnership was a two-man affair; it usually had its 'office' member and its 'court' member."[52] It was after the turn of the century that larger firms began to develop, and the periods of their greatest growth were the 1920's and the 1930's. The development of these firms, then, seems to be conditioned by the same factors that account for the growth of corporate legal departments: the growth of corporate clients and the increase in government regulations concerning these clients. In the United States the response of the bar to these economic and political developments was to increase the facilities of firms in private practice, while in Germany similar changes have resulted in a stronger role of house counsel. Whether in the future "inside lawyers" will in America, too, increasingly limit the part played in corporate law by large private firms remains to be seen.[53]

### PATTERNS OF SPECIALIZATION

Specialization is most likely to develop in larger firms. Here a fairly continuous flow of complicated legal tasks can be expected, requiring special expertise and warranting higher expenses if standardization does not reduce costs sufficiently. Here, too, some of the most important obstacles to specialization are removed or reduced in importance: referral to another lawyer does not involve the risk of losing the client; the typical desire of the client to keep things in "one hand," if not with one lawyer, is satisfied; and maintaining a volume of specialty work does not, because of the visibility of the large firm, require advertising, which meets with resistance in the profession at large since it tends to increase competition and since it has become one of the most important symbolic distinctions of the profession from the business world.[54]

If specialization in the largest German firms is less detailed and less widespread than in their American counterparts, one should expect a similar contrast between the two bars as a whole. Full-blown specialization, however, is not typical of either bar. In both countries, most lawyers can be said to be in "general practice." At the same time, most have a few more or less broad fields of practice to which they devote most of their time and from which they derive most of their income, although they typically will accept other matters, too, as they come along. These rather vague forms of specialization are based on the geographic distribution of lawyers and clients with different types of problems; they, furthermore, grow out of contacts with clients and other lawyers at the beginning of a law career, and they are stabilized with the accumulation of experience, success, and reputation. Only in a minority of cases does the development lead to full specialization, clearly distinct from general practice and accepted by a large number of colleagues.

Geographic limitations are formally emphasized in Germany by admission to one *Landgericht*, and the principle of admission either to a *Landgericht*, the court of first instance for commercial and civil litigation excluding small cases, or to an *Oberlandesgericht*, the appellate court for *Landgericht* cases, constitutes another formal base of some specialization. Without the same formal restrictions American lawyers in private practice show a similar differentiation by jurisdictions and specific courts.[55]

Initial contacts and connections are probably more important in the American than in the German bar. Ethnic and racial heterogeneity of the American bar and its clientele is one factor that contributes to this, since it

is related both to many lawyers' access to clients and to the kinds of problems clients typically have. Equally or more important is the fact that the
metropolitan American bar is, as we shall see, highly stratified, with
mobility chances tied to the educational and home background of the
aspiring young lawyer. Both conditions are much reduced in importance in
Germany.

The relation between professional success and specialization rests on
several patterns. The pattern most frequent in Germany and of only
slightly less importance in the United States is that success of a general
practitioner gives him a certain freedom to choose among the cases offered. His choice typically leads him into those fields where remuneration
is higher, clients both richer and more prestigious, work more complex and
better regarded in the profession. Associates and junior partners often deal
with other matters that come along. The general business practice is in
both countries the "special field" of the successful general practitioner.
Such opportunity of choice is, of course, related to the type and quality of
initial training, and it requires fairly early success. Legal competence and
skills are maintained only by constant experience; lacking the latter, they
are likely to whither away if they ever were present.

Some shifts of emphasis come without special success, they virtually go
with seniority. An example would be estate and probate work, which is
likely to increase with established client contacts and age. In about half the
German bar, the *Notariat*, to which one is appointed only after many years
in practice, provides a focus of work for some lawyers in the second half of
their careers.[56]

The reverse pattern, where success is built on specialization, may seem
obvious in other occupations, but it encounters many obstacles in the law.
These are centered around the problems of getting sufficient business and
of satisfying clients who want the same lawyer for all their problems. As
argued before, such obstacles play a lesser role for large firms, and specialization within these firms is one of the different types falling into this
pattern. Another type, benefiting from similar circumstances, is the lawyer
or the small firm which may be called a "satellite" of the large firms,
handling the "over-flow" of their business or other referral work these do
not care to engage in.[57] In these cases, which appear to be more frequent
in the United States, the problem of clients' preference for one lawyer or
firm handling all their business may exist, but it is overcome because of the
highly technical character of the work, because of the initially retained
firm's inability or unwillingness to do the work and because of its
respected sponsorship of the "satellite." A similar type is found wherever
one source of referrals—such as a trade association, an insurance firm, a

bank or a title company—provides a lawyer with a fairly large amount of business in one field.

Aspiring specialists in no such way "affiliated" will encounter greater difficulties in sustaining a sufficient volume of specialty work, given the limited opportunities for legitimate advertising and the reluctance of many lawyers to refer clients. However, problems of particular legal complexity and special institutional arrangements may put certain fields out of reach for the ordinary practitioner and secure a steady flow of referral. Trial work, especially in the higher courts, and brand-name and antitrust work are examples of this in both countries, although the latter tends to be monopolized by established large firms in the United States, while in Germany there is a greater chance of success for the excellent individual specialist who then may build a firm. Work under the jurisdiction of special courts and agencies also tends to generate specialization, although it appears that in Germany, where special courts exist for public administration, revenue matters, labor law, and social security, specialization of the judiciary goes much further than that of the bar.[58]

A field may be for one or another reason unattractive to many lawyers, and this may constitute the basis of specialization for a minority, often reached by default. In the American metropolitan bar, criminal law, negligence work, matrimonial matters, and work that involves local political institutions are often examples of this. These fields sometimes have a reputation for unethical and illegal practices, a reputation which may occasionally be exaggerated, but which does have a foundation in reality. Conditions are reinforced, in a vicious circle, by the facts that these fields often go together in the practice of a lawyer and that this kind of work is largely done by the part of the bar which is least economically secure. Not infrequently, lawyers with higher standards could not easily break into the criminal and personal injury fields, if they wanted to, because of the very effective use of illegal solicitation.[59]

It appears safe to say that in the German bar no field of practice is stigmatized by a reputation or actual prevalence of serious and persistent violations of legal ethics. In criminal law, the relative absence of organized crime, the lesser involvement of courts and prosecuting attorneys in politics and its network of "connections" and "debts," and the rather hobbled role of counsel in criminal trial are likely to have contributed to this result, and the wider spread of criminal work among lawyers who work mainly in other fields sustains it secondarily. Though most lawyers may prefer to do other work, criminal cases are handled on the side by many if not most German lawyers and firms. That, on the other hand, criminal law is the main field of practice for 5 to 10 percent of the German bar appears due to some dislike of the clients involved, but mainly to the peculiar nature of the work—the different legal knowledge required, less written work, and more straining litigation.[60]

When it is permitted to announce a specialty in letterheads, door signs, and lists of lawyers and when the requisites for this competitive advantage are not too demanding, one is likely to find many self-pronounced "specialists" who may have some training and the wish to specialize in the advertised field but who have neither particularly great experience nor a large volume of business in their specialty. Rather than indicating the extent of real specialization, such self-designations are in many cases not much more than an embellishment of the shingle, a moderate form of advertising. The "tax attorney" in Germany often is a case in point.[61]

It is the same kinds of conditions, then, that lead in both countries to specialization, but the incidence of these conditions varies. By and large, specialization is more frequent in the American bar than in the German *Rechtsanwaltschaft*. This is true both for full-blown specialization and for the concentration on one or a few fields which is not in any sense exclusive and is not acknowledged by colleagues as specialization. The difference between the two countries is mainly due to the situation in large American cities, while conditions in smaller American cities and towns come closer to the German overall picture.

In New York City, 70 percent of all lawyers in private practice spend half of their time or more in a single area of practice and 40 percent spend more than three-quarters of their time.[62] Less extreme concentration of work in one field was found in a sample of 100 lawyers drawn from three metropolitan areas and two cities with less than 100,000 population. Still, only a quarter spent less than 40 percent in one area of practice and, at the opposite end of the scale, one-quarter spent 70 percent or more of their time in one field.[63] Comparable data from Germany are lacking, but even in the centers of greatest concentration of lawyers and legal business specialization is not likely to exceed the level found in the second study, which we tentatively take as representative for general urban conditions in the United States.

The existence of specialty associations and committees within general bar associations can be taken as another indication for the development of specialization. The American Bar Association has fifteen sections which concern themselves with major areas of specialized interest, and each section has a number of committees.[64] In addition to these divisions of the major national association and their counterparts in state and local general bar associations, there are a number of special associations of lawyers such as the American Trial Lawyers Bar Association, the Federal Bar Association, the American Patent Law Association, the Association of the Customs Bar, the Association of Life Insurance Counsel, the Federal

Communications Bar Association, the Association of General Counsel (i.e., of house counsel), the Judge Advocates Association, and the Maritime Law Association.[65]

In Germany, both the *Deutsche Anwaltverein*, the voluntary association of *Rechtsanwälte*, and the *Bundesrechtsanwaltskammer*, the national integrated bar association set up by statute, have committees. However, these have the character not of specialty associations but of work groups charged to develop the association's position on diverse legislative matters. Even if the diversity of these committees is tentatively taken as some indication of what is considered a field of special competence, it would indicate still a lower level of differentiation.[66]

Finally, the different degree of specialization in the two countries can be gauged by looking closely at one field of specialization in a metropolitan area characterized by a high level of differentiation of legal activities. Johnstone and Hopson asked members of the "elite group of Manhattan real property practitioners" to indicate the various subspecialties of real estate practice in New York City and to name specialists in these fields. A common criterion used in answering was whether the specialists received referrals from other lawyers. "The fields most frequently mentioned were condemnation (eminent domain), real estate tax reduction, rent control, tenant relocation (and obtaining possession, including eviction), zoning, Title I (urban renewal), cooperatives, leasing, large mortgage loans, institutional lenders, builder owners, investors, and operators."[67] By contrast, what is found in the German "real property" bar, which is less set off from the *Rechtsanwaltschaft* as a whole in the first place, seems to be basically some differentiation according to type of client and amount of money involved (e.g., tenant-landlord matters versus construction) and in terms of the decision-making agencies concerned (regular courts versus local administration and courts for matters in public administration).

The diversity of specialized work in conjunction with the large number of lawyers has in the largest American cities important consequences for the perception of the profession by its members. Their image of the bar is highly fragmented; it focuses on those working in the same field of specialization, those one has referred clients to, and those one is associated with in the same firm.[68] The visibility of lawyers to each other in New York is more comparable to the degree of mutual knowledge of German lawyers as a whole than to conditions on the local level, the largest cities not excluded.

## STRATIFICATION OF THE BAR

Any group that is fairly differentiated tends to show some forms of stratification, that is, stable differences in evaluation as well as in control

over valued resources. Both differentiation and differential ranking find
the more favorable conditions the larger the group in question. These considerations would lead us to expect that the two bars show definite inequalities in the distribution of income and prestige as well as of such associated factors as professional competence and access to high-status clients.
At the same time we should anticipate that stratification is more developed
in the metropolitan centers in both countries and exhibits the most extreme
forms in the large cities of the United States.

Nearly 40 percent of all American lawyers practice in cities with a
population of 500,000 or more. The equivalent proportions of German
lawyers in private practice as well as of the population at large are
somewhat higher.[69] However, these similar distribution patterns mean
vastly larger absolute numbers of lawyers and a much higher lawyer-
population ratio in the largest cities of America. In New York City alone,
there are more lawyers in private practice than in all of Germany. The
three largest local bars in Germany—those in Munich, Hamburg, and
Berlin—had in 1963 between 1,250 and 1,500 attorneys who were admitted to the courts, and six of the twelve cities with a population of 500,000
or more had less than 500 *Rechtsänwalte*. Of the twenty-one American
cities with populations over 500,000, fourteen had more than 1,500 lawyers
in private practice, five had between 1,250 and 1,500, and even the
smallest, San Antonio and San Diego, had more than 500 lawyers in
private practice in 1960.[70]

In the largest American cities the bar is characterized by a rather rigid
division of strata which show great differences in professional prestige,
type of work, type of client, income, and general social standing. The
evidence available comes mainly from New York City, Chicago, and
Detroit,[71] but we may assume that similar though attenuated patterns
are found in most cities with populations over 500,000 or 750,000.

The top of the stratification system in the metropolitan American bar is
held by the partners of large law firms, while the bottom, which is very
large, is occupied by the majority of individual practitioners and small-
firm lawyers.[72] By and large, these two groups work and live in different worlds in virtually every respect. Lawyers in large firms have a different clientele than small-firm lawyers and individual practitioners. Large
corporations and well-to-do individual clients of higher status ethnic
background predominate on the one side, small business firms as well as
middle- to lower-class individual clients of lower ethnic status are characteristic on the other. The firm with a large number of clients who provide a
steady flow of business is in contrast to one with a predominance of clients
who come and go, so that among individual practitioners and small-firm
lawyers a pervasive sense of insecurity is often combined with a depen-

dence on the few clients with recurrent business. The differences in type of client are reflected in different kinds of work. The lawyer at the very bottom appears to be little involved in specifically legal work.[73] This is not true of all individual practitioners and small-firm lawyers. However, while elite lawyers specialize in business law and trust and estate work, individual and small-firm lawyers show a heavy concentration in the fields of personal injury, criminal, and matrimonial matters. Actually, for the latter group, too, business law is most frequently the main area of practice, but its character differs radically from the business practice of large-firm lawyers. Typically, it involves far more routine work, smaller amounts are at stake, and less legal competence in the technical sense is required.[74] Large-firm lawyers, furthermore, spend far less time in courts and administrative agencies, and if they do their contact is much more likely to be with higher level agencies and courts.

As will be expected from the differential distribution of types of clients and kinds of law work, the two groups contrast sharply in income. Table 3 gives a rough indication of the magnitude of income differences in New York. It also shows that size of firm is closely related to income independent of type of work and kind of client. The reputation of established firms attracts more associates working for relatively low fees and allows the charging of higher fees. In addition, the larger firms have probably more possibilities for cost-saving rationalization.[75]

There is little doubt that income differentiation along the lines of firm size, type of work, and kind of client is paralleled by similar differences in prestige and professional regard, although no study has systematically documented this prestige hierarchy—its span from top to bottom, the way it is linked to different positions in the structure of the bar, and its division into more or less sharply distinct strata. One aspect of the prestige hierar-

TABLE 3. *Percentage of Lawyers with more than $35,000 Annual Income by Size of Firm, New York, 1960.*

| Type of practice | All partners | All lawyers including associates | Lawyers with "high-status practice" only [a] |
|---|---|---|---|
| Large firm | 70 | 35 | 75 |
| Individual and small firm | 13 | 11 | 44 |

*Source:* Carlin, *Lawyers' Ethics*, p. 27 and p. 38, note 19.

[a] "Handling probate and business matters for a high status clientele, and having contact mainly with upper-level courts and agencies" (p. 27).

chy is, however, fairly clear, and it is crucial for the structure of the metropolitan bar in America. The stratum at the very bottom is accorded not just lesser prestige; it is viewed in distinctly negative terms. Lawyers in this category are not seen simply as less competent colleagues, less well connected and less lucky; they are considered to operate below a minimum line of competence and of honesty in dealing with clients, colleagues, and officials. Serious breaches of professional norms are thus seen as characteristic of certain groups and not only as the failure of certain individuals—the proverbial few "bad apples" to be found in any group.

The findings of Carlin in New York show that these views are not mere inventions of prejudice. Small-firm and individual lawyers do violate basic norms significantly more often than other members of the profession. This is specifically true of lawyers in the fields of criminal, matrimonial, and personal injury law, of attorneys with a low status and unstable clientele and of lawyers who have frequent contact with lower level courts and agencies.[76] These differential frequencies of violation of professional norms are to a large extent an outcome of the very system of stratification in which they function as one further element of cleavage and social distance. Not surprisingly under such conditions, the stratification pattern is reflected also in the professional and social contacts lawyers have with each other. The huge size of the local bar and the high degree of specialization facilitate and support the effects of stratification. Most lawyers in the highest and in the lowest stratum have no contact whatsoever with their opposite numbers. Parallel local bar associations appeal to different strata of the bar, and elite control of the leading associations is resented by lawyers of lower standing.[77]

A very low level of mobility between strata further accentuates the divisions within the metropolitan American bar. In New York, less than 2 percent of those who did not start out in large firms ended up working there. Downward mobility is more frequent. Some upward mobility into higher status practice occurs without a change in firm size. However, the association between firm size and type of client, kind of work, and amount of income is such that the chances of lawyers in smaller firms to acquire a high-status practice appear severely limited, especially if lawyers and firms indirectly connected with large firms are excluded from consideration. Finally, career patterns are closely related to socioeconomic background and ethnic origin. Considerable differences in the quality of college and law school education correlate highly with social origin and are decisive for one's career chances.[78] Thus, the whole life experience of lawyers at the top and the bottom of the American metropolitan bar differ radically.

The vast social distance between the top and bottom groups of the

American metropolitan bar is reflected in the views either group holds of the other. Smigel speaks of a "series of mutually derogatory images." The opinions of individual practitioners and small-firm lawyers frequently express the dissatisfaction arising out of the fact that they have reached professional status but are deprived of much of its reward. However, their judgments of large-firm lawyers do not simply grow out of resentment; they represent, too, a variant ideal for the profession's role. According to Smigel, "The solo practitioner sees himself ideally as the defender of the poor and the needy, an independent man with real responsibility. He is the spokesman for the people, not the mouthpiece of big business."[79] He is the "real lawyer, or more of a real lawyer than his colleagues in the large firms" because he still goes to court and is not a cog in the wheels of a big office. The success of the top lawyers is often seen as based on extraneous advantages like family connections and wealth rather than ability.[80]

Large-firm lawyers are less aware of their counterparts at the bottom of the barrel. They also lack the intense dissatisfaction characteristic of a good number of solo practitioners. Smigel says that those "who would talk about the solo lawyer did so with more tact and less emotion. They could not see how the law could be adequately practiced by the single lawyer . . . Some large firm lawyers felt that there were more unethical people among solo lawyers, although they hastened to add: 'Perhaps they are forced into it.' "[81] That these images held by the most and the least successful lawyers about each other are not too different from stereotypes about the bar frequently found in the wider community—"servants of big business" and "petty shysters"—may be seen as one indication of the fact that the American metropolitan bar does not constitute a distinct community with a well-developed subculture of its own which is insulated from the wider public and in particular from the "neighboring" strata of the middle classes, a phenomenon that will concern us at several points below.

In describing the stratification of the American metropolitan bar I have focused on the extreme groups. Lawyers in medium-sized firms constitute together with those lawyers in smaller firms, who have a better than average practice, a middle stratum. They form an intermediate group in terms of their clientele, kind of work, income, prestige, compliance with professional norms, and various background characteristics. We may be justified in concluding that practice in medium-sized firms, together with high-status practice in smaller firms, constitutes the highest level of success for the average attorney who is upwardly mobile, and that it provides at the same time a training ground for a large minority of small-firm lawyers and individual practitioners. These members of what we took generally to be the lowest stratum of the metropolitan bar are likely to be better off and more respected than the rest of individual practitioners and small-firm lawyers.

The professional and social contacts lawyers in medium-sized firms have with lawyers outside their own office spread more into other strata than is true for large-firm lawyers and lawyers in smaller practices.[82] In assessing the softening effects this may have on the cleavages which separate the top and bottom strata, one has to bear in mind, though, that the size of this group is relatively small and that the contacts are likely to be selective. Medium-sized satellite firms and lawyers who started their careers in large firms on the one side, and the attorneys who moved between the medium-sized firms and smaller practices on the other are likely to account for a good deal of this wider spread of interaction. It appears unlikely that lawyers at the very bottom of the system share significantly in this interaction across stratum boundaries. In sum, the metropolitan American bar is steeply and rigidly stratified. Large differences in privilege and standing, relatively low mobility, and a subjective social distance between subgroups which merges at the extremes into mutual hostility combine to create deep social cleavages in the professional community of the American metropolitan bar.

Little is known about the bar in smaller American cities and towns. The evidence available from a few scattered studies can, however, profitably be compared to the more detailed sketch of the stratification of the metropolitan bar just given. Two patterns which contribute greatly to sharp and rigid divisions in the metropolitan bar are much less developed in smaller communities. Large firms are virtually unknown in communities with populations under 200,000. And it appears from the single most systematic study of a nonmetropolitan local bar that law firms are less specialized and that specialization is generally far less developed.[83] Desirable clients, different types of law work, income, and professional prestige are unequally distributed in the nonmetropolitan bar, too; but the span of inequality seems narrower, there is more overlap in the kind of work done by lawyers of different standing and income, and the lowest stratum is not stigmatized as a virtual "outcaste" group which violates persistently basic standards of competence and honesty. The patterns of social and professional contact within the bar are surprisingly dense and extend across income differences which in the absence of strong professional bonds would in all likelihood prohibit close association. Such professional community is supported by a greater homogeneity of the bar in terms of social background and training. There are fewer members with lower ethnic and social class backgrounds and a smaller proportion has studied law on a part-time basis. Thus we may say that divisions within the bar in these smaller communities are to a lesser extent built on and reinforced by major divisions in the society at large and an uneven pattern of professional education.

This picture of stratification in the bar of smaller American cities shows remarkable similarities to the patterns which prevail in the German bar as a whole. Previously, similarities in firm size and degree of specialization were noted, and the likeness in these two respects accounts to a large extent for the similarities in the patterns of inequality. On the whole, differences in clientele, type of work, income, and prestige appear to be somewhat less pronounced in the German bar. Furthermore, inequalities in one dimension are not as closely associated with differences in another; the division into several strata is less rigid, and the differences which exist seem to be less divisive in their consequences.

The contrast between income distribution in the two bars seems signifi-

TABLE 4. *Income Distribution in the German and American Bars
in Private Practice.*
(Estimated Deciles and Quartiles)

| Percentage of lawyers who earned less than the indicated amount | Annual incomes, dollars | |
|---|---|---|
| | Germany, 1954 | U.S., 1954 |
| 10 (1st. decile) | 2,000-2,200 | 1,800-1,900 |
| 25 (1st. quartile) | 3,500-3,700 | 3,800-3,900 |
| 50 (2d. quartile, median) | 6,100-6,300 | 7,200-4,400 |
| 75 (3d. quartile) | 11,000-11,300 | 13,000 |
| 90 (9th. decile) | 18,000-20,000 | 21,000-21,500 |
| Ratio | | |
| Third to first quartile | 3 - 3.2 | 3.3 - 3.4 |
| Ninth to first decile | 8.2-10.0 | 11.0-12.5 |

*Sources:* Liebenberg, "Income of Lawyers," p. 4, table 2 (reporting a survey of the Office of Business Economics), and *Anwaltsblatt*, 12:206 (1962) (reporting income tax statistics). Both sources give the total income of those who derived most of their income from independent legal practice. German incomes were divided by 2, rather than by 4 as the exchange rate of the dollar and the Deutsche Mark would suggest; this corresponds approximately to the costs of living in the two countries and also to the average incomes of lawyers in private practice ($10,294 and DM 18,910). Deciles and quartiles had to be extrapolated from the data available.

cant, but not particularly strong. Table 4 shows that the dispersion of incomes in the American bar is somewhat stronger at the extremes. The contrast may actually be greater, since the data used for Germany—statistics of the internal revenue administration—seem to overstate the dispersion of incomes in the German bar.[84] While this difference in income distribution may be interpreted as reflecting the conditions in the metropolitan American bar, the basic similarity between the two income distributions deserves attention. Which factors counteract in the German bar the divisive effects one may expect from considerable income differences? The answer to this question is found, it seems, in the lesser importance of established firms and the lower level of specialization in the German metropolitan bar, in the character of prestige differentiation and its relation to differences in financial success, and in the recruitment and training patterns of the German bar. Each of these aspects will be considered in turn.

Firm size, in Germany too, correlates with type of work and professional success.[85] The crucial question is whether firm size in the German metropolitan bar is as strong a determining factor of financial success as it is among American lawyers who work in large cities. Since, as was discussed above, German partnerships are often junior-senior arrangements, the differences in income, clientele, and type of work appear largely to be an outcome of shifts in the career of moderately successful attorneys, with only a modicum of stability across "generations." A larger partnership, especially one with internal specialization, does provide competitive advantages. It is a visible symbol of success, it makes certain economies possible, and the cooperation of competent specialists results in superior service for the client whose problems warrant such expertise and who can afford to pay for it. However, firms of this kind are not as frequent and not as well established in Germany as they have been since the turn of the century in metropolitan America. E. J. Cohn seems on safe ground when he asserts that in Germany larger firms do not monopolize the "better and bigger type of work."[86] The partner in a two- or three-man firm is often found among the top lawyers in any local bar and even in the highest ranks of national reputation; and being an individual practitioner by no means creates the presumption that one is near the "bottom of the barrel."

Specialization in certain fields as well as the less exclusive concentration on some broad areas of the law is also associated with considerable income differences. Table 5 gives the rank order of different types of practice in terms of income. It contains as "major fields of work" clearly defined fields, such as antitrust work, tenant-landlord matters, or criminal law, as well as broad characterizations of a lawyer's practice, such as business or commercial law and civil law. Since the survey on which the table is based

TABLE 5. *Percentage of Lawyers with an Annual Income of More than DM 36,000 by Major Field of Work, Germany, 1965.*

| Field to which "most time" was devoted | Percentage of those who earned more than DM 36,000 annually [a] | |
|---|---|---|
| Antitrust work and law of competition | 83 | (6) |
| Advice on contracts | 75 | (8) |
| "Business law" | 70 | (10) |
| "Commercial law" | 68 | (31) |
| Tax law | 62 | (21) |
| Tenant-landlord matters | 60 | (5) |
| Real estate and construction | 58 | (12) |
| Traffic and personal injury | 50 | (32) |
| "Notariat" | 44 | (16) |
| "Civil law" [b] | 43 | (93) |
| Labor law | 38 | (8) |
| Criminal law | 38 | (21) |
| All lawyers in sample | 46 | (240) |

*Source:* "Ergebnisse der Befragung deutscher Juristen 1965" (MS), Forschungsinstitut für Soziologie of Cologne University, p. 3. Data from 240 replies in a mail survey of Wolfgang Kaupen addressed to a random sample of 632 lawyers.

[a] Figures in parentheses give the number of lawyers on which each percentage is based. These figures add to more than 240: several respondents indicated more than one field.

[b] "Zivilrecht," also referred to as "BGB" (initials for the civil code), is a broad category excluding business law and criminal law. It may be taken as indicating lack of specialization.

included syndic-attorneys who maintain an office on their own but work predominantly in salaried employment, the data exaggerate the degree of specialization in the German bar. It is likely that among the lawyers in independent practice a far smaller proportion work in the more lucrative fields, but those who do have an even better chance of earning a high income than indicated. What emerges, then, for the bar in private practice is a very small top group of attorneys who do real specialty work in corporate law. A somewhat broader group in less specialized business work is also highly successful in financial terms. The financial chances of general practitioners with little business work, more than 50 percent of those in independent practice, are considerably lower than those in the two top groups, but one has to keep in mind that no sharp specialty lines separate this group from the general practitioner who has predominantly business clients and indicates "commercial law" as his main field; the division is based on locality, stage in one's career, and access to clients of different types as much as on specialized competence. Several specialties fall between this large group of general practitioners and the top groups of business lawyers, and the category with the lowest chances for financial success is that of lawyers whose main field is the criminal law.

There is some evidence that this rank order of specialties in terms of income chances does not coincide with the rank order of prestige and attractiveness in the profession. Specialty work in the field of business law, followed by general business work, carries the highest prestige with most lawyers, too, but the general practitioner without a strong business practice is highly regarded at least in a large segment of the bar. Certain specialties which are moderately lucrative do not seem to be deemed particularly desirable; tenant-landlord matters and personal injury work may serve as examples. Finally, criminal law has a better overall standing than the financial status of its specialists would suggest.[87]

In assessing the nature of the prestige hierarchy of the German bar it is of paramount importance that no status group is stigmatized as "unprofessional," as characterized by widespread dishonesty and devious behavior toward colleagues, clients, or the judiciary. Even in the largest German cities, where there is a clearer distinction between a lower, a middle, and an elite stratum, the lowest positions are clearly seen as inside the professional community, and deviant behavior is basically viewed as unrelated to the structure of the bar—an individual phenomenon. The small size of most local bars in Germany, and by comparison with American metropolitan conditions of all bars, contributes notably to this end. Given the solid standing of general practice, the broadest stratum in all bars, the limited number of lawyers in any one community permits individual evaluations and judging a man on more subtle criteria than financial success, firm size, and specialty. Reliability, devotion to his work, legal competence, professional attitude, and honesty are likely to be taken into account, and opinions not relating to legal work at all will also enter such judgments. The effect of this is to reduce the tendency toward stereotypical prestige rankings hinged on a few visible criteria, and to prevent the crystallization of more sharply defined prestige strata.

It appears, however, that something more than such situational factors is involved in the contrasting character of the prestige hierarchies in the German and the American bar. The criteria determining the standing of an attorney, a specialty, or any subgroup in the profession seem to carry different weights in the German than in the American profession. It appears in particular that financial success is definitely less important for the professional standing of a German lawyer. Table 6 shows the rather drastic deemphasis of "external" rewards, of income and prestige, as well as the strong positive evaluation of professional craftsmanship. These findings cannot directly be compared to any research results in the United States,

TABLE 6. *Ranking of Rewards, Germany, 1965*.
"Which of these things should a person in your
professional position value higher? Please rank."

| Evaluated rewards | Percentage giving first rank | Percentage giving last rank | Percentage giving first minus percentage giving last rank |
|---|---|---|---|
| Objective recognition of work done | 40 | 6 | 34 |
| Fulfillment, personal satisfaction | 35 | 19 | 16 |
| Gratitude and trust | 20 | 28 | −8 |
| Income and reputation | 4 | 43 | −39 |
| | 99 (261) | 96 (261) | |

*Source:* "Ergebnisse der Befragung deutscher Juristen 1965" (MS), Forschungsinstitut für Soziologie of Cologne University, p. 2.

but there is little doubt that the pattern of value orientations in the American bar is considerably different.[88] Public references to any kind of invidious comparison—be it in terms of income, prestige, or even reputed competence—are not frequent in Germany and are frowned upon by many. According to Weyrauch, "The hearsay ratings of members of the bar, as shown in the Martindale-Hubbell Law Directory, are an American undertaking that would be hardly acceptable to lawyers in Europe."[89]

Finally, with fewer established firms dominating the market for legal services and with specialization less developed than in the American metropolitan bar, the chances of mobility into higher status practice seem to be greater for German than for American lawyers. Of course, in Germany too, career chances are influenced by social background. However, if such characteristics make a difference among German lawyers, too, it should be noted that the *Rechtsanwaltschaft* is less heterogeneous in its social origins than the American legal profession. Ethnic differences are negligible, and there are fewer attorneys from lower class backgrounds. Finally, in contrast to the United States, where legal education varies considerably in quality and prestige, all German lawyers have shared the same type of education: studies in the law division of a state university and an extended period of preparatory service.

To sum up, the metropolitan American bar is highly stratified. The different dimensions of rank and privilege—remuneration, prestige in the community, and moral and technical esteem in the profession—are closely linked. Mobility is at a relatively low level, and wide subjective social distances separate the different subgroups. This stratification reflects to a large extent the patterns of the wider society. Education and recruitment into different statuses in the bar vary with class and ethnic background, and the criteria of evaluation do not seem to be differentiated from those of the American middle and upper middle. In smaller cities, the internal stratification of the bar is considerably attenuated and its divisive effects are furthermore counteracted by the small size of the local bars.

Stratification in the German bar is more distinct from the stratification system of the wider society. Recruitment and education are homogeneous; professional esteem is less based on remuneration, or at least less directly so, and invidious comparisons are deemphasized generally. The lesser development of specialization and of large firms even under metropolitan conditions allows for more mobility within the bar. Finally, the number of attorneys in a local bar is virtually never large enough to encourage significantly the development of a rigid system of impersonally ranked subgroups separated by lack of interaction and stereotypical images of each other. Thus, an income distribution which nearly approaches the dispersion of income in the American profession does not result in as deep cleavages as are characteristic of the American metropolitan bar.

### BAR ASSOCIATIONS

A discussion of the social organization of private legal practice would not be complete without a consideration of bar associations. Following is a cursory review, designed to highlight some features of the associations of the bar which correspond to the contrasting social patterns discussed above. Generally, the German *Rechtsanwaltschaft* displays a far tighter organization than the American bar in private practice. The more complicated array of associations in the American case and the looser grip these have on the vast numbers of attorneys correspond to the greater diversity of the membership of the profession, to the heterogeneity of backgrounds, and to the deeper cleavages in its status structure. This looser pattern of organization appears to be both consequence and further cause of a comparatively weak sense of professional community. It also seems related to the lesser uniformity of government organization in the United States and to the weaker role of government in American society. Some of these background factors will be discussed in connection with the historical development of the two professions.

The German *Rechtsanwaltschaft* has its own distinct associations, while a general association for all lawyers does not exist in Germany.[90] All *Rechtsanwälte* are by virtue of their admission to practice members of *Rechtsanwaltskammern* established by law in the jurisdiction of all courts of appeal. The *Kammern* are institutions of public law and are subject to formal supervision by the state ministries of justice. At the same time, they are the officially instituted framework for the self-government of the profession. An elected board carries out the major functions. Among these are the duties to advise and supervise the members in matters of legal ethics and etiquette, to mediate in disputes between members as well as between attorneys and clients and to prepare opinions advising public administration in matters concerning the bar. Guidelines for professional behavior expressing the common opinion in the *Rechtsanwaltschaft* are established by the national federation of regional *Kammern*. The state ministries of justice appoint members of the courts enforcing legal ethics, which in the first instance are composed of *Rechtsanwälte*, while the two courts of appeal have a mixed bench of attorneys and regular judges. Proceedings are initiated and the case against the accused is conducted by the office of the prosecuting attorney. In appreciating these arrangements one has to remember that both judges and prosecuting attorneys are career civil servants who only in rare cases have been members of the bar in private practice. Control of professional behavior thus lies to an important extent in the hands of outsiders who represent the state rather than the professional community. In general, the *Kammer*-organization constitutes a compromise between state supervision and professional autonomy.[91]

Besides the *Rechtsanwaltskammern* there exists a voluntary association, the *Deutscher Anwaltverein*. More explicitly concerned with the pursuance of the interests of the profession, it devotes its energies to other matters, too; for instance, its committees prepare advisory opinions on pending legislation, whether directly related to the interest of the bar or not. Another field of activity is continuing legal education.

About two-thirds of all *Rechtsanwälte* are members of this association, which has local chapters in most important communities. Membership is somewhat higher in cities with a population of less than 500,000, among middle aged and older attorneys, and among those with a higher than average income.[92] It seems that these differences do not so much reflect cleavages of stratification but rather are accounted for by syndic-attorneys, who seem to belong far less often to the *Verein* than do regular attorneys. Office in either association is an honor of considerable repute. The comparatively close integration of the German *Rechtsanwaltschaft* through its associations is finally underlined by the limited size of the *Rechtsanwaltskammern*, which in 1960 varied from 100 to 2,300 members. The law empowers the state ministry of justice to divide a *Kammer* if more than 500 attorneys are admitted in its district.[93] This seems of some importance for the social control of professional behavior, since it increases the visibility of any one lawyer, while the role of the prosecuting attorney diminishes the leniency that may grow out of acquaintance and intimacy.

The American bar in private practice does not have a distinctive association of its own, but because of its size and the career structure of the other branches of the profession it dominates most associations. The American Bar Association as well as most bar associations on the state and local level are general organizations for all branches of the profession. On the other hand, there are a number of more specialized associations, such as the American College of Trial Lawyers or the Federal Bar Association, which comprises mainly employees of the federal government and lawyers practicing before federal agencies; and there are, as noted before, a considerable number of sections of the A.B.A. which are in effect sub-associations of lawyers with specialized interests.[94]

The American Bar Association claimed in 1965 a membership of more than a third of all lawyers and more than half of those actually engaged in law practice. It appears that the percentages are substantially lower in the larger cities and that membership is strongly related to status in practice.[95] The cleavages in the status structure of the bar are also, as noted above, reflected in membership in local bar associations. In some cities, different associations serve essentially different strata of the bar.

About half of the state bar associations are "integrated," with compulsory membership of all lawyers admitted in the states. However, only one-third of all lawyers practice in these states; such important states as New York, Illinois, and Massachusetts have voluntary bar associations only.[96] Even in reference to the integrated bars Corinne L. Gilb's general comment applies: "The renascence of professonalism for the American bar came, not as an outward flowering of the bar's growing cohesion, but rather as a weapon to counteract the bar's growing disunity. It arose out of a desire to restore traditional standards in the face of many hostile forces."[97] Both the integration movement and the resistance to it are in part based on considerations that refer to the same actual conditions. On the one side it is argued that integration gives a better chance to unify and to control the profession, on the other that the integrated bar cannot be more professional than the bulk of its members or, alternatively, that elite control is to be expected and that it is incompatible with compulsory membership in a highly differentiated and stratified profession.

National, state, and local associations as well as various specialty associations are interrelated in complicated ways which do not have to concern us here in detail. Neither does it seem necessary to discuss the various bar activities and policies which are basically similar to those of the German associations. The American Bar Association has formulated a code of professional ethics which serves as a guide for the regulations in most states.

Of particular interest in this comparison are the institutional arrangements for professional discipline, although here, too, a short description of the typical pattern has to suffice. Basically, the power to control and discipline the bar rests with the courts, usually the state supreme courts. Committees of the state or local bar associations investigate complaints, and often they are empowered to take evidence, to hold formal hearings, and to recommend action to the court.[98] The courts are often said to be more lenient than the association committees. Discipline of the profession seems to be somewhat more effective in states with integrated bar associations, although the evidence is not conclusive. Speaking generally and comparatively, a tendency toward leniency seems to prevail, and, according to one interpretation, "there seems little doubt that it is explained by the loose organization of the American legal profession and the complex social variety of its membership."[99]

The function of the regular courts in disciplinary proceedings may seem to indicate stronger outside control in the American than in the German case. Actually, the de facto role of the bar associations is at least as important as in Germany and it is a role free from administrative supervision; the prosecuting attorney's office is only rarely involved in disciplinary proceedings, and, again, the different relation between the bar in private practice and the judiciary gives a different meaning to the latter's part in professional discipline.

In conclusion, the professional associations of the American bar organize the profession less systematically and inclusively than the associations of the German *Rechtsanwaltschaft*. They seem to control professional behavior less effectively and have greater autonomy from governmental supervision. These differences in organizational patterns correspond to the general role of government in the two societies, to the larger size and the greater heterogeneity of the American bar, and to the sharper distinctions between the different branches of the German legal profession as well as to the differences in specialization and internal stratification of the bar in private practice. On the whole, the German bar in private practice comes closer to the model of a "professional community," although the higher degree of government supervision deviates from most formulations of that model.

# 3

# THE BAR AND ITS SUBCULTURE
# IN THE CONTEXT OF SOCIETY

This chapter will examine four interrelated aspects of German and American society as they bear upon the legal profession: (1) the distribution of income and prestige, (2) the structure of power and politics, (3) contrasting elements in the overall value patterns, and (4) the educational system. These analyses will provide a more detailed picture of the larger sociocultural contexts of the two bars and permit an assessment of the two professional subcultures. In the conception of "reference groups," modern sociology has developed a tool for the analysis of subjective orientations as they relate to social structures. The basic idea is that the development of attitudes and values is closely intertwined with and influenced by a person's relations to various social groupings seen as holding or rejecting a given set of orientations.[1]

## INCOME AND SOCIAL PRESTIGE OF THE BAR

While there are great individual differences, lawyers, like members of other professions, have on the average a relatively high income in both Germany and the United States. However, as Table 7 shows, German lawyers in private practice are considerably better off than their American colleagues when their incomes are compared to the average incomes of other professions and to those of workers in industry. In the early fifties German *Rechtsanwälte* had a higher average income than any other profession and earned nearly four and a half times as much as workers in in-

TABLE 7. *Average Annual Income of Lawyers in Private Practice and of Selected Other Occupations.*

A. Germany

| | 1954 | | 1961 | |
|---|---|---|---|---|
| | Income in DM 1,000 | Multiple of Workers' Income | Income in DM 1,000 | Multiple of Workers' Income |
| Attorneys | 18,3 | 4.4 | 38,0 | 5.5 |
| CPA's and tax consultants | 16,4 | 3.9 | 39,5 | 5.6 |
| Physicians | 18,2 | 4.3 | 40,3 | 5.7 |
| Dentists | 11,5 | 2.7 | 28,1 | 4.0 |
| Workers in industry | 4,2 | 1.0 | 7,0 | 1.0 |

B. United States

| | 1940 | | 1951 | | 1954 | |
|---|---|---|---|---|---|---|
| | Income in $1,000 | Multiple of Workers' Income | Income in $1,000 | Multiple of Workers' Income | Income in $1,000 | Multiple of Workers' Income |
| Attorneys | 4,5 | 3.5 | 8,7 | 2.6 | 10,3 | 2.8 |
| Physicians | 4,4 | 3.4 | 13,4 | 3.9 | — | — |
| Dentists | 3,3 | 2.5 | 7,8 | 2.3 | — | — |
| Production workers in manufacturing | 1,3 | 1.0 | 2,6 | 1.0 | 3,4 | 1.0 |

*Sources*: Germany 1954: Bundesminister für Wirtschaft, *Bericht über die Lage der Mittelschichten*, Deutscher Bundestag 3. Wahlperiode, Drucksache 2012, 1960, p. 122; Statistisches Bundesamt, *Statistisches Jahrbuch für die Bundesrepublik Deutschland* (Stuttgart, 1955), p. 469. Germany 1961: "Die Anwaltschaft in der Statistik," *Anwaltsblatt*, 16:56 (1966); Statistisches Bundesamt, *Statistisches Jahrbuch für die Bundesrepublik Deutschland* (Stuttgart, 1964), p. 497. United States, income of professionals: Albert P. Blaustein and Charles O. Porter, *The American Lawyer*, p. 15; Maurice Liebenberg, "Income of Lawyers in the Postwar Period," *Survey of Current Business*, December 1956, p. 27, table 1. United States, incomes of production workers: U.S. Bureau of the Census, *Statistical Abstract of the United States*: 1955 (Washington, D.C., 1955), p. 211.[2]

dustry. Between 1954 and 1961 their income more than doubled, and while they have lost, by a small margin, the lead position among the professions, their income in 1961 was on the average five and a half times that of industrial workers. American attorneys earned in the early fifties only two-thirds of the compensation of physicians, while ten years before they still had a slight lead over the medical profession. In comparison to industrial workers' incomes, American professionals in general earn less than their German counterparts. Lawyers in particular had in the 1950's an average income which was less than three times as much as the income of production workers in manufacturing. In the respective economic stratification systems, then, German *Rechtsanwälte* rank considerably higher than American lawyers in private practice.[2]

Lawyers rank high in prestige in both countries. In the United States they rank with architects and dentists behind doctors and college professors; their standing is similar to that of bankers, members of the board of directors of large corporations, and owners of medium-sized factories. For Germany, the prestige rank of lawyers in private practice has not been directly ascertained. From what is known about closely related positions, their standing appears to be similar to that of lawyers in the United States, the main determinant being in both cases their accepted status as a liberal profession.[3]

The position of lawyers in a *rank order* of prestige does not, however, tell the whole story that is of interest here. There are indications that qualitative differences between the two status systems are of great importance for the place of lawyers in the two societies. It appears that the German prestige structure contains much stronger "ascriptive" elements.[4] This does not only mean that a man's lifetime status is in larger measure determined by his status at birth; it means that an acquired status such as membership in a learned profession tends to assume the character of an ascribed quality, somewhat independent of continued performance. A person who has become a member of a profession in Germany will gain more prestige, more deference, and more trust from that fact alone, independent of his personal success, than his American colleague.

This greater emphasis on ascription in German social culture seems to be in part a consequence of Germany's feudal past and of the peculiar combinations of modern and traditional features which German society has retained long after full-scale industrialization. That ascriptive tendencies have become progressively weaker does not make them irrelevant. Observers as different in theoretical perspective as Talcott Parsons, Ralf Dahrendorf, and Erwin Scheuch agree on their continued salience for the German status structure. Parsons formulates the aspect I have in mind most precisely when he argues that the societal value orientations he sees as characteristic for Germany create a "tendency to ascribe qualities to the whole group to which an individual belongs" in contrast to a dominant emphasis on differential individual achievement.[5] One example of this tendency was noted in the previous chapter, namely, the disdain of German lawyers for the public invidious comparisons which are commonplace in the American bar.

Collective prestige is especially high for university-trained professionals in Germany. While their place in the rank order is similar in the United States and in Germany, the subjective distance to the ranks of other occupations is not necessarily the same; and although no precise measure of these social distances exists, it seems safe to assume that a university education in Germany creates a greater social distance than study at a professional school in the United States.

Two considerations are pertinent here. First, a much smaller proportion of Germans than of Americans reaches higher education of any kind. The proportion of high school graduates of the German population is smaller than the proportion of Americans who graduate from college.[6] In Germany the sphere of education is marked by stronger inequalities than many other dimensions of the stratification system, while the much more inclusive and still rapidly expanding American system of education has been judged as "probably the most important single factor in creating the American feeling that social-class differences are not very important".[7]

The second consideration appears to be of nearly equal importance for the social distances created by education. The American educational system exhibits many more graduations, a fact which makes a given educational achievement less distinctive and less readily recognized. On any level—high school, college, and postgraduate study—American institutions of learning vary considerably in quality, and, furthermore, the broad college level stands between high school education and graduate or professional studies. By contrast, this middle level between high school and professional university studies is lacking in Germany and—at least by reputation—most institutions of learning are fairly similar in quality. University-educated people in Germany, then, are seen as a rather homogeneous social category, and they are distinctly set off against the next category of high school graduates.

These latter differences between the two educational systems support the stronger emphasis on ascription in German social culture. The greater homogeneity of the different levels of education in Germany makes evaluation on the basis of academic attainment and of membership in a profession more realistic, while the qualitative diversity of the American system of education inhibits ascriptive imputations around the mere fact of a certain level of higher education.

What inferences can be drawn from these contrasting conditions in wealth and prestige about the reference group orientations of lawyers in the two countries? Which social groupings provide guideposts for judgment and attitude, and how strong are the identifications with these reference groups? Given its higher relative income and a prestige position which probably establishes a greater social distance from most of the population, the German bar is likely to be a more influential reference group for its members than the bar in the United States is for American attorneys. Furthermore, in Germany membership in a profession as such, independent of individual success, gives—at least in many social contexts —greater prestige than in the United States to its members.

While education is a crucial determinant of prestige in both countries, the greater homogeneity and the lesser accessibility of higher education in Germany make the social categories of people with whom this education is shared more likely and more forceful reference groups. For German attorneys in private practice, university-trained lawyers in general (*Juristen*) and all university graduates (*Akademiker*) are therefore probably important reference groups. American lawyers do have similar reference groups, the legal profession at large and the whole family of the professions; but these categories are fragmented in terms of their educational qualifications, and educational categories are less visible and constitute less forceful reference groups in the large number of cases where college and professional education was received at less distinguished schools.

These hypotheses have important implications for the relations of attorneys to their clients. The clientele of a lawyer always constitutes an important reference group because it stands in direct interaction with the legal practitioner and because it wields some measure of sanctioning power. The impact of this reference group appears to be counterbalanced to a greater extent in Germany by the conditions noted above. The presumed stronger identification of the *Rechtsanwalt* with his own profession and with the broader community of university-trained professionals limits his assimilation into the business culture represented by the majority or at least a sizeable minority of clients. Furthermore, the superiority in economic position which the German *Rechtsanwalt* enjoys relative to a larger part of his clientele in comparison to his American colleague, as well as the greater social distance created by the nature of the German status structure, limit his susceptibility to the value orientations of a different, though overlapping segment of his clientele.

This "protection" of the German *Rechtsanwalt* may finally be reinforced by a phenomenon which has not been documented through systematic research but has been noticed and commented upon by numerous observers. It appears that in Germany contacts with others in a professional capacity tend to be more specific, more limited to the business at hand than in the United States. This pattern inhibits the development of the quasi-friendships which are said to be characteristic of professional and business associations of some duration in the United States. Such specificity should considerably reduce the chances of intentional or unintentional influence of a client on the attorney's behavior and especially on his basic professional orientations.[8]

## LAWYERS IN THE POWER STRUCTURE

The nature of power, the ways in which it is exercised in modern societies, and its distribution among different groups and strata in the two countries being considered are problems on which there is little agreement in modern sociology.[9] Neither the theoretical nor all the empirical issues under debate need to be considered in any detail. The main question here is whether American and German lawyers have a different place in the structures and processes of power in the two countries.

Of all the professions the legal profession is most likely to participate in the exercise of power in any modern society. Its very professional competence concerns the norms which define positions of authority, prescribe and proscribe various types of behavior, and regulate the conditions under which the might of the government can be invoked in solving disputes. Every modern society has an elaborate system of such norms which has to be articulated and interrelated for a large number of typical situations, and it has to be continuously developed so that new types of situations are covered without seriously disturbing old patterns. The need for interpretation and the inevitable, if mostly infinitesimal innovation in the legal order through interpretation and adjudication means that lawyers "make a difference": a system of general legal norms can never be fully determinate with regard to all situations which it is supposed to regulate.

Power can, of course, be exercised outside or even against the institutional structure of authority and legal norms. However, in most typical situations in modern societies the stability of power relationships and their smooth functioning are enhanced if they are well integrated with the framework of legal norms and agencies or at least hedged against interference by parties which have the backing of the legal order.

Legal advice and advocacy form the core of the lawyer's service to the incumbents of positions of power as well as the basis of his participation in power processes. However, the lawyer's role will often broaden beyond his sphere of immediate technical competence. Legal counsel of policy-makers is likely to acquire organizational and interpersonal knowledge and skills which enlarge his opportunities for influence. Being simultaneously a spokesman for "the law" as a cultural tradition and as a system of values as well as for particular interests and power positions, the lawyer is often in a position to gain broader assent to the actions and policies of his client, to gain, in other words, "legitimacy" beyond mere legality; this, too, will increase his importance in the development and the exercise of power. If for such reasons counsel takes a particularly crucial place in the staff of policy-makers of all kinds—in corporations, trade associations, unions, government departments, and legislative bodies—he will, finally, also have a good chance to be recruited out of his staff role into decision-making positions. From these general considerations one would expect a disproportionately large number of lawyers in the power elites of both countries, and this is what we find.

### LAWYERS IN JUDICIAL OFFICE

That lawyers in both countries have a monopoly on judicial positions and enjoy a high degree of autonomy in these positions is a trivial observation, but one which is of great importance for the aggregate share lawyers have in the exercise of power. Judicial autonomy appears to rest in part on the belief that adjudication is basically an application of existing rules and that therefore the policy-making opportunities of the judiciary are rather limited. Judicial autonomy is further buttressed by the fact that it appears in some measure indispensable for dispute solution between parties which are in principle equal in standing and rights. Finally, with increasing complexity of the system of legal rules and a persistent moral authority of "the law," open and continuous interference with judicial decision-making by outside lay parties has become intolerable in modern societies, since it would seriously disturb the predictable functioning of the legal system, a matter of practical as well as intense moral concern.[10]

While all these elements contribute to the legitimation of judicial independence in both countries, their relative weight differs. In the United States, the requirements of dispute solution have been a specially salient consideration through various political periods. The fact that the government, more precisely its executive and administrative branch, was never seen as standing as radically "above" the partisan disputes of "private" parties as in Germany goes far to explain the greater organizational differentiation of the American courts from other governmental agencies. Election and political appointment of judges match in the United States the more open acknowledgment of opportunities for policy decisions in the application of legal rules, a greater distrust of the proclaimed impartiality of judges, and a lesser reliance on a professional ethos which at the same time asserts prerogatives such as professional autonomy.[11]

By contrast, the autonomy of the German judge is more strongly based on the postulate of a virtually complete system of legal norms anticipating most possible cases and on the respect for presumably impartial learned professionals devoted to the common good. This respect is not impaired—if anything it is reinforced—by the fact that these professionals are civil servants, since a commitment to the interests of "the state" is not seen as prejudicial to the impartiality of magistrates. This at least has been the dominant position in the past when a government run by a corps of professional civil servants and subject to weak popular controls defined itself as the guardian of the common good above the partial and conflicting interests; and such notions continue to have wide currency in many quarters.[12] An institutional expression of this trust in professional civil service judges is the dominant role allocated to the judiciary in German procedure.

Precisely because, and to the extent which, judicial decisions involve policy decisions, some integration with the political process should be expected. The openly political recruitment of American judges from the practicing bar ensures a fair measure of responsiveness to a broad, if by no means inclusive spectrum of political demands, although the processes involved are very complex and sharp tensions occur with some frequency.

The German judiciary is subject to similar but less manifest controls. German judges are career civil servants with life tenure. Their appointment and promotion are open to some direct political influence, but what seems more important is the control of a nucleus of senior judges and higher administrative lawyers in the departments of justice, the presidents of courts being not infrequently drawn from administrative positions.[13] By and large political influence on recruitment and promotion of German judges appears to be mediated through the administrative bureaucracies.

The organizational situation of German judges tends to segregate them from political process. Their relatively insulated subculture appears to explain why the radical constitutional changes in 1918-19, in 1933 and in 1945-49 were taken with relative equanimity. It also may be one major factor in the changing patterns of reserve, hostility, or loyalty shown by judges during different phases in German political history. "The German judge . . . was the more loyal to the law, the more authoritarian the constitution of the German state; to the degree in which the country became more democratic, the binding validity of the law became problematic for the judge," is the conclusion of one study of this subject.[14] There is little doubt that such authoritarian reserve and hostility toward the democratic

70

process is weaker today than it was during the Weimar Republic. There is considerable doubt, however, whether it has been replaced by stable commitments to a democratic framework for the struggle of political forces.

### LAWYERS IN POLITICS

The prominence of American lawyers in politics is proverbial. The list of percentages is familiar from presidential addresses at bar meetings and from numerous writings on the legal profession: Nearly half of the signers of the Declaration of Independence and more than one out of two members of the Constitutional Convention were lawyers. Nearly two-thirds of all presidents and a higher proportion, at least in recent decades, of vice presidents and cabinet members came from the bar, and so did nearly every other state governor between 1870 and 1950. In the legislatures, lawyers have held similar proportions of all seats. In the United States Senate the percentage has varied from 55 to 75 in recent decades, in the House of Representatives from 50 to 65, and among state legislators a quarter has been a typical average proportion, covering considerable variations from state to state.[15]

In Germany, lawyers are also overrepresented among the incumbents of both executive and legislative political positions, whether their numbers are compared with their share in the total labor force or with the size of the legal profession relative to other upper middle class occupations. However, their proportion is considerably lower than in the United States. Characteristically, it is highest in executive political positions. Somewhat less than half of the ministers in federal cabinets from 1949 to 1963 have been lawyers, with a higher proportion for secretaries of ministerial departments (58 percent in 1955) and a slightly lower one for prime ministers of state governments (40 percent in 1955).[16] Among German legislators, the proportion of lawyers is considerably lower. In the *Bundestag*, the lower house of parliament in the Federal Republic, the figure was 15 to 16 percent (1963), and among state legislators about every eighth was a lawyer in 1960.[17] In the legislative branches of government, then, the share of German lawyers was less than half that of members of the American legal profession.

Most important for an explanation of these differences appear to be two major factors. First, elections and political appointments as modes of recruitment for various legal offices, of which those of judge and public prosecutor are the most important, bring a larger part of the legal profession into contact with party politics in the United States than in Germany. Second, the facts that in Germany the Social Democratic Party and to a certain extent even the Christian Democratic Party have close organizational ties with unions and other working class associations and that voting is to a larger extent based on class position than in the United States limits the chances of lawyers to become candidates and to be elected. Conversely, where, as in the United States, no party is uniquely identified with working class associations and where voting is as much based on regional, ethnic, and religious loyalties as on class loyalties, the chances of lawyers to become political representatives are considerably higher. Both factors have, furthermore, reinforcing secondary effects. First, political connections are the more important for lawyers in general the more offices crucial for their work are involved in politics.[18] Second, if in a party or a whole country lawyers have held political mandates in large proportion over a long period of time, party officials and the electorate may come to consider lawyers as natural candidates for political office and a number of persons will enter legal studies with a political career in mind.[19]

The two major factors proposed in this explanation deserve some further consideration. A large proportion of American lawyer politicians have held law enforcement offices at some time during their career. Joseph A. Schlesinger concludes from a study of state governors: "It would appear that for these lawyer governors the law enforcement position rather than their occupation was the significant factor in their advancement to the governorship."[20] Popular election of law enforcement officers involves, of course, many more lawyers in politics than just those who succeeded in attaining prominent political positions. By contrast, German law enforcement officers are not particularly prominent in politics. Less than 5 percent of the lawyer politicians in the federal parliament were judges in 1960, and members of the *Justizdienst* (judges and district attorneys) tend to be less frequently members of political parties than do lawyers in private practice.[21]

The other main explanation of the different proportion of lawyers among political office-holders in the two countries involves the willingness of the electorate to vote for lawyers and the readiness of party organizations to nominate lawyers, considering in both respects the availability of alternative suitable personnel. The chances of lawyers to attain political office seem lowest (1) where voting is strongly based on class position, (2) where leftist parties take a large part of the vote, (3) where leftist parties have a developed organizational apparatus and/or are closely linked to unions and other labor associations with such an organization, and (4) where lawyers—because of their education, profession, and clientele—are viewed as a conservative group. In regard to this hypothesis, an admittedly limited comparison of the four major English-speaking democracies reveals interesting patterns. The contrast between the United States and Canada on the one side and Great Britain and Australia on the other is clear-cut as far as type of major "left" party, index of class voting, per-

TABLE 8. *Lawyers in National Parliaments and Related Indices for the Four Major English-Speaking Democracies.*

| Country | Lawyers in national parliament, (percent) | Character of major "left" party [a] | Index of class voting [b] | Working-class legislators, (percent) [c] | Estimated rank in terms of "elitist values" [d] |
|---|---|---|---|---|---|
| United States | 50-65 [e] | center-left | t  16 | 3 | 3 |
| Canada | appr. 33 [f] | center-left | 8 | 1 | 2 |
| Great Britain | 15-20 [g] | social democratic | 40 | 19 | 1 |
| Australia | 12 [h] | social democratic | 33 | 19 | 4 |

[a] For the characterization of the political parties in these four countries see Robert R. Alford, *Party and Society: The Anglo-American Democracies* (Chicago, Rand McNally, 1963), pp. 11-17.

[b] This index is arrived at by subtracting the percentage of nonmanual workers voting for "left" parties from the percentage of manual workers voting for "left" parties; Alford, *Party and Society*, pp. 79, 86, and 102. The figures are based on several polls in each country between 1952 and 1962.

[c] See Alford, *Party and Society*, p. 98.

[d] These estimates are Seymour M. Lipset's; see *The First New Nation* (New York, 1963), p. 249.

[e] House of Representatives, see note 15.

[f] House of Commons in 1945, similar percentages in the 1930's, higher ones in the first two decades of the century; see Norman Ward, *The Canadian House of Commons* (Toronto, 1950), pp. 56, 132, 135.

[g] Depending on definition of lawyer, the percentage has varied since 1918 from a low of 13 percent to a maximum of 23 percent; see J. F. S. Ross, *Parliamentary Representation* (London, 1948), pp. 77, 271; also the comparative table in G. Loewenberg, *Parliament in the German Political System*, p. 109.

[h] See W. Farmer Whyte, ed., *The Australian Parliamentary Handbook* (Sydney, 1952), pp. 252-300, for data on the House of Representatives and the Senate.

centage of working class legislators and percentage of lawyer legislators are concerned, and it is consonant with the hypothesis advanced. The interpretation is reinforced by the fact that in Great Britain and Australia it is the labor parties which have the fewest lawyer legislators while in the United States and Canada the percentages are similar in both major parties or even higher in the "center-left" parties. The smaller differences between the two countries on each side of this contrast are inconsistent with this hypothesis. The lower proportion of lawyers among Canadian legislators than among American legislators is most likely due to the fact that judiciary positions are not filled by popular election.[22] As to the other two countries, although the estimate of differences in elitist orientations given in Table 8 is based on rather impressionistic evidence, the greater role of deference toward established status groups in Great Britain may well be the major distinguishing factor between Australia and the United Kingdom.[23]

The proportion of lawyer legislators in Germany is very similar to that in Great Britain—between 15 and maximally 22 percent, depending on the definition of lawyer used; and with regard to all other characteristics used in Table 8 Germany also resembled Great Britain more closely than any of the other countries.[24] As far as this limited comparison goes, then, the data support the hypothesis advanced.

How many lawyer politicians are or have been private practitioners? The question is difficult to answer because the distinction between private practice and other branches of the legal profession is more fluid in the United States than in Germany. In the German federal parliament 7 to 9 percent of all members have been *Rechtsanwälte* in recent years.[25] While German private practitioners are thus more strongly represented than any other subgroup of the legal profession, their proportion among legislators is still far lower than that of their American colleagues. For the United States, it can be argued that virtually all lawyer legislators are in some sense private practitioners; a large majority have been in private practice at one time in their careers, and a return to private practice is a realistic possibility for a still larger proportion. If a third is subtracted from the number of lawyer legislators as having no private law experience for all practical purposes, American attorneys in private practice still hold four to six times as large a share of the seats in Congress as their German counterparts have in the *Bundestag*. With the same reasoning the percentage of private practitioners in American state legislatures may be estimated at 15 to 20, while German *Rechtsanwälte* have held between 5 and 7 percent of the seats in the *Landtage*. For city councils, I do not know of any comprehensive American statistics. In Germany, the share of *Rechtsanwälte* averaged here 1.6 percent in 1957, decreasing with the size of the community.[26]

The political involvement of the average American private practitioner, largely concentrated at the local level, is vastly greater than that of the German *Rechtsanwalt*. It is grounded in an intense participation in civic associations and other voluntary organizations. Wardwell and Wood have argued that such civic and political participation is part of the "extra-professional role of the lawyer" in America. Not among his specific technical obligations, it is nevertheless strongly encouraged as befitting a lawyer.[27] The level and the character of this involvement vary with region, size of the community, and position of a lawyer in the stratification system of the bar. Generally, activity in community affairs is most common among lawyers in small communities, but even in large cities a substantial proportion is active.[28] Individual practitioners tend to be more active in local politics and less active in nonpolitical associations than partners in well-established firms; "some nonpolitical associations . . . demand high social qualifications," while politics is an area open to the socially not distinguished man. Conversely, established lawyers prefer to maintain worthwhile contacts and to fulfill their obligations of "community service" in nonpolitical clubs and associations, "since politics is often distasteful or closed to them." The lowest level of participation in either political or nonpolitical associations is found among associates employed in law firms.[29] The very top of the American bar has been quite considerably engaged in political life, but its participation was characteristically through high appointive office rather than through involvement at the local level and in electoral politics.[30]

German lawyers in private practice appear on the average to be less active in politics than even the least involved segments of the American bar. Although far more active than the average citizen, they do not seem to surpass the general level of political participation as much as their American colleagues do.[31] Data from one local survey suggest, furthermore, that the participation of German attorneys in other voluntary associations is somewhat less common and intense than that of their American colleagues and that especially their involvement in community service organizations is less strong.[32] At all levels, then, the German private practitioner, while surpassing other categories of *Juristen*, is less often found in elective office than his American colleague, is less involved in grass-roots party politics, and also seems to participate less in voluntary associations with varying relations to political life.

### LAWYERS IN PUBLIC ADMINISTRATION

The role of lawyers in the third, the administrative branch of government, can be treated more concisely. Public administration has gained in importance and power with the tremendous increase in range and complexity of government services characteristic of all advanced industrial societies. This gain has been modified but not eliminated by constitutional arrangements which explicitly subordinate administrative bureaucracies to legislative bodies and elected executive officials. While these generalizations hold true for both Germany and the United States, there is little doubt that public administration plays a greater and more autonomous role in the structure and the processes of power in Germany than in the

United States. This appears primarily to be due to three major conditions: (1) the historical background and resulting traditions, (2) the character of the civil service and the internal organization of public administration, and (3) differences in volume of government activity relative to the size of population and economy.

Popular control of public administration through elected officers and legislative bodies was firmly established in the United States long before the modern expansion of government services. In Germany it was not until 1919 that it became similarly strong and the autonomy and influence which administrative elites had enjoyed in the last decades of the Empire were reestablished in the Weimar Republic, when democratic politics did not result in stable coalitions capable of mobilizing and sustaining support for decisive policies. Generally, the German civil service was least influential when political decision-making was in the hands of leaders who enjoyed strong popular support but were subject to little or no control by elected officials. The names of Bismarck and Hitler indicate the two major constellations of this kind. The strong leadership of Adenauer, based on the electoral success of the Christian Democratic Party, may have opened a period of effective control by democratic political elites.[33]

The historical background also accounts for major differences in the internal structure and subculture of government administration in the two countries. Very briefly, German public administration appears to have a more streamlined organization, especially as far as interagency relations are concerned, and it has a body of higher civil servants which is more homogeneous in social background, training, career patterns, and broad ideological orientation. Shared ideological orientations are particularly important for the kind of power that is in question here: power not so much of individuals, but of organizations. According to Deutsch and Edinger, "By tradition and training, [German administrators] were imbued with the image of the civil and military services as the politically neutral guardians of the 'national interest,' the defenders of the state against 'selfish' interests of political factions and pressure groups."[34] These orientations have no doubt been diluted and diversified in recent decades. The experience with the Nazi regime, which many misjudged as a modern restoration of older authoritarian patterns, the limited purges of nazification and denazification, the increase in the proportion of Social Democrats, and the differentiation of agencies all have contributed to this effect. Nevertheless, in attentuated and less self-confident forms the old ideological syndrome survives.

Finally, differences in the volume of government activity should be considered when the place of public administration in larger society is

TABLE 9. *Government Revenues and Expenditures*
*as Percentage of Gross National Product.*

| 1. General government [a], 1959 | Revenues | Expenditures |
|---|---|---|
| West Germany | 36.4 | 30.1 |
| United States | 25.3 | 23.8 |
| 2. Expenditure on defense, 1961 | | |
| West Germany | | 3.8 |
| United States | | 9.6 |
| 3. General Government, social security and public enterprises, 1959 | | |
| West Germany | 41.3 | 38.8 |
| United States | 27.4 | 27.9 |

*Source*: Bruce M. Russet et al., *World Handbook of Political and Social Indicators* (New Haven, Conn., 1964), p. 58, 59 (1.), p. 79 (2.), p. 63 (3.).
[a] ''General government'' includes the national, state, and federal levels.

discussed. Table 9 presents some global indicators. Both social security institutions and public enterprises play a larger role in Germany, but even without these funds and in spite of the higher defense expenditures in the United States, the relative size of German government transactions surpasses that of American government activities considerably.

Lawyers dominate in the general administrative positions of the German higher civil service, while they constitute only a minority among the higher civil servants in the United States. American lawyers in public administration are, more than their nonlegal colleagues and more than German lawyer administrators, involved in the political process.[35] The relations of administrative lawyers to the bar at large, especially to lawyers in private practice, are relatively close in the American case and rather tenuous in Germany. American government lawyers more often work as legal experts, not infrequently consider the government as their ''client,'' and are far more likely than their German colleagues to go into private practice after some years in government service. Many of them are thus a part of the bar at large in a sense in which the largest number of German administrative lawyers definitely are not. According to Bader: ''Of all the branches of the legal profession, administrative lawyers have without doubt done least for the unity of the profession. Most of them forgot as soon as possible that they were lawyers 'by origin,' so as to cope even with those problems in a pragmatic framework of expediency [Zweck-mässigkeitserwägungen] which could not be solved in any but a legal manner.''[36]

## LAWYERS IN THE BUSINESS ELITE

The role of lawyers in the exercise of power cannot be gauged by looking only at the three branches of government, that is, at the formal organization of collective decision-making at the national, regional, and local levels. Although neither available evidence nor space permits a detailed assessment of the part lawyers play in the patterns of informal influence and power, some comments on business elites will give a partial insight into these matters. Large business corporations have a crucial, if not *the* crucial influence on societal policy formation outside the formal institutional framework in both countries. Aside from their function as legal counsel, which in itself is of considerable importance, but does not concern us here, what role do lawyers play in business corporations? In both cases, the proportion of lawyers among business executives—about 6 percent in the United States and 6 to 8 percent in Germany—is fairly low compared to their role in government bureaucracies. This proportion, however, increases considerably when executives of the largest firms only are considered. Two roughly comparable studies found that 15 percent of American business leaders in this category and 21 percent of their German counterparts were lawyers.[37] These proportions have not remained constant over time. In a crude way, the variations in the occupational composition of the business leadership seem to reflect the dominant problems corporations encounter in society as well as trends in organizational complexity, technology, and the educational system.[38] If in both countries a slight overall decline can be noticed, the increasing competition from other, newly professionalized occupations like business administration and engineering appears to be the most likely explanation, a factor which is counterbalanced to some extent by the continued growth of government regulation and intervention.

It is difficult to say what kinds of lawyers these lawyer executives are. A few estimates can be made, however. First, some proportion of the German lawyer executives are lawyers by professional education only, so that the share of lawyers by professional experience is likely to be more similar in the two countries than the available data show;[39] it may actually be lower in Germany than in the United States. Second, the percentage of those who at one point in their careers have been in private practice appears to be higher in the United States than in Germany, especially if only executive positions are considered and supervisory officers are excluded. The proportion of lawyers in the latter is particularly high, and we may assume that in both countries it is here that private practitioners are concentrated.[40] Third, a considerable proportion—possibly well over one-third—of both executive and supervisory lawyer businessmen in large German firms are government lawyers by primary occupational experience—a reflection of the much greater involvement of government, local as well as state and federal, in the German economy.[41]

Business associations are crucial for the exercise of power through welding the interests of different firms and branches together, establishing coalitions with other aggregate interest groups, and influencing the governmental process in all its branches. The extent of this influence of private pressure groups on the political process in different countries and the relative strength of business interests compared to other pressure groups and to political parties is a matter of debate. While it seems likely that both the judiciary and the civil service are by virtue of tradition and organization in Germany less open to outside pressure than in the United States, it may well be that the greater publicity and the greater acceptance of pressure group activities in the United States create an exaggerated picture of their power. In any case, there is some agreement among experienced observers that the *associations* of business are in a stronger position in contemporary Germany than in the United States.[42]

There is little doubt that in both countries the staff of these associations includes a considerable number of lawyers, although no precise data are available. The same is true for the overlapping group of people who act as intermediaries between political institutions and business firms and associations, whether they are employed or retained as outside agents for the special purpose.[43] It is likely that these groups are more closely linked to the practicing profession than the previous category of lawyer businessmen. In Germany, many of the syndic attorneys are found in these positions, and the legal departments of various trade associations cooperate closely with house counsel of affiliated firms.

Although the role of the legal profession in the structures and processes of power does not easily fit into one coherent picture, some general conclusions may be drawn. A few observations on the power elites and the character of politics in the two countries will provide the background for the major differences noted in the role of the two professions and their subgroups.

Both countries lack a socially homogeneous, established elite. Rather, in both we find a number of elites in various institutional and functional spheres which differ in social character, characteristic political orientations, and dominant interests. None of these elites dominates all others so much that it can be characterized as *the* power elite.[44] A major difference in the character of the two polities concerns the handling of antagonisms. In the United States, special interests are asserted more openly and with more self-confidence and conflicts are acted out with considerable vigor, while members of the German elites, in the opinion of one analyst, at least, "lack the confidence needed for leadership and conflict"; Dahrendorf characterizes their mutual relations as a "cartel of anxiety." While I tend to concur with this judgment, I disagree with Dahrendorf's explanation, which simply points to the social heterogeneity and lack of social cohesion of the German elites. These are supposed to undermine "that self-confidence which is a necessary condition of lively competition."[45] Such an explanation may have a certain plausibility when German social structure is compared with British conditions; it falls flat when the case of the United States is considered. A more adequate explanation must take into account historical aspects of societal power which are relevant for the part played by the legal profession in them.

There is first the obvious contrast in the constitutional history of the two countries, with a competitive framework for the political process institutionalized for generations in the one case, and a shift from a highly monopolistic framework to a competitive one by legislative fiat, followed by a breakdown of the latter, a totalitarian regime, and a reestablishment of a still recent competitive pattern in the other case. Put in sociological rather than historical terms, this means that in the United States expression of conflict and competitive politics has a more stable basis in shared ultimate value orientations which are anchored in such institutions as the systems of liberal education, the framework of the common law and autonomous courts, and traditions of an aggressively autonomous press. In addition, it appears that social and political conflicts, with the exception of racial conflicts, are less polarized in the United States because of a greater degree of overlapping interests and group solidarities. Open expression of conflict and assertion of particular interests thus have been less disruptive of a societal solidarity the definition of which is in turn bound up with shared values.

The historical background also gives a second major clue to a comparative analysis of the power structure in the two societies. If we go back two generations, it seems fairly clear that business and its allies were dominant in American society with government administration in a relatively weak and decidedly instrumental role, while Germany—Imperial Germany, that is—was dominated by a "troika" of administrative elites, traditional aristocratic groups and business elites, the latter having the most precarious support from dominant value orientations. Both societies have undergone far-reaching changes in converging directions, but in both cases the older patterns of power and legitimation have significant aftereffects. Considerable strains are associated with the rise in importance of national government administration in America and of the business community in Germany.[46] In both countries, the older dominant groups—business in America and administrative elites in Germany—still derive a particular strength from long-standing legitimation and from their organizational advantages in successive phases of the long-run change. They have "infiltrated" the more recent nuclei of power, shaped the mode of organization of the latter, and colored their dominant outlook and orientations. Since competitive politics, assertive leadership, and open, if regulated conflict are more congenial to business elites than to civil service elites, this legacy of the past, too, is a factor contributing to the contrast under discussion.

Lawyers constitute a considerable minority in the power elites of both countries, whether formal position or reputed influence is taken as an indicator of "membership," and their share is high on the national as well as on the regional and local levels. But this similarity conceals differences in the kinds of positions held with particular frequency by lawyers and differences in the types of legal careers that lead to these positions. It is here that the above discussion of certain general aspects of the two power structures becomes relevant; the role of the legal profession exemplifies in prototypical manner the major contrasts noted.

American lawyers are strongest in those parts of the power structure where positions are reached through involvement in party politics and, at least in theory, open competition: in the legislatures, in party offices, in community associations indirectly related to politics. Judicial and prosecuting offices, by their nature a preserve of lawyers, are filled in close and unconcealed connection with party politics. German lawyers are strongest in elite positions which are reached through bureaucratic careers, that is, in the higher civil service. Judges and public prosecutors are tenured government officials in separate bureaucracies, and the major link of the administration of justice to the rest of the political system is through government administration rather than through political parties and electoral politics. The basic tendencies in the two countries can be discerned even among the incumbents of the respective "nontypical" positions. Many of the American lawyer administrators reached their positions "politically": their appointments are part of the complex network of political debts which links party structures, legislators, and administrative units. In turn, a considerable minority of German lawyer legislators are tenured civil servants.[47] It is probable that similar differences exist between American and German lawyers who hold top positions in business firms and associations.

These differences mean at the same time that German private practitioners are less strongly represented in the various power elites than their American counterparts. Although their share in the legislatures is considerable and exceeds that of any other branch of the legal profession, it is far lower than in the United States. In addition, they are not a significant source of recruitment for positions in government administration and the courts. Even in leading business positions their role seems weaker than that of their American colleagues if supervisory roles with superficial involvement in the conduct of corporations are excepted and if permanently employed house counsel is considered separately. Finally, participation and influence in community affairs, whether through parties or voluntary associations, is at a substantially lower level. In sum, German *Rechtsanwälte* stand more aloof from the political process in all its ramifications and exercise less influence than American private practitioners.

In considering some implications of these different involvements in structures and processes of power for modal attitudes and value orientations within the two professions, we will focus again on the reference group behavior of lawyers in private practice.

The much greater participation of American lawyers in civic affairs and politics is likely to make them more responsive to a variety of interests and orientations and to "public opinion." These reference group orientations should have divisive effects for the American bar, since constituencies as well as motives and modes of political and civic participation vary for the different segments and strata of the profession. Political and community involvements thus seem to contribute to a lesser sense of a distinctive and cohesive professional community.

One might infer a counterinfluence from the fact that American lawyers can take pride in the considerable number of members of the bar who have attained, in the past as well as today, positions of power and nationwide eminence. Certain power positions are too well concealed from public view and contemporary leadership in public life is often too much involved in issues over which the bar is divided to have such a unifying effect. However, the American bar does derive a measure of collective pride and prestige from the fact that judges, including many outstanding judges in appellate courts, are recruited from its ranks and remain identified with the broad community of the profession. The prominence of lawyers in the national elite of the past may be assumed to have similar effects for the collective self-image; but taking pride in national heroes may at the same time contribute to a blurring of the lines that set the professional character apart from national traditions.

The relationships between the German *Rechtsanwaltschaft* and other subgroups of the legal profession at large are very different from the American case, and the contrasts can in part be explained by differences in

82

the place of lawyers in the structure of power. It will be remembered that the four major groups—*Rechtsanwaltschaft*; lawyers in business, lawyers in public administration, and the judiciary—are in Germany roughly equal in size. The latter two are most obviously involved in the exercise of power. Their power and authority are not strongly individualized; rather bureaucratic anonymity is characteristic of it in both groups. Collectively, however, they wield a substantial amount of power. The power and influence of business lawyers are less visible and also less legitimate. If we consider that all categories of lawyers share a common education and that private practitioners are in many ways dependent on the decisions of judges and administrators, we may conclude that lawyers in the civil and judicial service constitute a forceful reference group for the German *Rechtsanwaltschaft*.

What makes this constellation distinctly different from the American situation is the fact that judiciary and civil service represent a subculture which contrasts strongly with that of the private practice of law. In spite of ambivalences generated by these differences and the formal dependence of the *Rechtsanwaltschaft*,[48] the influence of these reference groups strengthen a professionalism conceived in the image of civil service virtues, emphasizing reliability, objectivity and, in the extreme, quasijudicial attitudes; negatively, it limits tendencies to identify with the clientele and the subcultures they represent.

## CONTRASTING VALUE ORIENTATIONS IN THE TWO SOCIETIES

Social values are conceptions of what is desirable for a society or a part of society. They are at the same time a highly elusive subject of sociological inquiry and of paramount importance for stability and change of social structure. The difficulties of ascertaining value orientations are a direct consequence of the ways in which they relate to routine social life. People do not continuously talk about, are not even clearly conscious of, their image of the "good society." Value orientations do become salient, however, under certain conditions—in various phases of socialization and wherever people become aware of discrepancies between different normative demands as well as between highly visible behavior patterns and strongly held values.

Values shared by all those the bar in private practice deals with are patently of special significance especially since the bar is otherwise exposed to many divergent influences. These are the orientations reinforced in otherwise divergent contexts, and they will often tip the balance of

83

cross-pressures. This effect is even likely if certain values are not fully shared throughout a community or society but are seen as the dominant ones, those held by the most prestigious, authoritative and/or influential groups.[49] The latter suggestion would make it more defensible to rely on relatively impressionistic and interpretative assessments of prevalent value orientations by different observers, a procedure we have to follow in the absence of more detailed, systematic and reliable evidence.

The following analysis is confined to value orientations of the middle and upper classes, for it is with them that the bar has to deal for the most part; furthermore, only those values will be considered which appear relevant for the place and function of the legal profession in society, and finally, orientations which are common in both societies will receive passing attention only. There are four more or less clear-cut contrasts in value orientations, shared by the middle and upper classes, which affect the interplay of influences impinging on the two bars. These concern (1) the moral status of economic success and of a set of orientations actually or supposedly characteristic of the business world—risk-taking, private initiative, and the competitive pursuit of private interests; (2) the attitudes toward open conflict between individuals and groups; (3) basic ideas about the function of law in society; and (4) the relative strength of egalitarian and elitist values.

1. A strong positive evaluation of economic success and the pursuit of private interests is in Germany more than in the United States limited to certain spheres of social life. "Free enterprise" is in Germany neither part of an image of the glorious past nor an ideal cultivated in educational institutions. Although widely accepted as the *modus operandi* of the economy, it does not have a strong "halo-effect," shaping value orientations in other areas. It is the modus operandi of a sphere which, for many Germans educated in the humanities and related fields, is a lower realm of life, a realm that may be granted its own "laws," but that is not accorded primacy in determining societal values.[50] In this tradition, which persists today, although it was stronger in Imperial Germany, the valued features of the business world are technological efficiency, organizational achievements, and the overall contribution to national welfare and strength rather than the competitive pursuit of private interest. By contrast, the "values of the businessman" according to many analysts "dominate and permeate national life" in the United States. This means not only that monetary success constitutes one central symbol for achievement as such. It also means that the pursuit of individual goals is given moral sanction with relatively few qualifications involving direct and specific obligations to the "common good" and the order of society.[51]

In both societies, these contrasting value orientations were strongest in the two generations before World War I, reflecting and reinforcing the dominance of different elites as discussed in the previous section. During that period, and for some time to come, American protest movements accepted and defended the same individualist values, while in Germany both conservative and socialist movements espoused ideals radically different from the "business creed." In both countries, structural changes in a direction of convergence have taken place in more recent decades. These changes have made the contrasts in value orientations less sharp and less pervasive in each case, but they have not—perhaps not yet—eliminated them. While even those analysts of American society who stress most the new emergent patterns still refer to "the economic emphasis in our system of values," their counterparts in Germany note strong elements of defensiveness in the public posture of German business and a variety of reassertions of the older ideals of order.[52] Furthermore, the business subculture that gained ascendancy in the last two decades in Germany has never given to economic individualism the same priority it had in the traditional American business creed.

2. In the concluding discussion of the place of lawyers in the societal power structure it was suggested that inter-elite relations in Germany are characterized by a stronger tendency than in the American case to avoid open conflict. This difference was related to the greater value consensus underlying the American institutional framework and to a dampening of the intensity of conflicts resulting from overlapping interests and group loyalties which are more characteristic of American society.

The argument can be generalized beyond the realm of politics. The value orientations dominant in the German middle and upper classes show little tolerance for the open acting out of conflict in any sphere. This tendency to question the legitimacy of conflict is intimately linked to strong beliefs that contended issues would find their right solution if only sufficient good will and expert knowledge were mobilized. While the paramount role of science and scientific expertise in modern society and culture makes such a "spillover effect" of a trust in systematic empirical knowledge into areas of value judgment and choice likely in all modern societies, it has an additional base in Germany in authoritarian traditions of rule by an enlightened and supposedly neutral bureaucracy. It is further supported by the very strong value emphasis on technical occupational competence which pervades many different levels of the stratification system in Germany. For the power elites, specialized competence is a major factor legitimating elite status, both in the judgment of the population as a whole and in their own eyes.[53] If this conception is carried to its logical conclusion, an impasse results. Leadership and political decision-making necessarily transcend any specialized expertise. A collection of experts, mutually respecting the boundaries of their respective fields of competence, is as such incapable of decision-making and rule; as Max Weber long ago pointed out about bureaucracies, the top is necessarily non-bureaucratic. Of course, realities always diverge from ideal conceptions, and the conception described expresses only a dominant value orientation, not one held unanimously. Nevertheless, these orientations strongly encourage the fiction that there are no genuinely "open" problems, that everything has its "right" solution—right by unquestioned tradition, right by decision of unquestioned authority, right by a logically closed system of legal norms, or right by "natural law," whichever the case may be.

These considerations require one final comment. Only if the issues raised or the manner in which a conflict is acted out imply a serious indeterminacy of what is right would this German value syndrome put the legitimacy of conflict into doubt. Conflicts which are framed as the pursuit of one's rights in terms of an objective order are exempted from the odium of illegitimacy. While with this qualification the difference between the two countries may, in many cases, be one of interpretation and verbal form only, it subtly colors the atmosphere even around routine legal and nonlegal social conflicts. It reinforces, and is reinforced by, institutional differences such as those between case law and codification or between the contrasting types of court procedure. This leads us to a consideration of contrasting ideas about the place of law in culture and society.

3. We can leave open whether the popular stereotype that Germans are especially law-abiding is true or not.[54] There is little question that the value placed on law-abiding behavior in German normative culture is very high indeed. That this may be paralleled by a much lower level of actual conformity is a possibility which need not concern us here. Respect for the law was throughout the nineteenth century one of the meeting grounds between modernized authoritarian traditions and the *Rechtsstaat* (government under the rule of law) ideals of the liberal opposition. With the vanishing of the underlying constellation in the balance of power we may assume the corresponding value orientations to have weakened, too, and the abuses of respect for the law under the Nazis most likely had a similar effect; but it is still a safe guess that the emphasis on obedience to the law and respect for the law is stronger than in the United States, particularly among the more conservative groups and strata.

Of the place of law in American culture there exists a similarly simpleminded stereotype that is based on the notion of the lawless frontier. A more adequate conception may be one of ambivalent and sometimes strained attitudes toward the law. J. W. Hurst states: "People in the United States of all social levels and at all times mingled respect for the law and for doing things in a legal way with an unashamedly practical attitude toward the law as an instrument. They would use it when it effected a purpose and otherwise dispense with it more or less openly.''[55] Hurst's characterization of pervasive American attitudes toward the law could as well serve to describe the orientations of the authoritarian bureaucracies in continental Europe and particularly in Prussia during the eighteenth and well into the nineteenth century. The crucial difference is that the law in the one case is seen as an instrument of many groups and individuals and of compromise, while in the other it was first an instrument of order and of policy determined largely by one center of power and then became a means to restrain and regularize this central power, largely retaining, however, the character of an objective order independent of changing constellations of interests and influences.

These differences in the place law holds and held in popular attitudes and value orientations are strongly reflected in the conceptions prevalent in legal scholarship and in the subculture of the legal profession. Max Rheinstein, one of the most knowledgeable and perceptive observers of the two legal cultures, states: ''In the European view law is . . . a set of norms and principles of behavior addressed—by whom is not always made clear—to the individual members of society.'' By contrast, in the United States, ''law is that set of rules and principles which tell judges how they have to decide those disputes which private individuals choose to submit to them for decision, or, even more realistically, tell the judges under what circumstances they are to order, or to authorize, sheriffs, prison wardens, and other governmental 'force officers' to go into action against some individual. In such a view, law is addressed to the judges rather than the individuals. The norms by which individual human beings are expected to direct their behavior are primarily those of religion, ethics, and social convention.''[56]

The state upholding, in the form of the law, an objective order transcending the moral worlds of diverse groups and strata which make up modern society—this conception brings us back to the idea of objectively ''right'' answers in matters of value, choice, and conflict. Walter Weyrauch, like Max Rheinstein versed in both legal cultures, states the idea explicitly when in summing up his interviews with German lawyers he says: ''Many subjects professed an image of law as some form of ultimate truth and of the lawyer as a person detached from emotions and the trivialities of life. They tended to rationalize their decisions by high sounding language, statements of general principles, or sublime intuitive revelations and did not tolerate contradiction.''[57]

4. Seymour M. Lipset is only one in a long line of analysts of American society to assess equality and achievement orientation as key values in American normative culture.[58] We speak of equality when differen-

tiations and hierarchies existing in other areas are not permitted to shape interaction in a given dimension of social life; this may concern the respect accorded to people or any other aspect of social life. To emphasize equality as a central value, then, means to give preference to equality in as many ways as possible. Achievement orientation designates a stress on goal-oriented activities and on success in such activities. Differences in the evaluation of economic success and the competitive pursuit of private interests, as discussed above, can be interpreted as one aspect of contrasting substantive definitions of achievement orientation and the relation of these definitions to different conceptions of societal order. When achievement orientation becomes the predominant basis of social evaluation and of the distribution of rewards and facilities for future performance, it merges into one form of equality: equality of opportunity.

Together with equality in social intercourse, with what has been called "democratic manners," equality of opportunity has been a stronger ideal for a longer time in the United States than in Germany, particularly if certain conditions such as the racial and ethnic composition of society are hypothetically held constant. As one major expression of this the greater encouragement of talented youngsters from all backgrounds to go into higher education may be cited. The differences between the two countries, however, are far from clear-cut and simple, even at the level of value orientations. All modern industrial societies elevate achievement orientation to a major place in the system of values. Yet all not only have stable arrangements for "protecting the inept" and for keeping many people with superior talent out of higher positions but affirm competing values—of consideration for a man's needs or of loyalties irrespective of performance, to cite a few—which make the protection of the inept and various forms of discrimination more or less legitimate.[59] Similarly, in all industrial societies the ideal of equality has risen to a higher place in the hierarchy of values, higher in comparison to the pre-modern value systems in the same countries, but in all there are tendencies toward a diffusion of rank from one dimension into others; and again these are not just factual tendencies supported by those who are in advantageous positions, but they are buttressed by more generally held value orientations competing with the ideal of equality.

The contrast between Germany and the United States, then, is one found in the "mix" of elements, particularly in the strength of value orientations competing with the ideals of achievement and equality. When discussing above certain contrasts between the two status systems we noted the major difference that is relevant here: a stronger emphasis on ascription in Germany. This emphasis is qualified by its coexistence with strong achievement orientations. A stress on competent performance as one's obligation in whatever station in life can be combined with rather ascriptive ideas about social rewards. Still, ascription of status just by virtue of birth is not any more considered legitimate. On the other hand, the idea of equal opportunity independent of parental status, while of considerable appeal, founders against a multitude of institutional and attitudinal blocks. Without overt discrimination against lower-class students, German high schools and universities manage to have far fewer graduates from working-class backgrounds than has the American system of higher education. Aside from education, though linked to it, movement from working-class backgrounds into upper middle-class and upper-class positions is far less frequent in Germany than in the United States.[60]

Even if other mobility rates, such as those measuring movements across the "blue collar-white collar line," are much more similar in the two countries than popular mythology about the "old European countries" and the "land of opportunity" has it, it seems that status and mobility in the stratification system have quite different meanings in America and in Germany. In the United States, particularly in the American middle classes, status and mobility tend to be viewed as primarily dependent on talent and effort, on "achievement." In Germany, mobility within the status structure is seen as something much more equivocal than the result of differential ability and hard work; it could as well be an expression of ruthlessness, of luck, of a better start due to the resources of one's family.[61] The differentiation of high and low statuses retains thus much of the character of a grid of ascriptive positions in contrast to the image of occupational prestige stratification in the United States as an expression of capability and performance.

Aside from their consequences for equality of opportunity, ascriptive value orientations encourage the generalization of status from one dimension into others. To take the most strongly contrasting sphere, patterns of deference in social intercourse outside the occupational context in Germany are more closely tied to occupational and educational status than is the case in the United States. While to some extent respect is, of course, due to all people simply as human beings, "democratic manners" are far less characteristic of Germany than of American society; particularly membership in the professions—privileged in income, occupational prestige as well as education—carries a special kind of "honor," based on respect for the expert yet vaguely reminiscent of older, feudal types of stratification.[62]

The four complex contrasts between dominant value orientations in the two societies are not four isolated sets of differences. On the contrary, each pattern can be said to form a syndrome. A summary may reveal this systematic character more sharply by emphasizing the characteristic features of each pattern.

In the American case, achievement orientation is the overriding value, an achievement the goal of which is, in secular terms, individual fulfillment. Yet at the same time, achievement is a moral duty for the individual, a duty not owed to this concrete society or "the state," but a duty in terms of a moral order which transcends the concrete shape of the status quo. The ideal which makes achievements ultimately worthwhile is the building of the "good society" of the future, the social framework for the "good life" of individuals; it is a relatively open-ended ideal of progress. The historical religious roots of this value orientation are, of course, found in ascetic Protestantism with its injunction against indulgence, its affirmation of disciplined action and its vision of the "kingdom of heaven."[63]

This individualist activism engenders strong supports for egalitarianism. It also requires a high level of tolerance for social conflict, especially once dogmatic substantive formulations of what the kingdom of heaven on earth is had lost much of their binding force. What remains, however, is a particular anchoring of the idea of order. If we distinguish different levels of normative patterns, we may say that there is a characteristic tendency to see societal order primarily grounded in ultimate moral aspirations on the one hand and in the mores, conventions, and shared opinions of diverse groups on the other. The law has primarily an instrumental function mediating between these more salient levels; as a system of norms it is relatively open to consideration of and influence from these other normative orders.[64]

The German case may, in one sense, be understood as a modification of this syndrome, but again the modifications have a systematic character. Achievement is valued highly, but it is combined with and limited by the idea of an ascriptive social order. Accomplishment and effort are, while strongly emphasized, to some extent contained within narrower subsystems, membership in which acquires an ascriptive character. The ultimate worth of effort and achievement is seen in their contribution to the "common good." Individual fulfillment may be considered a rival criterion; however, in its forms of highest moral standing it is divorced from societal reality and becomes a private idea encompassing the close primary environment but remaining indifferent to the wider social structure of secondary associations and relationships.[65] In this form, the ideal of individual fulfillment is compatible with the ideal of doing one's duty in contributing to the "common good."

The substantive meaning of the "common good" is derived more from ideals of solidary integration of society and of justice than from an open-ended idea of progress. In the Hegelian tradition, which still permeates much of German social and political thought,[66] as well as in many quarters apparently outside this tradition, it is the state that guarantees or even represents this order. The order instituted through the law and governmental authority becomes thus imbued with the sanctity of ultimate values. Moral ideals outside this order tend in such perspectives to be relegated to the status of private concerns, and the traditions, established practices, and the interests of diverse groups are merely instruments or obstacles to the "common good." Conflicts within and between them may be tolerated as long, and only so long, as they do not question the objective order.

In this sketch of some value orientations relevant for the place of law and the legal profession in the two countries I have stressed the contrasts between Germany and the United States. These contrasts between two structurally rather similar societies were strongest in the last third of the nineteenth century. Today, different ideals are important in both societies and full-fledged professions of the ideals described tend to be perceived as conservative or "rightist" in the United States as well as in Germany, especially when they are aggressively formulated and when their advocates insist that operating norms and institutions be made strictly consistent with these value orientations. However, "conservative radicalism" may be understood as the extremist version of value orientations which are pervasive in the center, too, albeit in less systematic form, and some of these orientations may even be found in different formulation at the opposite, the "leftist," end of the ideological spectrum. One underestimates the resiliency of value orientations in the face of institutional change if it is assumed that value patterns of long standing are simply discarded and replaced by others in the course of one or two generations. A toleration of inconsistencies between changed operative institutional norms and retained ideals, simultaneous commitments of different strength to incompatible values, often combined with feelings of ambivalence toward either, and a partial suspension of or a greater haziness about ultimate commitments appear more likely than swift change of basic value orientations, especially in those groups and strata which are, unlike intellectuals, not primarily concerned with value orientations, their interrelations and their implications.[67]

What inferences about the reference groups and the subculture of the two professions do these considerations about dominant value orientations suggest?

Client loyalty and partisan involvement in the actual and potential conflicts of clients with other parties are universal components of the role of private counsel. So is a commitment to the integrity of the system of law and the administration of justice. It appears from the above that the tension between these components is greater in the German case because the public component, the "officer of the court" aspect of the private practitioner's role, receives in Germany stronger support from dominant value orientations in the community at large than in the United States.

The function of the bar in private practice, when viewed in terms of the ideal conceptions of society, is of lesser importance in Germany than in the United States. The elite of the American bar is legitimately involved in conflicts and disputes the outcome of which may change the order of public life, while ideally—if not necessarily in reality—the work of the *Rechtsanwalt* is confined to participation in applying an established order to disputes which may arise.

Both the conceptions of law and order and the greater weight of ascriptive orientations render the German *Rechtsanwalt* in various ways more immune to outside influences. Invoking the established legal order gives the German lawyer a greater authority in relation to clients. His role as expert, also strongly supported in pervasive orientations, puts him similarly into a more authoritative position and renders his relation to clients more specific, and the greater generalization of occupational prestige adds to the same effects in relation to role partners of lower standing.

Aside from this generally stronger insulation of the bar against outside influences, the lower standing of the business world in the view of the more conservative elements in German society diminishes the impact of the business community as a reference group at least for important segments of the German bar. The social categories of university-educated people (*Akademiker*) and of all persons trained in the law (*Juristen*) are for a variety of reasons, discussed in previous sections, powerful reference groups for many private practitioners, and the values outlined as dominant in Germany find a particularly strong resonance in these groups. These reference groups, then, strengthen conservative orientations and reinforce a reserve toward the world of business. Since on the other hand most lawyers in private practice are to some extent involved in business matters, and a considerable minority predominantly so, we are led to expect a good deal of ambivalence in the reference group relations of many private practitioners as well as some tensions between different segments of the bar concerning these contradictory orientations.

In the United States, the business community should be a far more powerful reference group for the bar in private practice than in Germany. Counterweights to this influence are found here, too; the ideals of professionalism and the integrity of the law are the most important ones. The substance of these ideals, however, is in America more compatible with the traditional values of the business world.

The contrasting value syndrome in the two societies finds its clearest expression in two groups, businessmen and civil servants, respectively. Insofar as shared or predominant value orientations determine reference group behavior, one would expect businessmen and civil servants to be important reference groups for many different categories of people in the two societies. For lawyers, both groups would appear to have added salience because they are, as clients and administrators, respectively, immediate role partners.

While many questions about the precise impact of business groups of various kinds and about the consequences of structural changes in the economy remain open in the American case, there is little doubt that the business community represents a powerful if complex reference group. To speak of the civil service subculture as a model for diverse groups in German society and for lawyers in private practice especially raises, however, serious objections which deserve closer consideration.

In the image Germans have of German society civil servants occupy a place of extraordinary prominence. They were named by half of the respondents in a representative sample as one of the—typically four to five—strata they would distinguish in German society, that is, more often than any other broad occupational group with the exception of workers.[68] This salience of civil servants in the images of German society can be interpreted in part as a result of the congruence between the syndrome of dominant values and their function, their style of life, and their value orientations. For many lower-class people the conspicuously secure and respectable existence of a lower or middle civil servant has been the hope for their children, and a good deal of mobility into the German upper middle and upper classes originates, as we will see in the next section, in the lower and middle ranks of the civil service.

Civil servants are not, however, generally admired and respected. Peter R. Hofstätter even concludes from several findings that the *Beamten* are generally disliked and seen as "un-German." A closer reading of his data on student attitudes suggests, however, some important qualifications. The label "civil servant" appears to have been understood frequently as a minor official concerned with routine work, a position university students are unlikely to aspire to or have much respect for. Furthermore, there is evidence of a variety of subimages of the civil servant, one of which virtually coincides with the positive image of "the German."[69]

If these attitudes are not to be interpreted as outright rejection and hostility toward the civil service subculture, they at least betray a strong ambivalence. This ambivalence may be partially resolved by differentiating between different kinds of civil servants and by concentrating negative attitudes on those of lower levels and most representative of the rigidities of red tape and dependent subordination, while more positive orientations are reserved for other public officials. A civil service role relatively free of these restrictive aspects and yet representative of the dominant value syndrome is that of the judiciary. In this context it should also be remembered that a large proportion of both *Akademiker* and lawyers serve the government as civil servants, and an indentification with them as university graduates and as *Juristen* may bypass the rejected and resented connotations of the bureaucratic world.

Self-employed *Akademiker* finally, the members of the *freien Berufe*, are likely to be an important reference group for the *Rechtsanwaltschaft* precisely because they stand "in the middle" between bureaucrats and businessmen, combining the autonomy of the latter with the devotion to the "common good" of the former. Even where the civil service subculture is overtly rejected, then, it looms large and colors the identifications with other groups, introducing subtle differences of meaning into reference group relations which seemingly are similar in both the American and the German case like the orientations toward professions in private practice, the *freien Berufe*.

## PATTERNS OF RECRUITMENT AND EDUCATION

Recruitment and education constitute a major link between the subculture of any status group and the wider social structure and broad cultural orientations. Social background, which gives a rough indication of the conditions of early socialization, and the various phases of formal education are particularly important for the professions because the professions, especially those involving private practice, largely rely for the control of performance on internalized personal commitments and the informal social control of colleagues. To anticipate the major conclusion of the following discussion, the patterns of recruitment and education found in the two professions tend to reinforce those value and reference group orientations which were suggested by our discussion of the place of the two bars in the stratification system and in the structures of power and of their relation to contrasting societal value patterns.

### THE SOCIAL BACKGROUND OF GERMAN AND AMERICAN LAWYERS

Professionals in all modern societies tend to be recruited from higher strata of origin than any other broad occupational category. This tendency is, however, far less strong in the United States than in Germany. The proportion of people with working-class backgrounds, a rough indicator for the openness of upper middle-class occupations, is negligible among Ger-

TABLE 10. *Socioeconomic Background of German and American*
*Students in Different Fields.*

A. *Fields of graduate study chosen by American college*
*seniors ranked in terms of association with high socio-*
*economic status (SES) of parents, 1961*

| Field of study ranked | Q | Percent high SES |
|---|---|---|
| 1.   Law | +.408 | 73 |
| 2.   Medicine | +.382 | 72 |
| 3.   Humanities | +.235 | 64 |
| 4.   Social sciences | +.175 | 62 |
| 6.5 Biological sciences | * | 58 |
| 6.5 Business | * | 57 |
| 6.5 Other professions | * | 53 |
| 6.5 Physical sciences | * | 48 |
| 9.   Education | −.165 | 48 |
| 10.  Engineering | −.177 | 45 |

B. *Percentage of German university students with fathers*
*in upper middle-class and working-class occupations*
*by field of study, 1958-1959*

| Field of study ranked | Upper middle class | Working class | N |
|---|---|---|---|
| 1. Medicine | 66.2 | 2.1 | 19,241 |
| 2. Law | 54.1 | 3.5 | 18,729 |
| 3. Business admin., Economics and social sciences | 44.2 | 5.1 | 19,180 |
| 4. Humanities | 42.5 | 6.5 | 31,809 |
| 5. Natural sciences | 42 | 6.9 | 10,432 |
| 6. Theology | 34.6 | 12.5 | 6,055 |
| Total | 43 | 5.3 | 151,173 |

*Source*: Part A, James A. Davis, *Undergraduate Career Decisions. Correlates of Occupa-*
*tional Choice* (Chicago, 1965), p. 65. The study was based on a total of 33,982 individual
questionnaires. Q varies from +1 through O to −1. A positive value means that students
with high parental socioeconomic status are more likely to choose the occupation indicated.
A star (*) indicates that the value of Q was smaller than +.15 and larger than −.15. High
SES is a far more inclusive category that "Upper middle class" in section B of this table;
it includes all white collar occupations with the exception of those who earned less than $7,500
*and* who did not go beyond high school in their education (19 percent of the white collar
group); of the blue collar and farm groups it includes those 4.5 percent who both earned
more than $7,500 and had at least some college education; James A. Davis, *Great Aspirations.*
*The Graduate Plans of America's College Seniors* (Chicago, 1964), p. 19f.

Part B, recalculated from Statistisches Bundesamt, *Statistische Berichte*, VIII/4/40, Wiesba-
den, pp. 24-29. The category of upper middle class comprises children of *Akademiker*, high
civil servants, white collar employees with management status, manufacturers, and wholesale
merchants. The category of working class comprises children of workers of all skill levels.

man *Akademiker* while it constitutes a sizeable minority among professionals in the United States. [70]

The American legal profession has long been thought of as a particularly open occupation. This has been of special importance because of the bar's close relations to politics in a democratic and egalitarian society. As Toepfer has said, "The bar and the law schools, too, have always taken pride in the belief that anyone with intelligence and industry could become a lawyer."[71] In comparison to the German bar, the American legal profession is indeed fairly open to the lower class. About one of every five American lawyers comes from a working class home in contrast to only 2 or 3 percent in the German legal profession.[72] The evidence on student backgrounds presented in Table 10 suggests that in comparison to other professional fields in America law, together with medicine, recruits its practitioners from relatively affluent families. These data are likely to give an exaggerated picture for the American bar as a whole, since, as we will see below, a large, though declining, proportion of American lawyers did not complete college and lawyers without a college degree are likely to come more often from lower-class homes. Furthermore, for many questions the public image of the bar as a relatively open profession is as important as the actual patterns of access, particularly if it is congruent with widely held value orientations.

As Table 10 (B) shows, the recruitment field of German law students is high, too, when compared with the origins of all German university students, though law ranks clearly behind medicine in this respect. This represents a decline of the recruitment field of law students since the turn of the century when law students came from families of higher status than any other group of students.[73] These comparisons *within* the two countries should not conceal the fact that the recruitment of German university students in general is far more exclusive than that of American students in professional and graduate school. Neither the law nor any other field of university studies has in Germany a reasonable claim to be open to "any one with intelligence and industry."

Equally important, and possibly more so, is another difference in the recruitment structure of the two bars. German lawyers come disproportionately from families of university graduates and of civil servants. *Akademiker* and *Beamte* are very strongly represented among the fathers of all German university students, and this tendency is even somewhat stronger among law students (Table 11). Judging from student statistics, the best source for estimates about the profession at large, 40 to 45 percent of all German lawyers have grown up in families of *Beamten,* and between 30 and 35 percent are children of university graduates. Considering tendencies toward self-recruitment, the overrepresentation of the latter is

TABLE 11. *Selected Background Groups of German University Students, Percentage.*

| | 1) *Akade-miker* | 2)Higher civil servants | 3)All civil servants | Father's status 4)1+3 exclud-ing duplica-tions | 5)Business self-employed | 6)Employ-ees of manage-ment status | 7) 5+6 |
|---|---|---|---|---|---|---|---|
| All students, 1928-1929 | 23.1 | 16.9 | 47.7 | 54 | 23.9 | ? | ? |
| Law students, 1928-1929 | 25.0 | 19.4 | 46.9 | 53 | 27.1 | ? | ? |
| All students, 1958-1959 | 32.5 | 16.3 | 35.1 | 52.5 | 15.9 | 15.9 | 31.8 |
| Law students, 1958-1959 | 38.6 | 20.8 | 39.9 | 59.4 | 14.4 | 17.0 | 31.4 |
| Students in business admin., economics, and social sciences, 1958-1959 | 21.2 | 9.7 | 27.2 | 39.8 | 26.7 | 17.3 | 44.0 |

*Sources*: W. Richter, "Die Richter der Oberlandesgerichte der Bundesrepublik," *Hamburger Jahrbuch für Wirtschafts-und Gesellschaftspolitik*, 5:248 (1960), and Statistisches Bundesamt, *Statistische Berichte*, VII/4/40:24-29 (1960).

of course less remarkable than the overrepresentation of civil servants, more than half of whom are in the middle and lower ranks of government service, which do not require university degrees. German civil servants and their children thus show an extraordinary inclination toward—and success in—advancement through higher education. Both groups of origin together account for 55 percent or more of all German lawyers (column 4 in Table 11).

We can compare lawyers from professional and civil service backgrounds with those with business origins. As Table 11 indicates with rough accuracy, the latter of these subculturally distinct groups provides only half as many members of the German legal profession as the two major nonbusiness groups.[74] In assessing the significance of these relative proportions it may well be argued that the sons of *Akademiker* and *Beamte* are not only numerically dominant but represent in comparison to other groups a more homogeneous set of attitudes and orientations, which should increase their influence on the subculture of the profession. By con-

TABLE 12. *Selected Background Groups of American Lawyers and of College Seniors with Preference for Legal Studies, Percentage.*

| | Father's status | | |
| | Professional occupations | Proprietor or manager of business firm | Number of individuals studied |
| Category | | | |
| --- | --- | --- | --- |
| College seniors with preference for Law | 36 | 30.5 | 1,731 |
| Lawyers in small city (50,000), New York | 24 | 31 | 79 |
| Lawyers in "Prairie City" (80,000), Midwest | 29 | 37 | 75 |
| Lawyers in middle-sized cities (150-350,000) | | | |
| (a) Massachusetts | 16 | 39 | 100 |
| (b) Ohio | 26 | 45 | 100 |
| (c) Texas | 25 | 38 | 61 |
| Lawyers in New York City | 21 | 50+ | 801 |

*Sources*: For college seniors, Seymour Warkov, *Lawyers in the Making* (Chicago, 1965), p. 4. Since the data on college students are of recent date and since college graduation is not a universal prerequisite for admission to the bar, these proportions cannot be generalized to the contemporary bar. For lawyers in a small New York city, Thomas J. Matthews, "The Lawyer as a Community Leader," unpub. Ph.D. diss., Cornell University, 1952, p. 19; for lawyers in "Prairie City" Joel F. Handler, *The Lawyer and his Community* (Madison, Wis., 1967), p. 182; for lawyers in two middle-sized cities each in Massachusetts, Ohio, and Texas, Stuart Adams, "Regional Differences in Vertical Mobility in a High-Status Occupation," *American Sociological Review*, 15:231 (1950); for lawyers in New York City, Jerome E. Carlin, *Lawyers' Ethics* (New York, 1966), pp.28 and 190, and Bureau of Applied Social Research, Columbia University, "A Brief Progress Report on the Metropolitan Law Office Study," multilithed, 1961, p. 2.

trast, the strongest background group in the American legal profession are the sons of businessmen, of proprietors and of managers, who account for about 40 percent of all American lawyers (Table 12). They are followed in numbers by those who grew up in professional families. This category— about 20 to 25 percent of American lawyers—is far more heterogeneous in education, type of work, occupational prestige, and characteristic value orientations than its German counterpart, the *Akademiker*. While the latter are all university graduates, grew up in middle- and upper middle-class families and are recognized as a distinct and high-ranking status group, the American "professions" include occupations of semiprofessional status such as librarians and elementary school teachers, are highly unequal in their training and are recruited from a wider range of strata. Thus, the argument about subcultural homogeneity and impact on the orientations of the profession advanced above about the German bar can be reversed in the American case: sons of professionals are in the American bar not only numerically second to lawyers of business origins, they also do not represent as sharply distinct and homogeneous a subculture as *Rechtsanwälte* from *Akademiker* and *Beamten* families.

In terms of class background and occupational subcultures, then, the American bar is recruited from more heterogeneous origins than the German legal profession. This heterogeneity is increased and reinforced by ethnic diversity, which is, of course, much greater in the United States than in Germany. While the number of Black lawyers is extremely small, law is more open and/or more attractive to other minorities than other fields of graduate or professional study.[75] That length of family residence in the United States and national descent as well as the related factor of religious affiliation make for considerable differences in professional orientation has been demonstrated in Jerome Carlin's study of lawyers in New York City.[76]

In conclusion of this review of recruitment patterns, the question has to be raised whether the compositions discussed for the two professions as a whole hold in a similar way for the bar in private practice. In the American case, lawyers in private practice account for nearly four out of five members of the profession at large so that they may be taken to reflect the general pattern.[77] In Germany, however, one might expect that the four branches of roughly similar size which make up the legal profession— judges and prosecuting attorneys, administrators, lawyers in private practice, and lawyers in private employment—attract people in highly selective fashion so that the latter two groups would include more lawyers from business backgrounds and fewer from *Beamten* families. Although such a tendency exists, Table 13 shows that the German bar in private practice—here all *Rechtsanwälte,* including syndic-attorneys—still is dominated by the same background groups as the profession as a whole. We have detailed data on different background groups only for *Rechtsanwälte* and the *Justizdienst* (judges and prosecuting attorneys). It seems that lawyers in public administration resemble by and large the judiciary in their recruitment pattern,[78] while those in private business employment appear to be the group with the highest share of members from business backgrounds.

Two contrasting aspects of the German and American educational

TABLE 13. *Selected Background Groups of Different Branches of the
Legal Profession in the United States and Germany, Estimated Percentage.*

| | Germany | | | United States |
|---|---|---|---|---|
| Father's status | Persons trained in the law | Judges and public prosecutors | *Rechts-anwälte* | Private practitioners |
| Working Class | 2-3 | 1 | 1 | about 20 |
| *Akademiker/* Professionals | 30-35 | about 45 | about 45 | 20-25 |
| Civil servants | 40-45 | 54 | 37 | ? |
| Civil servants and *Akademiker* combined | 55-60 | about 65 | about 60 | ? |
| Business: proprietors, incl. self-employed craftsmen | 15-25 | 19 | 28 | ? |
| Business: proprietors and managers | about 30 | about 25 | about 33 | about 40 |

*Sources*: Estimates in the first column are based on the same sources as those used in Table 11. Estimates in the second and third columns are based on Wolfgang Kaupen's national survey of *Rechtsanwälte* (N-259) and judges and prosecutors (N-188) in Germany; see his *Hüter von Recht und Ordnung*, p. 78. Estimates in the fourth column are based on data in Table 12.

systems have been discussed above, when the place of the bar in the structure of economic and social stratification was considered: (1) access to higher education is much more limited in Germany than in the United States, and (2) American educational institutions vary on all levels much more in quality and prestige than German high schools and universities. The smaller proportion of Germans who attain a higher education is recruited in highly selective ways—though not manifestly and intentionally so—from certain sectors of German society; this is the basic condition which makes the German bar more homogeneous in terms of social origins than the American legal profession. The diversity in quality and orientation of American high schools, colleges, and professional schools builds on and reinforces the heterogeneity introduced by a wider field of recruitment, while the similarity of German high schools and universities in character and standing contributes further to the homogeneity of the German legal profession. We will see that this is not only true in respect to the composition of the student body and the quality of instruction, but that the character of the faculties and the value orientations inculcated in advanced German education also reinforce patterns dominant in the typical family backgrounds of students.

#### THE EDUCATION OF GERMAN LAWYERS

The vast majority of German lawyers receive an education that can be described in fairly clear-cut fashion. After four years of elementary school the prospective lawyer parts with his classmates and moves, if successful in admission tests, to a high school, where he studies for eight or nine years, passing at the end a final examination, the *Abitur,* which entitles him to enroll at any German university irrespective of his grade level. Most of the students with whom he started out in the first year of high school have by then dropped out.[79]

The vast majority of German elementary and high schools are public schools. Their faculty members are *Beamte,* with university degrees in the case of high schools and teachers' college degrees in that of elementary schools. Roughly half of the teachers on both levels in turn grew up in *Beamten* families.[80] The peculiar character of German high schools—in part a result of this composition of their faculties, in part based on continuing, though modified traditions which go back to the neo-humanist reforms of the nineteenth century—is difficult to describe in a few words. More than American schools they seem to limit their responsibility for the success of students rather narrowly, emphasizing the importance of family education and relying strongly on the students' autonomous motivation—one reason, it appears, for the high rates of drop-outs from an already highly selected student body. German secondary education, especially in its more conservative forms, tends to foster attitudes of concern for the "common good" as well as neglect and aversion toward social conflict based on material interests and toward the world of commerce and business. The German high school teacher often sees it as his mission—poor and uninspiring as the implementation may be—to impart beyond specialized knowledge and an ability to integrate such knowledge meaningfully "a moral responsibility toward the values that sustain our lives"; these values are typically "cultural" values that are idealistically separated from technical developments and modern "civilization."[81] It is here that the value orientations discussed above have a strong institutional anchorage, and that, aside from family traditions, the role and the self-image of *Akademiker* begins to be developed. Such tendencies are probably strongest in the classical high schools, and these have of all types of high schools the largest proportion of graduates opting for legal studies.

Wolfgang Kaupen found that nearly half of all *Rechtsanwälte* in a national sample graduated from classical high schools and that these—in comparison to their colleagues who graduated from other high schools—show more generalized conservatism, are underrepresented in the field of business law, and are somewhat less successful economically while their grades in legal examinations were noticeably better.[82]

"On the whole they come by default," is the judgment of Felix Frankfurter about the ways in which American students arrive at the decision to go to law school, and German law students have the same reputation. Dahrendorf interprets this as a "renunciation of specialized knowledge" and relates it to a "very consistent desire for an elite education": "Elite positions always require interchangeability; at the top the specialized qualification counts for less than the general qualification for leadership."[83] While this may be true for a small segment of law students, a more adequate interpretation would emphasize on the one hand that law is after all a field rather removed from the early life of most persons and on the other hand that legal studies may be attractive for a variety of reasons—offering diverse professional possibilities, they allow to delay occupational choice; they are compatible with elite ambitions as well as with hopes for affluence; and they also may lead to relatively secure positions serving the maintenance of social order.

The law divisions of state universities are the only law schools in Germany. As in the case of high schools, their faculty members have *Beamten* status, and nearly half of them grew up in *Beamten* families.[84] During his three and a half to four and a half years of university studies the prospective lawyer is exposed to a system of lecture and discussion courses, both often crowded by hundreds of students, which imposes few sanctions against underachievement. Competitive, hard study is not particularly characteristic of German law students—a fact that corresponds to the secondary role of competition in the ideals and the actual life of the profession. The combination of sudden academic freedom after highly regimented high school studies with a completely new subject matter, which is not presented in ways to make it attractive to the uninitiated, often leads to a crisis that is resolved by most students in one of three ways: they leave the university altogether, they change their field of studies, or they stay in law school, but they withdraw their energies more or less from the offerings and ideals of the university and turn to commercial cram schools and correspondence courses.[85]

It seems likely that this pattern reinforces certain selective mechanisms observed previously—sorting more lower-class than upper middle-class students out of legal studies. Those who stay get typically—against the ideals of the university—a highly examination-oriented legal education.

On the other hand, extracurricular activities and interests, such as participation in student fraternities and, less frequently, student government, attendance of courses in other fields, interests in theater, literature, and politics, are of considerable importance among German law students. This latter, "unofficial" aspect of law school study may be seen as an effective preparation for the generalized status of *Akademiker*.[86]

Organizationally, student fraternities are a major focus of this socialization into the upper middle-class role of *Akademiker*. Fraternities respond to the needs of students for company in a highly impersonal and unstructured situation; individual off-campus residence, large classes, and the strains of untutored study make these needs particularly urgent. Socializing, cultivation of proper forms of etiquette, student camaraderie, and a vague conservative and elitist orientation in political and social matters appear characteristic of most fraternities. Alumni of these associations frequently keep in contact with one another and support their old fraternity. Their social position often enables them to further the early career of the younger "brothers," which adds to the attraction of fraternity membership, although it is difficult to assess whether such "connections" are really significant.

Both initial recruitment patterns and the impact of legal education are revealed in the distribution of career preferences among the four major branches of the legal profession. Table 14 shows that only one out of eight or nine first-year law students intends to go into business employment, a proportion which declines to 7 to 8 percent at the end of legal studies. Careers in the administration of justice are the only choice which steadily gains in attraction.[87] Whether this change is due mainly to patterns of self-selection of those who finish law school or to changes in individual preferences, we may conclude that German legal education is strongly oriented to judicial roles and that it does little if anything to encourage an orientation toward legal careers in business. In addition, university studies are concluded with a state examination under the supervision of the administration of justice. Passing it entitles law school graduates to enter a formal preparatory service, which again is supervised by the judiciary. Until recently of three and a half years', now two years' duration, this preparatory service is required for future judges, public prosecutors, *Rechtsanwälte*, and the majority of higher civil servants. It consists, however, mainly in practice periods in various courts; apprenticeship under a *Rechtsanwälte* accounts for less than half a year and administrative experience for six to twelve months.[88]

The first years of actual professional practice are known to be of great consequence for the formation of the professional self-image and of lasting attitudes and orientations. Thus, the facts that future *Rechtsanwälte* con-

103

TABLE 14. *Career Preferences of German Law Students
by Year of Study, 1959-1960, Percentage.*

| Branch of profession chosen | Number of semesters studied | | | | |
|---|---|---|---|---|---|
| | 1-2 | 3-4 | 5-6 | 7-8 | 9 or more |
| Judiciary (incl. public prosecutors) | 29 | 33 | 36 | 39 | 32 |
| *Rechtsanwaltschaft* | 30 | 30 | 28 | 30 | 32 |
| Public administration | 19 | 16 | 16 | 17 | 19 |
| Business employment | 12 | 11 | 11 | 7 | 8 |
| No answer | 10 | 10 | 9 | 7 | 9 |
| N | 3,419 | 4,012 | 4,208 | 4,038 | 1,989 |

*Source*: Statistisches Bundesamt, *Bevölkerung und Kultur* (10, V/5-59) (Stuttgart and Mainz, 1963), pp. 80-87 and 92-95.

stitute a minority among their peers who aspire to become judges, public prosecutors, and public administrators and that they spend several years of apprenticeship as if they were to become judges and civil servants should have a profound impact on the subculture of the German *Rechtsanwaltschaft*. We encounter here the last element of a syndrome fostering civil service orientations and loyalty toward "the State" which was also evident in the value orientations dominant in the German middle and upper middle classes, in the social backgrounds of university students in general and law students in particular, and in their pre-legal education.

Until 1959, young lawyers had to become apprentices after their second state examination for one more year with a *Rechtsanwalt* if they were to be admitted to the bar in private practice. Many still do so voluntarily today, although it seems that employment in trade associations and in business, as well as to a certain extent in government, is increasingly chosen as a first step. From this base the young lawyer may or may not succeed in moving out into private practice as an individual practitioner or a junior partner.

### THE EDUCATION OF AMERICAN LAWYERS

There is far less uniformity in the educational careers of American lawyers. Thus, the sequence of elementary school, high school, college, and law school by no means has been the experience of all lawyers. As late as 1951, only half of all lawyers had graduated from college and one out of five never had attended college. The same proportion, 20 percent, had not received a law school degree. Increasingly, the states require a law school degree as well as a minimum number of years of college education, so that in these formal terms the education of American lawyers is slowly becoming more homogeneous.[89]

The elementary and high school education of American lawyers differs in three major respects from that of their German colleagues. First, already we encounter greater heterogeneity in terms of quality which appears to be in large part a consequence of predominant local control over the school systems. Second, the student who later goes on to college and/or professional school stays longer in the same school and in the same classroom with his schoolmates who do not go on to higher education. Differentiation according to academic ability occurs later and the selection is not as narrow as in Germany. The equalization of educational opportunities inherent in this arrangement is limited, however, by local decentralization. Combined with residential segregation in terms of class and ethnic affiliation, decentralization effectively aligns parental status and quality of education. Similarly, the minority of secular private schools provide a special education for students with a higher average status of origin. Third, in spite of the high degree of heterogeneity in American primary and secondary education, certain themes seem to be pervasive in the orientation of American schools and in contrast to those of German schools, especially German high schools. According to Williams: "Emphasis is put upon the practical usefulness of formal education. Contemplative or speculative thought, art, highly abstract theoretic work are relatively little valued."[90] To the extent that humanistic ideals of the "well-rounded man" are pursued in American schools, they are not as much balanced against the realities of industrial society as in Germany, and social values of a liberal-democratic variety are strongly emphasized in contrast to the primacy of personal virtues and the cultural heritage of the past in German high schools. Finally, if the American public school is a "middle-class institution," it is "middle class" in a much more broadly defined sense than the German *Oberschule*, and its class character is mitigated by the ideology that every individual has a right to go as far in education as his ability and motivation will carry him.[91]

Colleges and universities are in America even more heterogeneous than primary and secondary schools. Vast differences in educational quality and orientation are to some extent paralleled, to some extent cut across by differences in social prestige and in the social origins of students.

However, schools that once were clearly selecting their students in terms of social criteria have shifted in recent decades consistently toward a primacy of academic entrance standards, so that today's differences in the social composition of the student body are increasingly due to background-related differences in earlier phases of socialization. The diversity in quality and reputation of institutions of higher learning introduces a strong element of competitiveness into secondary education which continues at the higher levels. Although all high school graduates who care to may be able to gain admission to some college, high academic achievement is necessary to get into the best and most renowned.

Since a college education typically involves a separation from one's family and home community on the one hand and more or less intense association with other undergraduates on the other, it should have profound socializing effects. However, while there are common "cultural themes" similar to those of secondary education, though with emphases shifted, the heterogeneity of American colleges and universities in recruitment, educational goals, quality, and prestige prevents this intense experience from contributing to the formation of as cohesive, and subculturally distinct, a status group as the German *Akademiker*.

Legal education, typically accomplished in three years, exhibits not surprisingly the same, if not even greater heterogeneity.[92] In quality, law school schools range from night schools and correspondence courses through a broad middle level, often associated with state universities to the top group of not many more than half a dozen "national law schools," of which Harvard, Yale, Columbia, Chicago, Berkeley, and Michigan are the best known. Part-time study is considered with ambivalence in the American legal profession: on the one hand, night schools and correspondence courses have been tagged the "problem children of legal education," and there is some evidence to support this judgment; on the other hand, there is a fair consensus that the bar should not be closed to those of limited means and that part-time study should be available.[93] This latter judgment is supported by the tradition of nonacademic legal education through apprenticeship with an experienced lawyer, which was replaced by law school education only in the decades around the turn of the century, as well as by democratic and egalitarian ideals, which are deemed to have particular urgency in the case of the legal profession because of its interrelations with politics and the judiciary.

All law schools force the student to work hard; they can build on the competitive achievement orientation which most students have developed in their pre-legal educational career. In many better schools, the top 10 to 15 percent of the students are invited to edit the school's law review, a distinction that results in exceptional learning opportunities as well as considerably better career chances. A number of other law-related extracurricular activities like moot courts, legal aid clinics, legislative drafting groups, and summer employment serve to reinforce the general emphasis on intensive specialized study. A by-product of this emphasis is that law students tend to be relatively isolated from students in other fields. This should aid the development of specific professional identification in contrast to the more diffuse socialization of German law students. However, as far as the consequences for the cohesiveness of the American profession are concerned, it has to be remembered here again that different types of law schools foster the development of self-images quite different in content and orientation.

If we could conclude that German law training is primarily oriented toward the education of future judges, American law schools may be said to train primarily lawyers in private practice.[94] The "national schools" focus more than the others on complex legal questions encountered rarely in practice except by corporate counsel in larger firms and the bench and bar in appellate courts, while the training in night schools and in part of the middle-level schools tends to be geared more to standard legal problems. Related to this difference which, it should be noted, is one of degree rather than a radical dichotomy, is a parallel difference in the extent to which the law of the state in which a school is located is taught.

Administered unevenly in the different states, bar examinations prove to be an obstacle to a large minority when taken for the first time, but since most states allow many repetitions, about nine out of ten applicants eventually succeed. Bar examinations, then, do not substantially diminish the heterogeneity of the bar's personnel as far as legal education is concerned, although in the long run the system of examinations has been an instrument of enforcing higher standards of professional training through admission requirements.[95] After their admission to the bar, most American lawyers pass through a period of supervised practical training, but in contrast to the German preparatory service it is neither required nor formally organized, it takes place predominantly under private auspices, and its incidence and varying quality are closely related to the past education of young lawyers.

If the educational routes that lead into the legal profession are in the United States so much more open to people from lower social origins than in Germany and if, in addition, the education of lawyers has in America a less homogenizing effect, an interesting question arises in view of certain functions fulfilled by the legal profession in society. Are we really to assume that roles intimately associated with the exercise of power, with the pursuit of corporate business interests, and with the private affairs of the upper and upper middle classes are filled in a manner so relatively open and "loose"? The answer, a qualified no, is found in the internal stratification of the American bar, which, as we saw, is on the one hand associated with social background and type of training and on the other hand with a differentiation of functions. Corporate business is served by the best-trained lawyers, who also come from families with an average status higher than the rest of the bar. Similarly, while lower level political and judicial roles may be particularly open to the lower strata of the legal profession, social origins, type of education, and previous status in law practice are of far higher rank when the backgrounds of lawyers in more elevated political and judicial office are considered.[96] Thus, while formal admission to the American bar is relatively open, the interlocking of diverse educational routes with different types of legal practice makes for a greater selectivity in the recruitment for those legal roles which are most crucial for advice and decision-making in political and economic matters of great consequence.[97]

The contrasts in the social background and the educational experience of German and American lawyers can be summed up succinctly. The German profession is more homogeneous than the American bar—in social origin, family upbringing, general education, legal studies, and practical training. Substantively, the dominant influences in the formation of German and American lawyers are likely to reinforce, for these professional groups in particular, the contrasts in over-all value orientations discussed in the preceding section. A prevalence of business backgrounds, a system of secondary and higher education the orientations of which are pragmatic, pluralistic, and responsive to a variety of social forces, a relatively specific and intense legal education geared toward business law, and a strong competitive achievement orientation pervading the whole system of education are salient aspects of the American case. By contrast, the milieu of *Beamte* and *Akademiker* is not only dominant in the family upbringing of German lawyers, it also pervades much of their formal schooling. German secondary education is more insulated from various social forces "outside" the educational realm and tends to engender attitudes estranged from, if not hostile toward, many features of modern industrial society. Less competitive and intense, German legal education is primarily oriented toward the education of judges. It allows more leeway for extracurricular activities which contribute to socializing the law student into the diffuse role of *Akademiker*.

## THE SUBCULTURE OF THE BAR
## IN THE CONTEXT OF SOCIETY

We have considered in turn the place of the two bars in the societal structures of status and prestige, of differential wealth and of power, the impact of certain value orientations dominant or of considerable force in the middle classes of the two societies, and, finally, the ways in which social background and early socialization as well as the training in formal general education link up with legal studies and the first steps in legal practice. Although many of the contrasts were subtle—differences in degree between otherwise quite similar societies—and some parts of the evidence were impressionistic or inferential, the differences between the two societies and between their legal professions appear to be systematic; they are interrelated and reinforce each other.

About the orientations of each of the two bars in private practice we can ask the following questions: (1) How strong is the typical identification with private practitioners as a group? (2) What is the relation between this identification and identification with other, wider social categories, such as the legal profession as a whole, the professions, the upper middle classes? (3) How do these in-group orientations relate to other reference groups of lawyers in private practice of which they are not a part? (4) What can be said about the values of each of these reference groups? (5) What elements in the subculture of the bar in private practice can be said to be shaped by pervasive reference group orientations of its members?

### THE SUBCULTURE OF PRIVATE LEGAL PRACTICE
### IN THE UNITED STATES

The American bar in private practice is more heterogeneous than the German *Rechtsanwaltschaft* in terms of the social background of its members as well as of their socialization and formal education. Especially in the larger cities private legal practice is highly differentiated; a great deal of de facto specialization by field of law, by functions fulfilled for clients, and by social status of clientele is closely related to the internal stratification of the bar and to differential patterns of association among lawyers. This heterogeneity and differentiation is likely to result in a comparatively weak identification with private practitioners as a group. The attractiveness of the bar in private practice as a reference group should furthermore be weaker than in the German case, because in the United States the prestige and income of lawyers surpasses that of the population at large to a lesser extent than in Germany.

Although these conditions which diminish the cohesion of the American

109

bar and its attractiveness as a reference group are of considerable effect, there are a number of significant counterbalancing forces. In the realm of power, the American lawyer can look up to a galaxy of prominent members of the bar both in the past and in the present. Aside from eminent lawyer politicians and powerful men in the world of business, most members of the judiciary have risen from the ranks of private practitioners. Perhaps even more important is the related fact that the ideals of the nation were to a large extent shaped by lawyers. Hurst says: "Lawyers were leaders in the formulation of the symbols which expressed what the American community believed in; they were leaders in shaping and maintaining rituals which helped preserve these symbols."[98] Finally, and again related, there is a better congruence between pervasive values in American society and the basic tasks of the bar—its involvement in social disputes and its association with the promotion of private interests—as well as the professional values these tend to engender. These conditions, which foster identification with the profession, are by no means negligible. On balance, it appears, however, that the divisive influences, which are more grounded in day-to-day routines and in vested interests, outweigh these more symbolic factors.

American bar leaders, judges, and law teachers have insisted again and again that legal work is professional work and that it is this professional character, shared with doctors, ministers, scientists, and teachers, which underlies the specific moral duties of the lawyer. To cite an influential opinion of fifty years' standing: "For lawyers, the most important truth about the Law is that it is a profession . . . And so, as a profession, the law must be thought of as ignoring commercial standards of success,—as possessing special duties to serve the State's justice,—and as an applied science requiring scientific training. And if it is thus set apart as a profession, it must have traditions and tenets of its own, which are to be mastered and lived up to."[99]

This view has not gone unchallenged. The dissenting voices range from critics of the bar, who declare that "traditions of public service, such as are found in the medical profession, insensibly disappeared" and who describe the respect for the legal profession as "the respect for an intellectual jobber and contractor rather than for a moral force," to an incriminated attorney's defensive assertion that "no amount of preaching can alter the cold, indisputable fact that the law has ceased to be a sacrosanct profession and has become a highly competitive business," and to Harrison Hewitt's argument, developed in the *Yale Law Journal*, declaring: "The difference between the obligations of a lawyer and the obligations of some other men, is based primarily upon the fact that the lawyer is acting for others and dealing with their property, and, perhaps, with their lives. Any other man who is put in the same situation has the same obligations.''[100] Although the latter line of reasoning affirms most special duties of the lawyer, it explicitly refuses, for the sake of egalitarian ideals, to link them to the ''other and higher'' principles of the professions as a distinct cluster of occupations. The strength of this ensemble of professional occupations as a reference group is not only weakened by egalitarian sentiments. The very wide definition of the term in current American usage includes occupations differing as greatly in formal training, status, and traditions as nursing, medicine, the ministry, engineering, and even, of late, business management; this testifies to the moral appeal of the ideals of professionalism and to its social reputability, but it also dilutes the impact of ''the'' professions as a reference group.

The legal profession as a whole, as distinct from the bar in private practice, is a positive reference group for most American lawyers. Indeed, the bar as a whole may be more often invoked as a community, membership in which entails specific commitments, than the profession in private practice. However, since the other branches of the American legal profession are relatively small and more or less closely related in careers and self-image to the bar in private practice, the two reference groups are for most purposes virtually identical, and what was said about private practitioners applies to the bar as a whole as well. Special groups within the profession, such as the judiciary, law professors, large firm corporate counsel, the ''Washington lawyers,'' or the lawyers in government administration—groups that stand out by their controlling power, by their learned authority, or by their professional attainment—do have an appeal as models for the profession at large, an appeal that varies in degree and in the aspects of their status considered paradigmatic for the different groups. However, even these special reference groups within the legal profession are by no means internally homogeneous as comparisons of the higher and lower judiciary[101] or of law professors in night and elite schools may show. Furthermore, if all groups within the bar which stand out by their learning, authority, power, prestige, or wealth are considered together, their influence should often be mutually contradictory. As an example, the ''romance of government service,'' involving often an activist idealism and a dispassionate pursuit of public welfare,[102] may be compared with the overriding partisan loyalty or the legal technician's disregard for the social consequences of his work, prevalent in much of the private business practice. That in this case the latter orientations are likely to be of greater influence will be argued below.

Aside from those groups and social categories of which he is a member, the most important reference group of a lawyer in private practice is constituted by his clientele. Taken for the bar as a whole, this is of course an extremely diversified social category, although the vast majority of clients are members of the middle and upper classes. Businessmen and business organizations can be singled out as the most important client category, since they provide the bulk of legal business which is recurrent, lucrative, "interesting" in a technical sense, and, as a result of all these factors, prestigious. There is, of course, a great variety of "businessmen," the two most important distinctions probably being, first, that which divides upper middle-class and upper-class clients from lower middle-class businessmen and those close to poverty and, second, that which separates the owner-manager from the executive who reached his position, at least ideally, by virtue of occupational qualification rather than of family relations and who acts as a trustee for the owners.

While these characteristics of the bar's clientele are similar in both the German and the American case, it appears that the impact of the business community as a reference group is far stronger in the American bar. Financial standards of success, rejection of or negligence about distinctively professional norms, and generally a self-image of one's role, which is closer to that of a special kind of business role than to the idea of a "higher calling," would be symptoms of this influence. They are not predominant, but widespread in the American bar, especially in the bar in big cities.[103] Slogans such as "law—from profession to business" may be exaggerated and may—a more serious misjudgment—invert the direction of change during the last fifty years, but they do not merely express the jaundiced view of idealistic critics and of rejected crooks. From the various discussions above, the following factors may be adduced in explanation of the comparatively strong influence of business orientations on the American bar. (1) The dominant values of American society strongly legitimate the subculture of business and give it a prominent, if not the leading place in society. (2) Sons of businessmen are the strongest background group in the American bar, and later education does comparatively little to discourage the orientations engendered by such home backgrounds. (3) The greater involvement of American lawyers in business matters which have little relation to technical legal competence may be in part a consequence of the greater influence of the business clientele and an expression of a less restricted conception of the professional role, but it also reinforces in turn the impact of the business community as a reference group. (4) The fact that the relations between professional and client, and possibly occupational roles in general, are in America less specifically defined, less segregated from diffuse personal contacts, makes for a weaker insulation of the lawyer from his clientele and its orientations. (5) To the extent that American lawyers are more deeply involved in community affairs and in politics and to the extent that these activities increase their influence in various spheres, there will be a greater interest in influencing their attitudes and orientations on the part of various groups, of which different business groups are not the least important. On the other hand, the responsiveness to the demands of a variety of groups and to public opinion, which is likely to be engendered by such activities, may result in some degree of autonomy vis-à-vis any one influence; but this autonomy would rest on a different basis than the autonomy characteristic for the professional.

These conditions shaping the bar's relations to its clientele and its susceptibility to reference groups in the business community have to be seen together with the comparatively weak cohesion of the American legal profession. Weaker identifications with the bar and its traditions make for less of a counterbalance to outside influences; individual attitudes and commitments as well as formal and informal control within the profession are not as strongly grounded in a sense of corporate identity and responsibility as would be the case in a more cohesive profession. In turn, greater susceptibility to outside influences and to demands for generalized loyalty from different client groups further reinforces cleavages in the bar as far as self-image, value orientations, and professional behavior are concerned.

The latter point is worth some elaboration. It was emphasized repeatedly that the differentiation of the bar varies considerably by size of community and that in the larger cities specialization and stratification within the bar are closely connected to type of clientele. It is here that the distinctions made above between different kinds of business clients come in. The marginal businessman may want to "cut corners" where a large firm is under no economic pressure to urge such a course of action; to the contrary, its greater concern with long-term considerations may render it positively disadvantageous to gain short-run profits at the expense of reputation and "good will." Similar differences are likely to obtain between different branches of business which vary in degree of competition and in the conditions that foster a concern with moral reputation. The widespread separation of ownership and management in large corporations makes for client representatives whose role is in several ways similar to the role of the lawyer—fiduciary in character, allowing for some detachment and for a certain consideration of other interests involved in the situation. More generally, specialization and functional differentiation are typically more developed in large than in small business firms. This greater division of labor gives to outside experts, too, the opportunity to stay more exclusively within their specialized field, although it should be noted that such differentiation of function decreases toward the apex of the bureaucratic structure, and if legal problems are intricately involved in top executive decisions, legal counsel may be as much drawn into nonlegal business problems in large firms as the attorney who, in addition to his legal work, serves a smaller business client as financial broker and general advisor.[104] Finally, not only the pressures from clients but also the ability and the inclination to resist pressures are associated with the position of a lawyer in the stratification of the bar. The weaker his economic position and the greater his dependence on a few important clients, the greater the probability that he gives in to the clients' point of view and that he views the traditional professional norms with a critical and skeptical eye.[105]

Such variations in the meanings of "business mentality" and in the impact of various business subcultures on different subgroups of the legal profession contribute to diversity of orientation and behavior in the American bar in private practice and reinforce its internal cleavages and antagonisms. This assertion should not, however, obscure the fact that by comparison with the German *Rechtsanwaltschaft* American lawyers in private practice are generally closer to the world of business. The National Opinion Research Center study of college students planning to go into legal careers found that "to a considerable degree the future lawyer is a man with occupational values similar to the businessman"; furthermore, this similarity is greater among seniors than among freshmen, indicating a selection process that may be based in part on an increasing awareness of the actual professional culture. Future lawyers differ most from other college students by saying that they want to "make a lot of money" and by caring less for "moderate but steady progress rather than the chance of extreme success or failure."[106]

The norms and values that prevail most strongly in the "working philosophy of the bar," it was found by both historians and sociological analysts, are those which the professional tradition shares with the wider community, especially the business community.[107] More or less within this category, but of particular importance to the role of the lawyer are the norms and values defining the attorney's obligations to his client. In any formulation of the bar's ideals firm loyalty to the client and active pursuit of his interests have an important place. What stands out about the American bar is that the corresponding norms and values which prescribe some detachment from the interests and the demands of the clientele and which emphasize responsibilities for the proper functioning of the administration of justice, for the integrity of "the law" and for the impact of the bar's work on the welfare of the larger community have weaker support. In the extreme, these considerations are reduced to a concern of mere prudence, a concern to avoid penal sanctions and untoward publicity. Hurst speaks of the "subordination of the professional attitude to an absorbed concentration on the workaday world of client-caretaking, as this

114

appeared to men in the circumstances of their particular distance from or nearness to the seats of power."[108] As a revealing incident, he discusses the public debate surrounding the confirmation of Louis D. Brandeis as associate justice of the Supreme Court. "Brandeis," one banker testified, "not only had to be convinced that the proffered retainer was not conceivably inconsistent with his then current public activities devoted to exposing the financial mismanagement of the New Haven. He also required 'to be satisfied of the justness of our position.' 'It was an unusual experience,' the witness observed. 'I had occasion to retain other lawyers, and no one ever raised the question.' " It was precisely this "judicial attitude toward his clients" in contrast to just "being his clients' lawyer" which made Brandeis, in the view of leading members of the American bar, unfit for high judicial office.[109]

On the proposition that partisanship combined with technical excellence summed up the conception of professional obligation in the elite of the American bar in the decades from 1870 to the 1930's there is a good deal of unanimity among responsible analysts.[110] There is also some agreement that the balance of forces among which the lawyer is a mediator has shifted in recent decades, with increasing weight of government regulation, a consequently stronger support for law enforcement, and a greater concern for far-sighted, "intelligent conservatism" on the part of big business as the main developments. Hurst says: "By 1950 prudence alone, even without the promptings of any felt sense of professional obligation, required that consideration of public policy, at least of that policy expressed in official action, enter into counsel given to clients. Out of this situation the lawyer might find a new independence in dealing with clients who found themselves perforce reshaping their aims and in a measure accepting their values from the law, whose immediate interpreter was their counsel."[111] It is worthwhile to note that Hurst's appraisal is formulated with extreme caution and that it is largely based on changes in the situation and in the orientations of the corporate clientele. The perspectives of business interests have themselves been modified, but they remain a dominant influence on the orientations of a large part of the bar's elite. Eugene V. Rostow's formulation of the new ideals may be taken as indicative of this: "the conception of the [corporate] lawyer as an *intermediary between business and the public*, educating both sides in the general interest of compromise, mediation and progress is a challenging ideal."[112]

The greater receptivity of the American bar in private practice to the subculture of business as well as its greater involvement in practical affairs that are outside the specific legal sphere, whether in business or in community activities or in politics, appear to have a number of indirect correlates in the culture of the American legal profession. It seems that, in comparison to their German counterparts, American lawyers more often think of themselves as "men who bring things to pass" rather than as in a specific sense "learned lawyers."[113] Corresponding to this greater emphasis on practical efficiency, on "getting things done" in a fairly wide range of spheres, is a stronger development of empirical realism.[114] Both in individual cases and in their overall conception of the law American lawyers seem to give more open and more realistic consideration to the interests and social forces that underly specific legal problems as well as legal and political forms and developments. If this concern with the factual conditions of legal arrangements contributes to a conception of law and justice as a flexible order, more grounded in reason and social circumstance than in absolute moral principle, it is only in line with our appraisal of values concerning law and justice that have wide currency in American society.

## THE SUBCULTURE OF PRIVATE LEGAL PRACTICE IN GERMANY

The German *Rechtsanwaltschaft* is more homogeneous than the American bar in private practice as far as the social backgrounds of its members and their socialization and formal education are concerned. It is also less differentiated in terms of specialization and internal stratification. This greater homogeneity should be conducive to a stronger sense of corporate solidarity and identification with the profession. We also have seen that, relative to the rest of the population, the average *Rechtsanwalt* enjoys higher prestige and a higher income than his counterpart in the United States and that social prestige is in Germany to a greater extent attached to membership in occupational groups as such—factors which should strengthen the character of the *Rechtsanwaltschaft* as a reference group for its members. On the other hand, while German lawyers in private practice are more strongly represented in politics than any other narrowly defined occupational group, the role of the *Rechtsanwalt* politician in politics is—and has been in the past—much more limited than that of his American counterpart. The judiciary is not recruited from the *Anwaltschaft*. The contribution of the German bar in private practice to the cultural heritage of the nation has been that of a specialized profession; it does not by any means come close to the role of the American bar in this respect. Finally, there is some dissonance between conservative, if not common, values in German society and the basic functions of the attorney which involve him in the open acting out of social conflicts and in the promotion of private interests.

On balance it appears that the German *Rechtsanwaltschaft* is a more cohesive profession and a more attractive reference group for its members than the American bar in private practice. If we take a second look at the factors involved, however, we find that some of these are shared by the *Anwaltschaft* with all lawyers as well as all or most *Akademiker*. This is true for recruitment and socialization patterns, for prestige standing and—to a lesser extent—for relative income level. This suggests that German *Rechtsanwälte* would see themselves in many contexts as university-trained lawyers—as *Juristen*—or as *Akademiker* rather than as attorneys in private practice. The *Rechtsanwaltschaft* by itself, then, seems to be a fairly strong reference group for its members, but it gains further strength from the fact that it is embedded in the wider categories of the legal profession as a whole and of university-educated people, which function as more important reference groups for the German private practitioner than in the American case.

The defining characteristic of an *Akademiker* is not the character of his work but his graduation from a university. This makes occupational differentiation less salient, but in addition, the occupational pursuits of *Akademiker* are less diversified than those of the American professions. Owing to the nature of their work and education, their social origins, and peculiarities of the German status structure, they enjoy a higher and more ascriptive prestige than members of the professions in the United States. Two major distinctions between different types of *Akademiker* are relevant for present purposes, that between different fields of training and between private practitioners, the *freien Berufe* in the narrower sense, and *Akademiker* in private or public employment. I estimate that about one out of every four or five *Akademiker* is self-employed in private professional practice and that three to four out of ten are career civil servants—*Beamte*.[115]

The picture drawn of the characteristic self-image of *Akademiker* and their model value orientations applies most to those trained in the traditional fields of university study, while economists, scientists, and engineers share least in this peculiar subculture; the latter fields are least integrated with the conservative educational ideals. The conception of the *Akademiker* involves a less dynamic ideal than the American conception of the profession. The latter is more often invoked as a justification for reform and upgrading of requirements in an occupational group, while the former represents an insistence on dignity, a veiled claim to superior status and responsibilities, the acceptance and implementation of which is largely taken for granted. The German conception is the self-image of established professions, fairly secure in their standing in the larger community. Linked both to the neo-humanist traditions of German idealism and the memories of a quasifeudal social order with estate-like status groups, it is not easily extended to the newer economic and technical professions. The inadequacies of these traditions in a changed environment as well as their continuous attrition without the development of a vital substitute may be—as far as the professions are concerned—among the conditions for what Gabriel Almond has called "the spiritual poverty of the German business and professional classes."[116]

The more conservative image of the *Akademiker* is likely to be a strong reference point for lawyers in general and *Rechtsanwälte* in particular. Their profession is an old and established one; nearly half of the private practitioners grew up in *Akademiker* homes; they more often attended schools espousing traditional educational ideals than other students; their occupational choice crystallized relatively late, while the decision for university studies was often taken for granted; and they participated during their student days in fraternities and other extracurricular activities which may be seen as training grounds for the diffuse role of *Akademiker*.

The legal profession at large has a very important place in the system of reference orientations of the *Rechtsanwaltschaft*. The situation is, however, far more complicated than in the American case. On the one hand, all German lawyers share the same or a very similar education, and this common experience includes, significantly, a prolonged practical training period. Furthermore, all lawyers share the common status of *Akademiker*. On the other hand, the four major branches of the profession—judiciary, government administrators, lawyers in business employment, and attorneys in private practice—are in Germany more strictly differentiated from each other than in the United States as far as the type and institutional setting of their work as well as their careers are concerned, and all four are of roughly similar size. Lawyers in positions other than private practice, then, are—because of shared experiences and qualities—potential reference groups for the *Rechtsanwaltschaft*, while at the same time they represent distinct mentalities and subcultures of their own.

The most important among these reference groups is the judiciary. The thrust of legal education is a first condition which makes this likely. Secondly, judges have the dominant place in the role structure at court, especially in German courts. Here it should be remembered that trial work is still of greater importance for the German than for the American private practitioner. The general value orientations about the law as well as the more specific ones current in the legal profession should additionally give the judicial role a more secure and a higher moral standing. Some confirmation for these inferences is found in Table 15. When asked to evaluate nine upper middle-class occupations according to the prestige they should have based on their social importance, respondents in a national sample of *Rechtsanwälte* ranked judges overwhelmingly more often at the top of the scale than any other occupations, including physicians, substantial businessmen, and *Rechtsanwälte*; less than one out

TABLE 15. *Ranking of Nine Occupations by German Private Practitioners, Judges, and Public Prosecutors.*
(Ranking according to the "prestige which these occupations should have according to their social importance")

| Occupations ranked | *Rechtsanwälte* giving: | | | Judges and public prosecutors giving: | | |
|---|---|---|---|---|---|---|
| | 1 or 2 rank, percent | 8 or 9 rank, percent | 1 and 2 minus 8 and 9 rank | 1 or 2 rank, percent | 8 or 9 rank, percent | 1 and 2 minus 8 and 9 rank |
| Judge | 58 | 1 | +57 | 66 | - | +66 |
| Physician | 28 | 3 | +25 | 29 | - | +29 |
| *Rechtsanwalt* | 18 | 1 | +17 | 3 | 9 | − 6 |
| Minister/ priest | 30 | 17 | +13 | 37 | 8 | +29 |
| Entrepreneur | 15 | 17 | − 2 | 7 | 23 | −16 |
| Higher *Beamter* | 11 | 18 | − 7 | 7 | 7 | ± 0 |
| Engineer [a] | 4 | 15 | −11 | 2 | 14 | −12 |
| Artist, self-employed | 3 | 31 | −22 | 9 | 28 | −19 |
| "Manager" [b] | 5 | 56 | −51 | 4 | 65 | −61 |

*Source*: *Ergebnisse der Befragung deutscher Juristen 1965* (MS), Forschungsinstitut für Soziologie of the University of Cologne—a report on Wolfgang Kaupen's questionnaire survey of German *Rechtsanwälte*, judges, and public prosecutors.

[a] Graduate of technical institute with equivalent of university standing.

[b] Manager was the term used in German; it evokes associations of "Americanization" and has, possibly therefore, somewhat deprecatory connotations, although no moral inferiority is imputed. The German work *Unternehmer* is more commonly used than the English "entrepreneur"; it is the favorite self-designation of upper middle- and upper-class businessmen.

of five placed their own profession as high. Judges and public prosecutors concurred in the high evaluation of their own status, but only 3 percent gave the *Rechtsanwalt* first or second rank.[117]

The evaluation patterns of the two groups of lawyers can be viewed as expressions of their mentality and their reference group orientations. Judges and public prosecutors display a markedly conservative pattern of ranking; ministers and priests stand next to judges at the top of the list, while all economic and technical occupations occupy, together with the artist, the lowest ranks. *Rechtsanwälte* follow these evaluations by and large, but with characteristic modifications. Aside from their different self-evaluation, they rank the entrepreneur higher and the higher civil servant and the minister lower than judges do. We note, however, that it is precisely these three occupations on which disagreement among private practitioners is greatest, a fact that may be interpreted to reflect the impact of divergent reference groups on the bar in private practice.

We have seen above that the generic figure of *Beamter* evokes ambivalent and predominantly negative associations, while there was some evidence that special types of civil servants, and particularly higher civil servants, are viewed more positively. Evidently the judges constitute such an exception as far as the *Rechtsanwälte* are concerned, although their work setting and their mentality are similar to those of higher civil servants in general; E. J. Cohn asserts in comparison to the English case, that "their ideological and social background is more akin to that which is associated in this country with civil servants than that which we would expect from one who after all is a member of the legal fraternity."[118]

That lawyers in public administration are—as members of the legal profession—to some extent exempted from the ambivalent rejection of civil servants is a guess which cannot be confirmed by available evidence, although their evaluation by private practitioners is by no means uniformly low. Whatever the status of this particular reference group, there are several qualitative judgments by knowledgeable observers which indicate that the attitudes and values prevalent in the *Rechtsanwaltschaft* are strongly influenced by the ethos of the civil service. According to one study: "All lawyers in Germany have, to a larger extent than they have with us [that is, in the United States], the official point of view and attitude." And Bader says: "Great reliability, industry and faithfulness towards the clientele are the rule in the German Anwaltschaft, and in this the German private practitioner resembles exactly the German judge and other German lawyers; also common, however, are timid adaptation to the dominant temper and considerable respect for the authorities."[119] Both observations date back to the 1940's, but they still seem applicable today, at least to a sizeable segment of the German *Rechtsanwaltschaft*.

Businessmen are the most important group of clients. As such they should be a powerful reference group for a good many *Rechtsanwälte*. However, in comparison with the American case, a number of factors limit the impact of this reference group. The socioeconomic status of *Rechtsanwälte* is superior to that of a larger proportion of their business clients, which results in a greater social distance toward the clientele; German private practitioners appear to be generally—with the exception of syndic-attorneys—less involved in the nonlegal aspects of their clients' business, in problems of financing and of commercial policy, and the lawyer-client relationship seems typically defined in a more specific way, thus reducing the impact of the business milieu. Furthermore, *Rechtsanwälte* from business homes do not form the dominant background group in the professions. Value orientations held widely in the upper middle and upper classes give a more limited legitimation to orientations and practices typical of the business world; and these value orientations seem particularly strong among *Akademiker* of the traditional variety and *Juristen* as a whole—the major competing reference groups for the bar in private practice.

Still, business clients, especially permanent clients with lucrative matters whose employment can in addition confer prestige and offer the opportunity to participate in important decisions, do constitute a significant reference group for the German *Rechtsanwaltschaft*. Insofar as this reference group stands in contrast with the others of the profession at large and the *Akademiker,* some ambivalence in orientations and polarization of the *Rechtsanwaltschaft* are the consequence. An indication of this was found in the fact that the entrepreneur is one of the occupations in Table 15 on whose relative social importance private practitioners showed disagreement. There is, furthermore, some evidence on a division of opinion within the *Rechtsanwaltschaft* on a number of other relevant topics, a division which is related to financial success.[120] This polarization is, however, held within fairly narrow limits, which can be explained by a common and rather homogeneous pattern of socialization and education for the legal profession as a whole and by the factors listed which tend to insulate the German private practitioner from the subculture of business.

A special category of *Akademiker,* the *freien Berufe*, or self-employed professions, seems of considerable importance as a reference group for the German bar in private practice precisely because of the tensions that exist between orientations toward the business clientele and toward civil service groups such as the judiciary. In emphasizing his membership in a *freier Beruf*, the *Rechtsanwalt* can identify with other high-status professions, such as physicians in private practice. Such a self-image acknowledges the income chances as well as the insecurities of self-employment—points of pride and concern to a good many German attorneys—without likening the lawyer's role to that of the businessman. At the same time, it permits expression of the major qualification of what in a comparative perspective may be called the *Rechtsanwalt's* "civil service orientation," his pride in being his own master.[121] The *freien Berufe* are, however, like the

*Rechtsanwaltschaft*, embedded in the broader category of university grad-uates and participate to a greater or lesser degree in the peculiar sub-culture of the *Akademikerstand*.

The German *Rechtsanwaltschaft*, then, constitutes a professional com-munity that is more than the American bar in private practice insulated against influences from its clientele, and especially its business clientele. Differences in involvement in business matters introduce variations into the outlook and orientations of lawyers in private practice, but these do not seriously threaten the cohesion of the *Anwaltschaft*, in part because syndic-attorneys tend to be considered members in name only. At the same time, while taking pride in the independence of self-employment, the Ger-man bar in private practice has strong links to groups that stand for the ethos of service to the state and to the wider groups which represent relatively conservative ideals of the educated upper middle classes. If, in a sense, the subculture of the German bar in private practice is closer to the model of professionalism, distinct from the orientations and values of business, it seems largely due to the impact of these latter reference groups.

# 4

# PROFESSIONAL ETHICS:
# SIMILARITIES AND CONTRASTS

In this chapter the norms of professional ethics will be considered only from the point of view of whether the pattern of contrast and similarity in legal ethics fits with the picture drawn of the two professions and of their place in their respective societies. "Professional ethics" may be understood to involve many different types of norms—formally enacted statutes, professional codes, the body of precedent from court decisions or committee opinions, special treatises, opinions advanced at meetings and conventions, or the convictions about right and wrong lawyers express in the daily contacts of work more or less casually. These varied manifestations of professional norms differ from each other in content, in the manner of articulation, in binding authority, in acceptance as legitimate by various segments of the profession, and in the kinds of sanctions available for each type.

The present discussion will be concerned mainly, and nearly exclusively, with two sources—with the official norms laid down in the respective codes of ethics[1] and with major writings on the professional responsibility of lawyers which interpret the codes, report and discuss case decisions, state what they consider the *communis opinio* of the responsible elements of the profession, and advance their own reasoning. At various points an attempt will be made to arrive at estimates about the norms held less officially by the bar at large and about the amount and the patterns of deviance, but the main focus will be on the official norms.

This approach is likely to minimize the differences between the two bars. The core of the role of private legal counsel is virtually identical in

123

the two countries. Furthermore, the explicitly formalized norms have in the classic professions a long and cherished tradition which is shared across national boundaries; this should make them less responsive to the exigencies of different factual situations and even to divergent value orientations widely held in different countries.[2] Yet contrasts in legal ethics will be the more significant if they are found at this most official level of professional norms.

## THE COMMON CORE OF THE DUTIES
## OF PRIVATE LEGAL COUNSEL

The basic obligations of private counsel which are similar across the world provide a starting point for our discussion. The attorney is entrusted with certain phases of the administration of justice. He therefore owes a fundamental loyalty to the legal order and to the law. He is, in American terms, an "officer of the court," or in the similar, though somewhat broader German formula, *ein Organ der Rechtspflege*. At the same time, he is not an employee of the government or the court. He renders his professional services to clients at their expense and on a basis of mutual trust. He is the ally of the party, his loyalty limited only by his commitment to the law and due process and by his explicit duties to other role partners.

He furthermore owes certain obligations to his colleagues, to those he is in a direct relationship with as well as to his colleagues as a group: he has duties to his profession. The duty to maintain the dignity, honor, and reputation of the profession is often deemed especially crucial in the case of the legal profession because of the distinctive and in large part inevitable bases for popular suspicion and dissatisfaction and because of the particular importance of trust in the lawyer-client relationship.[3]

The different professional duties and obligations can come into conflict with each other. In comparison with other professionals this is especially true for the lawyer, who deals with actual and potential social conflict in a partisan way and yet is bound by his loyalty to the law. To strike the proper balance between these obligations is at the core of all of the more difficult questions of legal ethics. The need for this balancing of multiple loyalties constitutes the basis for one of the most elemental duties of the lawyer, the duty to maintain his independence.

These four, then, are the basic obligations of the attorney and counsel from which flow the multitude of more specific norms: to be loyal to the law and the administration of justice, to be loyal to his client, to be loyal to his colleagues and their professional community, and to maintain his independent freedom of judgment and decision.

124

## THE LAWYER'S DUTIES TO HIS CLIENT

Werner Kalsbach, the contemporary German authority on legal ethics, quotes Canon 15 of the former American code and calls it a standard "common to the bar across national boundaries": "The lawyer owes entire devotion to the interests of the client, warm zeal in the maintenance and defense of his rights and the exertion of his utmost learning and ability to the end that nothing be taken or withheld from him, save by the rules of law, legally applied. No fear of judicial disfavor or public unpopularity should restrain him from the full discharge of his duty. In the judicial forum the client is entitled to the benefit of any and every remedy."[4] While such a general proclamation is indeed universally acceptable to lawyers, we shall encounter significant differences in detail, differences that can be summarized as a stronger emphasis in the German bar on the lawyer's independence, which limits the demands and rights of the client, as well as a greater stress on the peculiarly professional and "official" character of the relationship.

### ACCEPTING OR REJECTING A CASE

In contrast to the physician, the attorney both in Germany and in the United States is free to reject any case, except where assigned by the court. Henry Drinker states this right poignantly: "The lawyer may choose his own cases and for any reason or without a reason may decline any employment which he does not fancy."[5] Again in contrast to the physician, the attorney in both countries is not permitted to accept every case that is offered to him. To take the two most important rules, the attorney is not allowed to accept a case (1) if doing so would aid pursuits of his clients that he recognizes to be against the law and (2) if accepting it would involve him in representing "conflicting interests." On the first rule, legal ethics in both bars agree in principle. The lawyer, not the client, is responsible for what the lawyer does. Theoretically, the German position is more restrictive, insisting that a case must not be accepted against the lawyer's personal conviction as to its legal justification and against those rules of law and morals that he ought to take into account. By contrast, American and, generally, common law opinion argues that the attorney's function is different from that of the judge and that his particular conviction is irrelevant.[6] In both countries, of course, the lawyer is not obliged to convince himself of the innocence of the accused before accepting his defense.

We find similar subtle differences between the two patterns of norms concerning "conflict of interest." To represent conflicting interests in the practice of law is in Germany a crime classified under the heading "Crimes committed in public office"—a legacy of the late eighteenth century, when attorneys were made into civil servants, employees of the court.[7] The definition of conflicting interests in Germany is extremely complicated, and we need not go into all details. Important in this context is a duality of rationale that underlies the detailed prescriptions. To represent conflicting interests would violate the trust of the client as well as the principle that the lawyer, as an officer of the court, should stand by the course of action once chosen. The emphasis in both the penal code and the code of ethics is on the latter violation. A consequence of this emphasis is that consent of the clients involved does not justify the *Anwalt*'s working for both sides. Furthermore, for reasons of the clientele's confidence and the image of public officers, it is a violation of legal ethics to create even the appearance of representing conflicting interests. In the United States, the emphasis is clearly on the protection of the client's interests. Ethical considerations and a disciplinary rule of the new code require on the one hand that counsel decline any employment "that will adversely affect his judgment on behalf of or dilute his loyalty to a client"; on the other hand, the Code allows for consent of the clients after full disclosure and provided that "it is obvious that the lawyer can adequately represent the interest of each."[8]

Seriously violating the trust of the client is considered in both professions a serious offense, whether we consult the official norms or the available evidence on the attitudes and the behavior of the run-of-the-mill practitioner. The official standards, in their definition of what constitutes conflict of interests, seek to fend off all temptations, but both from Germany and the United States it is reported that the relevant rules are very frequently objects of requests for advice.[9] Voûte and Hardenberg conclude from a statement of Drinker to this effect that there are many violations of the more technical aspects of the rule. This conclusion may seem hasty. However, it was corroborated by two survey studies, in New York City and in a middle-sized Midwestern city.[10] Similar evidence on Germany is not available. It appears, however, both from the literature and from occasional interviews that there may be a good deal of confusion about the details of the rules but that the vast majority of German lawyers are not at all inclined on their own judgment to cut down formal rules to the size they might deem warranted for the protection of their clients' real interests.

### WITHDRAWAL FROM THE CASE

Once the American lawyer has accepted a case his freedom to terminate the relationship to his client is severely curtailed. He may withdraw only under compelling circumstances. According to the old Canon 44, "even the desire or consent of the client is not always sufficient. The lawyer should not throw up the unfinished task to the detriment of his client except for reasons of honor of self-respect.'' Under all circumstances, he has to take "reasonable steps to avoid foreseeable prejudice to the rights of his client.''[11] The German lawyer, by contrast, is free to terminate his employment at any time. Although the guidelines for professional behavior state that he may not withdraw at a time disadvantageous to his client, except for compelling reasons, and that even in case of such reasons he has to do those things for his clients that do not allow for delay, Kalsbach argues that these duties derive from the law of contracts only and that professional ethics leave the attorney and counsel entirely free to withdraw at any time. The basis for this opinion is a peculiarly one-sided conception of the required trust between lawyer and client: "If this relationship of trust is destroyed or even if only one of the two parties to the contract do not want to maintain this trust, the unilateral dissolution of the contractual relationship by the lawyer does not violate the professional ethos.''[12] German legal ethics, then, impose a lesser duty on the lawyer to continue his service to the client than the general law of contracts does on the parties to any contract, a remarkable condition which I am inclined to interpret in the context of what was said above about the interpenetration of the subculture of the German bar with remnants of estate-like class relations, an authoritarian civil service ethos and an idealistic professionalism hostile to many elements in its social environment.

### PROFESSIONAL SERVICE TO THE CLIENT

The lawyer is a professional expert serving lay clients. He has a duty to give competent service, although his customer cannot really control his performance in all phases. He often acts in place of his client, he represents him, in a fiduciary capacity, and this in a situation of actual or potential conflict. "The lawyer is a fiduciary in the highest sense. The affirmative duty of loyalty . . . applies in the strongest way to him.''[13]

On the other hand, the loyalty to the client is limited in several ways. The lawyer may not aid the client in illegal pursuits; the more his service involves the designing and planning of future transactions, the more prominent become the duties derived from the counsel's commitment to law and justice which may force him to oppose the client. The second limitation of the lawyer's loyalty to his client, supportive of the first, is his duty to maintain independence of judgment and action. Finally, there are obligations to the court, the opposing party, the witnesses, and to his colleagues which in some ways limit the attorney in the pursuit of his client's interests.

Again, if stated in such broad outline there is no difference between the two professions in the norms regulating the lawyer's relationship to his client. Significant differences are found in relative emphases, in certain details, and probably in informal operating norms which are closer to actual behavior.

There is clearly a stronger emphasis in the German writings on legal ethics on the duty to maintain one's independence from the client. Kalsbach treats the duty to maintain this independence to all sides as one of the two central duties of the *Rechtsanwalt*, the other being to maintain the dignity, honor, and reputation of the profession. He emphasizes how easy it is to become dependent on the client, through financial relations or through incorrect behavior which the client may threaten to reveal. "In no respect as much as in this is the urgent demand *'Principiis obsta*! .'" It is here that Kalsbach draws a parallel between attorney and civil servant, worth quoting at length:

> The attorney is not a *Beamter*. The penal sanctions against taking bribes in public office cannot be applied to him. And yet his role makes it necessary to acknowledge in the regulations of professional behavior the nucleus of these norms of penal law: A fee that exceeds the limits of moderation contains the danger that a lawyer who does not want to lose this client is led to a behavior which he would not have considered right otherwise. The same can be true for gifts, social advantages and other similar things . . . If he only once "offers the little finger," he must not be astonished when "the whole hand is taken." If he gives up his freedom once it is lost forever; and he who once enters the "devil's circle" is in danger never to get out of it again. At the least, however, the lawyer has to understand clearly in such or similar cases of temptation that it is his professional duty to avoid the appearance of impropriety.[14]

Of course, the American legal profession does not approve of a lawyer being simply a tool of the client. On the contrary: "The usefulness and loyalty of the lawyer are too often measured by the degree of his subservience to the client's wishes and plans. Such a view degrades the legal profession."[15] However, there is clearly less concern that the lawyer in his daily work may become dependent on the client. If excessive fees and gifts are a matter of concern, it is because the lawyer may take advantage of the client, and discussions of professional independence are primarily concerned with safeguarding efficient service to the client: "The lawyer need not often be troubled by the question whether a tendered case is unjust. This is fortunate, for, if the lawyer were always troubled by the doubt whether he should take a case, and whether each step in the case was a proper one, he could scarcely act with the vigor and effectiveness to which his client is entitled. The principal reason that the lawyer is not often troubled by the injustice of an offered case is that most cases are not unjust. Basically, most clients are decent people, and most cases involving

128

disputes have something on each side.''[16] A discussion of the qualities which make for success at the bar comments on the "gift of sympathy to take the part of the client properly": "Almost anyone can learn in the old phrase 'to strive mightily' in court; but there is a vast difference between the man who strives by main force and the one who strives sympathetically. The young man who feels (and he soon learns to know the feeling) that he cannot like every client he would like to have, may find delightful and even lucrative professional occupation; but he will rarely if ever rise to the higher planes of advocacy.''[17]

Both of these statements of fact are likely to be true in Germany too. However, the second would not be stated without indicating that here is a major temptation to unprofessional behavior if not an attitude plainly at variance with the professional code, and with respect to the first, we saw that the major German text chooses to emphasize, one is tempted to say exaggerate, the opposite: "Supporting the interests of the client can easily come into conflict with the duties of the lawyer as an officer in the administration of justice [*Organ der Rechtspflege*].''[18]

The right of the German lawyer to terminate his relationship with the client at any time gives him more freedom to assert his position against the client than his American colleague has. "The [American] lawyer's privilege to determine what he is to do after the case is taken is narrower than his freedom in determining whether he will take the case at all. For after the case is taken, it may be his duty to present an honest, though unfair, defense, if the client insists on it.''[19] The difference in the principles governing the acceptance of a case is replicated in regard to the question of how far a lawyer may go in supporting the interests of his client, but the contrast is reinforced in this second respect through the divergent rules about withdrawal from the case.

From the wide range of detailed regulations and case decisions about the attorney-client relationship and its limitations only one topic will be discussed here, namely some of the rights and duties of counsel defending a client who confessed his guilt to the lawyer. In criminal cases the basic structure of criminal procedure in both countries makes it the burden of the state to prove the accused guilty. However, the German criminal procedure is not based on the adversary principle. The prosecution is held to consider all points in favor of the accused in a quasi-judicial manner. Conversely, counsel has to observe certain limits in his defense lest he commit a crime of intentionally favoring a criminal. Legal ethics require a lawyer in addition to avoid ill appearances. German criminal proceedings provide for two kinds of verdict of "not guilty": not guilty because of lack of proof and positively not guilty. Legal ethics prevent the defense counsel from pleading for the second kind if he "knows" that the client is guilty.[20] It is not infrequently counseled that a lawyer who receives a confession from the client after he has taken the case should withdraw from the case under some pretext. Such is not, however, considered his duty.

The American defense counsel is, like his German brother, left to his own conscience as to what precisely constitutes "fair and honorable means" of the defense. But he definitely may plead for a verdict of not guilty "regardless of his personal opinion as to the guilt of the accused."[21] Some American lawyers make it a practice to withdraw from the case if they learn after acceptance that the client is guilty. According to the majority in the American Bar Association committee they are justified in doing so, but only if they have informed the client of their intention before accepting the case: "A lawyer consenting to appear for a defendant accused of a crime has no right to receive the confidence of his client, invited by that relation if the lawyer has formed an intention undisclosed to his client, to retire from the case, if he becomes convinced of the client's guilt." The dissenting opinion holds that the lawyer should not reserve such a right of withdrawal.[22]

This particular instance of a contrast between German and American legal ethics suggests that all the differences in emphasizing client loyalty are due to the different procedural arrangements. The American adversary system of trial relies on the balancing effect of opposing partisan argument, providing only for those restraints that seem necessary as rules of the game. It must be noted, however, that in civil cases German procedure, too, is built on the adversary model, if in a modified way. Furthermore, the general injunctions regarding independence, client loyalty, and obligations toward the administration of justice cover much more than work at court. Although American writers point out that counseling and planning out of court should be guided by more restraints, it appears that in the United States the obligations toward the client are stronger throughout legal practice than in Germany. Differences that may have historical roots in contrasts in procedure appear, then, extended to the general ethos of the two bars, and such extension is in line with our analysis of the reference groups and the subculture of the two professions.

It may be argued that American writers on legal ethics are simply more "realistic" and that the operating norms of the German *Rechtsanwaltschaft* are likely to be quite similar to those of the American bar. I would maintain, however, first that it makes a difference which obligations are stressed by formal rules and their authoritative interpreters. Aside from that there are some indications that the normative convictions held by the rank and file members of the American and the German bar, as well as their actual behavior, make for an even greater contrast between the two professions. The two studies of lawyers in New York and in a

Midwestern city referred to before showed that substantial minorities, confronted with hypothetical situations, did not disapprove of bribery and fraud in the interests of their clients.[23] While again no comparable evidence is available for Germany, it is beyond doubt that there is no comparable distance between official norms and actual attitudes among the *Rechtsanwälte*. Informants stressed that even the lower strata of the bar show a fairly high conformity with the official norms. It would even be an extreme estimate to say that German metropolitan conditions approach those of the middle-sized city studied. About operative norms protecting serious interests of the client it is virtually impossible to arrive at a comparative judgment, although the survey in New York City shows that here the normative commitments of a small but significant segment of the bar have been undermined in this respect, too.

SETTING THE FEE

The most obvious rationales for provisions of legal ethics about fees are two—to give a minimum protection to the client and to limit competition among colleagues. Patently, these two considerations may easily come into conflict with each other. Professional tradition—common to all classic professions—adds further dimensions of significance to these regulations. The distinct character of a profession is in this tradition in large measure seen in contrast to the business world—a historical heritage which has changed from the ancient and medieval disdain for mere economic pursuits to an emphasis on values and orientation presumably required for, or at least supportive of, the discharge of a public service. It is argued that restraint in the pursuit of economic gain not only would protect clients who may be in a vulnerable position but that it would generally contain within tolerable limits one major source of pressures to violate the complex network of rules hedging the role of attorney.

In both countries such ideals are invoked by spokesmen of the profession. Roscoe Pound defines a profession as a "group of men pursuing a learned art as a common calling in the spirit of a public service—no less a public service because it may incidentally be a means of livelihood."[24] The German statute regulating private legal practice declares the profession of the *Rechtsanwalt* to be a *freier Beruf* and adds: "His activity is not a business." Werner Kalsbach comments: "The character of the *freier Beruf* . . . is in large measure defined by the fact that its members *do not let themselves be guided by the pursuit of profit*."[25] Yet in spite of this similarity in basic ideals there are fundamental differences in the specific provisions regulating fees in the two bars. While fee-setting is rather tightly controlled in the German bar, for the American attorney it is basically a matter of free contract between him and the client. Both the old and the

131

new American codes give some guidance as to what constitutes a reasonable fee, and state and local bar associations often suggest fee schedules. However, these schedules cannot define compulsory minimum fees. Price competition among lawyers is thus specifically, if often perhaps only nominally, protected. Further, while Disciplinary Rule 2-106 forbids "clearly excessive fees," an upper ceiling is not easily given a meaningful definition. Drinker comments deftly on the old Canon 12: "There is no ethical question involved unless fees are flagrantly excessive."[26]

The German bar operates under a statutory fee schedule, which is in principle binding for the attorney. The rationale given for this regulation by the commentator of the guidelines is noteworthy. Kalsbach argues that excessive differences in the fees charged could lead to the disintegration of the profession. In his opinion, official schedules and regulations "are indispensable if one is not to see the attorney's work as a purely individual matter but rather as intricately connected with the framework in which the profession integrates its members."[27] *Rechtsanwalt* and client may agree on higher fees, but the attorney has to make explicit that, and by how much, they are at variance with the fees set out in the official schedule; to demand a higher fee otherwise is punishable under the penal code. The guidelines demand that the fees thus contracted should "not exceed the limits of moderation." In most cases, no special agreement is made and the official schedule determines the *Anwalt*'s remuneration. To ask less than the statutory schedule provides for is not simply a matter of agreement between attorney and client. Guideline 39 allows for certain exceptions, especially for the indigent client, but these are again limited by the injunction to avoid price competition and even the suspicion of illegitimate solicitation.[28]

The point on which the regulations of the two bars differ most radically is the problem of the contingent fee. Until 1957, fees contingent on the success of the lawyer's work were in Germany prohibited by statute. Since then, the problem is left to the profession, and a definite consensus has not yet crystallized. The guidelines prohibit without exception agreements which set the fee as a percentage of the amount recovered, but allow in exceptional cases a fee which in other ways is dependent on the outcome. Kalsbach—who in 1956 still took an uncompromising negative position, arguing that any relaxation of the prohibition would quickly turn the *Rechtsanwalt* into a businessman, undermine his detachment and independence, and threaten the whole structure of the *Anwaltschaft* as a profession—today rejects the distinction made by the guidelines between different forms of contingent fees, but insists that exceptions to the prohibition of either variety must be justified on narrowly construed grounds and

132

that the amount of the fee must be within the limits of moderation, never exceeding 10 percent of the recovery.

The major field in which contingent fee agreements have become common in Germany are matters of restitution to victims of the Nazi regime. These are decided in the first instance by administrative agencies which have no provisions for legal aid to indigent parties, so that in many cases there are problems of paying the attorney. Furthermore, clients residing in foreign countries who are there represented by counsel on a contingent fee basis have little understanding for the *Anwalt's* refusal to agree to the same arrangement. Finally, representatives other than the *Rechtsanwälte* can appear for the parties so that the *Anwaltschaft's* refusal to take matters on a basis convenient to clients would lead to the loss of a field of work the size of which is not insignificant. Different customs in foreign bars, then, in conjunction with the needs of the clientele and the collective interests of the *Rechtsanwaltschaft*, have engendered a major break with the older position which rejected contingent fee arrangements completely. This has resulted in some uncertainty as to the principles concerning the matter, but the official position tends to remain one of extreme reserve.[29]

The American attorney is allowed to ask for, and takes regularly, contingent fees in many areas of work. Disciplinary Rule 5-103 allows for this exception from the injunction against acquiring a proprietary interest in the cause of a client, while Disciplinary Rule of 2-106 forbids contingent fees in criminal cases. Typically, the fees are far higher than in Germany, going up to 33 and even 50 percent of the net amount recovered.[30] Contingent fees are a matter of concern in the United States, too. The New York County Lawyers' Committee, to select this one from many voices, diagnoses the consequences of the contingent fee in its Opinion 141 and comes to quite similar conclusions as Kalsbach, but it does not reject the practice. "It develops both in the lay and in the professional mind a conception of the practice of law as a business, not a profession, and tends to lower the essential standards of the Bar."[31] More common, however, is the view expressed by Max Radin: "The case for and against the contingent fee, if we disregard considerations of history and what may be called snobbery, may be briefly summarized. The contingent fee certainly increases the possibility that vexatious and unfounded claims will be brought. On the other hand, it makes possible the enforcement of legitimate claims which otherwise would be abandoned because of the poverty of the claimants. Of these two possibilities, the social advantage seems clearly on the side of the contingent fee. It may in fact be added by way of reply to the first objection that vexatious and unfounded suits have been brought by men who could and did pay substantial attorneys' fees for

133

that purpose.''[32] Although this summary argument is quite simplified, it points to the crucial components of the problem. What is at stake is (1) whether the professional independence and the "disinterested" role of the lawyer must be strengthened or whether some weakening may be tolerated, (2) whether the "honor and dignity" of the profession, especially its distinctiveness from the business world, should be emphasized, directly as well as symbolically, or whether this is to be considered as a historical relic of medieval times, worse, as "snobbery," and (3) whether there is an alternative to the contingent fee for providing legal services to the poor and persons of limited means.

Against these three tests, the respective positions of the German and the American bar are entirely consistent with the overall patterns of legal ethics as well as with the institutional environment in which they operate. (1) The adversary system of trial and the general ethos of the American bar allow for a greater measure of identification with the client's cause. That even in this system there is a public interest in limiting the parallelism of counsel's and client's motivations, and that in some cases the effectiveness of the lawyer's advocacy may be reduced because he is considered to gain from what he asks for—for example, in the application for discretionary decisions of administrative bodies—seems to be a plausible explanation for the recurrent concern in the American bar about the consequences of the contingent fee. (2) "Honor and dignity" of separate groups defined by birth, education, or occupation have a weaker tradition in the United States. There is a competing and stronger tradition which considers any such claims to special duty *cum* privilege as "snobbery," if not an outright danger to the protection of the dignity of all. In addition, there is less incentive to distinguish one's group from business in a society where the business community is not only politically dominant but also "ennobled" by its involvement in education, large-scale charity, and "community leadership" than in a society where significant groups in education, religion, and culture share a subculture with the legal profession, which is distinctively set off from, if not hostile toward the business world. The ascendancy of the business community in postwar Germany may have eased recent adaptations which were, however, mainly the result of other factors. (3) Finally, the German and the American arrangements for legal service to the poor differ greatly and in such ways that Radin's controlling argument has a much weaker force in Germany as far as most fields of legal practice are concerned. This will be discussed presently.

## SERVING THE POOR

The original tradition in both professions is identical. To serve the poor without consideration has been considered a *nobile officium* in all classic professions since antiquity. There are good reasons to doubt the efficiency of this injunction from the point of view of the poor; but then their point of view was given scanty consideration only. Still, in both countries many attorneys individually give service to clients of inadequate means for a lesser or no fee, and in both countries the duty of counsel to serve the indigent client as conscientiously as the wealthy is stressed. Institutional arrangements providing legal service to the poor exist in both countries, but while the German system is uniform throughout the country and essentially government financed, the American pattern varies from state to state; there are various forms of charity-financed legal aid which were supplemented in the "War Against Poverty" by special, federally funded, legal services for the poor. It appears that the German system is far more effective.[33]

There is little need to go into organizational details. Carlin and Howard document in detail for the United States that the system of assigned counsel and public defenders in criminal law as well as legal aid in civil matters is far from adequate. In regard to legal aid, they list the following principal limitations: "(1) grossly inadequate resources, (2) vulnerability to demands of the local bar and local businessmen (which may and often do conflict with the best interests of the Legal Aid client), and (3) the tendency of Legal Aid to adopt a social-welfare orientation toward its clients and toward its overall goals."[34] All such assessments of the need for legal aid, it may be noted, take into consideration that many cases can be handled in regular fashion on a contingent fee basis.

Provisions for access to the courts by poor persons and those of limited means have a long tradition in Germany. "It is not only the traditional disapproval of contingent fees but long-recognized considerations of social policy that explain the elaborate provisions of German law which secure legal representation of indigent parties and otherwise facilitate civil litigation by the poor."[35] Fees for court and counsel are low in the first place if the amount at stake is small. In addition, the courts grant state legal aid liberally. Under this arrangement, the court asks a lawyer, usually the one chosen by the party, to serve the client for a fee paid by the state. Legal aid in matters requiring advice is less comprehensive, but "legal information offices" exist in all cities with a population of more than 100,000 and in many smaller cities.[36] If the legal needs of the indigent, whether recognized as such by the parties themselves or not, are measured by the standards of the average upper-middle class person, overall access to legal services is inadequate in both countries, but there can be no doubt that the German system of government aid in conjunction with the response of the bar serves the poor better than the American system, which relies more on

135

private charity. To what extent this is due to differences in ideals of the bar and their observance is difficult to judge on the basis of presently available evidence.

## THE LAWYER'S DUTIES TO HIS COLLEAGUES

The obligations of lawyers to each other include, first, a general "duty to uphold the integrity and the honor of [their] profession" as Ethical Consideration 9-5 of the new American code puts it. They include, second, a set of specific rules outlawing advertising and solicitation, urging candor, fairness, and courtesy to one's colleagues, and protecting the attorney-client relationship against interference by other lawyers. Finally, one might include here some items which also relate to the concern for the administration of justice, namely the rules about the lawyer's relations to neighboring occupations as well as to the unauthorized practice of law.

### THE HONOR AND INTEGRITY OF THE PROFESSION

There are subtle differences in the concern for the integrity of the profession. Kalsbach treats the "duty to uphold the dignity, the honor and the reputation of the profession" as one of the two basic obligations of the lawyer,[37] while Drinker gives only passing attention to matters of honor and dignity. The new Code of Professional Responsibility devotes its first canon to the subject matter, but its language—"A lawyer should assist in maintaining the integrity and competence of the legal profession"—differs significantly from Kalsbach's formulation by including a concern for competence and by less emphasis on questions of collective dignity and reputation. Such differences of emphasis in general principle are reflected in some more specific rules. In Germany it is a punishable violation of legal ethics to create the reasonable suspicion or appearance that one has acted against the law or major provisions of the guidelines. The new American code also urges lawyers "to avoid even the appearance of professional impropriety" (Canon 9), but the related disciplinary rules confine themselves to prohibiting a few specific actions considered liable to create ill appearances.[38]

A related problem is how one deals with known wrongdoing in the bar. It is often advantageous for the reputation of the profession to handle these things as much as possible *en famille*. The American and the German codes are in perfect opposition on this point. American lawyers are obliged, by Disciplinary Rules 1-102 and 1-103, to report to the proper tribunal or agency any knowledge they have of violations of disciplinary rules, of "illegal conduct involving moral turpitude," of "conduct involving dishonesty, fraud, deceit or misrepresentation," of "conduct that is prejudicial to the administration of justice," or of "any other conduct that adversely reflects on [a colleague's] fitness to practice law."

German legal ethics reject a general duty of the *Anwalt* to inform public authorities of wrongdoing in the bar beyond the obligation imposed by the penal code on all citizens. Guideline 13 states that "every *Rechtsanwalt* has to see to it that other colleagues, too, do not violate the honor of the profession and endanger its reputation," but this is, according to Kalsbach, to be understood as an injunction to warn the colleague in a serious case, not as a right to supervision and control. Before an *Anwalt* takes his case against a colleague to any public agency and especially before he initiates civil or criminal proceedings, he has to inform the board of the *Rechts-anwaltskammer* so that in suitable cases the board can intervene and "as far as possible, eliminate the basis of the complaints without letting the subject of such disputes become known to the outside."[39]

The German rules reveal an image of the legal profession that is quite different from the one implicit in the American Code. The German bar aspires to a higher degree of solidarity, it gives greater emphasis to the need to protect the reputation of the bar and it seems more confident that measures to prevent notoriety in cases of actual wrongdoing will basically be justified by a low level of deviant behavior in the bar. By comparison, the official norms of the American bar give less protection to the dignity of appearances and to the solidarity of the profession.

### ADVERTISING AND SOLICITATION

The official norms of legal ethics in both professions firmly reject advertising and solicitation. This is seen in both countries as crucial for the maintenance of the professional character of legal practice. Restrictions on advertising and solicitation have a number of functions, manifest as well as latent ones. They keep professional traditions alive by making a distinction between business customs and professional behavior; but there are more tangible consequences, too. To allow advertising as in business would presuppose that the client can adequately judge the quality of services offered by different members of the profession. On the one hand, it would give the uninformed choices of the clientele a controlling influence over the profession incompatible with the maintenance of high technical standards; on the other hand, the harm which results from less than honest advertising "would, in large measure, fall on the ignorant and on those least able to afford it."[40] Advertising would furthermore increase competition among lawyers who under pressure might give in to temptation to deviate from other professional norms; specifically there might be a temptation to fulfill with illegitimate means promises made in advertising. Finally, free advertising and solicitation would stir up litigation.

The official rules on advertising and solicitation in the two bars differ only in technical detail, but it appears that there are strong contrasts in their implementation. The German guidelines deny in meticulous regulations any individual advertising to the *Anwalt*. Kalsbach even rejects collective and purely informative advertising by bar associations, which the guidelines allow.[41] Drinker asserts for the United States: "The legal profession is not relaxing the standards."

> There has not, it is believed, been any weakening of the condemnation by the bar associations of solicitation. What they have done is to sanction and regulate reasonable advertising by bar associations, the publication of law lists designed to enable persons who need a lawyer to choose the best suited to their needs, and to condemn, without any relaxation, all other forms of advertising and solicitation.[42]

There is little need to go into the multifarious detail of regulations about shingles, letterheads, professional cards, announcements of opening of practice, etc. The law lists mentioned by Drinker, however, are not known in Germany and constitute a significant divergence in the norms of the two bars. Published outside the profession, although supervised by the American Bar Association, they contain information on the fields of law practiced by an attorney, his educational, professional, and public career, and the names of references and regular clients with their consent. Lawyers may—and are asked to—pay considerable sums for being included in such lists, and some lists revise their fees according to the volume of business received by the listees.[43] The German guidelines allow the *Anwalt* to inform the board of the *Rechtsanwaltskammer* of his competence in special fields of law and in foreign languages. While usually requests for information are referred back to the general directory of lawyers in private practice, specific inquiries are answered on the basis of specialty lists thus collected, giving each lawyer listed an equal chance.[44] The principal differences are that the American lists are composed and published by "lay" agencies, are more easily available to the public, contain more detailed information on which invidious comparisons can be based, and charge a fee to the lawyer which is more or less directly related to the commercial value of the listing. While the American practice better serves the interests of the clientele, it is also likely to reinforce more strongly the differentiation and stratification of the bar.

The existence of commercial law lists in the United States is also a major difference in the related regulations concerning specialization. In the present context the question is not whether lawyers should specialize, but only whether a lawyer may hold himself out as a specialist. Because of a variety of considerations and vested interests, the organized bar in both countries is resisting pressures for more liberal regulations. In both countries, announcing a specialty on shingles, letterheads, and in general directories is permitted for very few fields only—for tax and public administration matters in Germany and for admiralty and patent or trademark matters in the United States.[45] Aside from these exceptions, the German attorney has only the already mentioned opportunity to advise the board of his *Rechtsanwaltskammer* of any special competence. The American lawyer has more leeway. Disciplinary Rule 2-105 allows, in addition to advertising in law lists and public announcement of the historically excepted fields, to inform lawyer referral systems of fields in which he will accept referrals and to announce his availability as a specialist consultant to or associate of other lawyers in notices sent out to colleagues or in advertisements in legal journals.

Discrepancies between official norms and the moral convictions actually held in different subgroups of the profession may seem particularly likely in matters of advertising. The two studies previously referred to found that several violations of norms about advertising and solicitation were disapproved of only by parts of the bar. Among these were substantial referral fees paid to lawyers with little or no connection to the case referred, the sending of Christmas cards to clients, and gifts or free advice given to clients who referred cases; to reward clients with money for referred cases is, however, considered improper by most lawyers.[46] Furthermore, an analysis of disciplinary proceedings in New York over a long period disclosed that the most frequent type of violation (client solicitation) is least likely to constitute the main charge in the adjudicated cases. By contrast, all reports agree that the German committees and courts are "not ready for any concessions and maintain the proscription of advertising and solicitation at its strictest."[47]

While it appears to be rather limited in Germany, the level of deviance from these standards in the United States is generally considered high. The contrast goes far beyond the differences in the size of signs at attorneys' offices in America, which strike the visitor from Europe. As Johnstone and Hopson observe, "In some communities, illegal solicitation scoops up such a high percentage of the clientele in certain fields that few who do not solicit are consistently active in these fields." Although referral fees to laymen are generally considered improper, the practice "persists in the United States. It is more prevalent in the big cities, most notoriously in the plaintiffs' personal injury and criminal fields, and sometimes involves regularized relations between lawyers and runners or contact men employed by lawyers."[48]

139

Widespread violations of rules against advertising and solicitation, which are de facto tolerated, have consequences beyond the immediate sphere to which the rules apply. One might be inclined to brush these findings aside as relating to mere matters of etiquette, but the vast cleavage which exists between official standards, actual custom, and patterns of persistent deviance undermines the authority of other standards of legal ethics as well, and this effect may be more consequential than the direct outcomes of illicit solicitation.

## CANDOR, FAIRNESS, AND COURTESY TOWARD COLLEAGUES

The general ideal for the relations to colleagues is aptly stated by Drinker in quoting Shakespeare: "Do as adversaries do in law: strive mightily but eat and drink as friends."[49] While relations within the bar in industrial urban centers are far removed from the conditions at the Inns of Court in Shakespeare's time, the working on opposite sides of disputes makes some emphasis on "colleagueship" imperative for any bar. Both American and German legal ethics hold that an attorney cannot be excused in these matters by a simple reference to his client's instructions, but when serious interests of the client are at stake they take precedence over considerate behavior toward the colleague.[50] There is reason to believe that the generally stronger emphasis on loyalty to the client in the United States tips the balance, in case of such weighing, somewhat more in favor of the client's interest.[51] Proper respect and consideration for the colleague involve, among other things, the keeping of his confidences and standing by one's promises. They also require the attorney not to deal directly with another lawyer's clients and to observe the rules for superseding and superseded lawyers, which are essentially similar in both bars, forbidding the attorney to "steal another's clients" and leaving the decision about who is to be employed to the client.

## "DEFINING THE BOUNDARIES OF THE BAR
## AS A PROFESSIONAL GROUP"

In both countries, a lawyer is not allowed to enter into a partnership with members of other occupations or professions "if any of the activities of the partnership consist of the practice of law."[52] The German guidelines allow shared offices with certified public accountants, and some authors argue in favor of allowing a full partnership between members of the two professions, but this is not the position of the organized bar. While at first sight at odds with the comparatively conservative character of German legal ethics, this rule possibly finds its explanation in the fact that

German *Rechtsanwälte* are generally less involved in business matters than their American colleagues and that they therefore compete less with accountants.

Related to the question of forming partnerships with persons other than lawyers are two other problems: Is a lawyer barred from other occupational pursuits by virtue of his being a lawyer? and: Are there any restrictions as to the lawyer's contact with members of the lay groups? The American answer to both questions is free from special considerations of professional dignity. The controlling test with respect to the first problem is whether pursuing another occupation or business constitutes or leads to improper solicitation or advertisement. As long as the second business is in no way used "as a feeder to his law practice," nothing prevents the American lawyer from getting thus involved.[53] The American lawyer's relations to laymen are governed by two principles, none involving the protection of a special professional dignity. Disciplinary Rule 3-101 forbids aiding a layman in an unauthorized practice of law. The other principle, specified in Disciplinary Rule 5-107, insists on avoiding influence by others than the client.

While considerations of competition and advertising are not irrelevant, one guiding principle of German legal ethics as to the compatibility of other occupational pursuits with the practice of law is that the role of the *Rechtsanwalt* must be one's primary occupation and cannot be taken on as a sideline. Furthermore, any occupation that interferes with the independence of the bar as a *freier Beruf* is considered incompatible. And finally, other occupational pursuits must not detract from the reputation of the profession.[54] The admission of the syndic-attorney, who is as house counsel employed while devoting part of his time to the private practice of law, to the *Rechtsanwaltschaft* constitutes a partial exception from these principles. However, house counsel can be admitted only if the character of his position guarantees the required independence.

The social standing and prestige of an occupation also enter to some extent into the considerations concerning its compatibility. Kalsbach refers to public accountants and licensed tax advisers as "reputable occupations"; he considers subordinate public offices incompatible since they would detract from the reputation of the profession, and admission of house counsel requires a "high position" and a salary which gives him independence.[55] This interpretation receives some confirmation from the fact that in the not too distant past such considerations were made much more explicit and applied in more rigid fashion. A critic of the bar in the early thirties spoke of standards more applicable to the entrance require-

141

ments of an upper-class club than to admission to the bar.[56] By comparison, such extraneous considerations have virtually disappeared today. As to cooperation with laymen, the German rules are similar to those of the American bar. The primary regulation is that any professional connection with the unauthorized practice of law is against legal ethics. It may be mentioned, though, that in the rules about relations to legal advisers with a lesser training there are some regulations which seem based on invidious social considerations.[57]

## THE LAWYER'S DUTIES TO THE COURTS AND THE ADMINISTRATION OF JUSTICE

The central issues which arise as to the lawyer's obligations to the administration of justice have been dealt with from the opposite perspective above, when his duties toward the client were analyzed. If one allows for the different systems of procedure, the basic official obligations in this respect are the same in the two countries. The attorney has to speak the truth, to act within the bounds of the law, and to show candor and respect to the court. "Respect owed to the court," however, means something different when it is due, concretely, to members of what for all practical purposes is a different profession than when it is owed to "one of us," to a member of the bar in a particularly honored position. The major strains on agreeable relations between court and partisan counsel arise of course from the advocate's zeal for the cause of his client. One might expect these tensions to be greater in the German case, since the German judge participates more actively in the proceedings. Yet, as we have seen above, the limits to the lawyer's zeal are drawn somewhat wider in the American case, a difference which particularly in court proceedings is related to the ethos of the adversary system of trial.[58] The duty to act with candor and respect toward the court is a more elusive one than the other two—to speak the truth and to act within the law. Concerning the latter, the lines are, in theory at least, clear, and the attorney faces in both countries the same demands. It is likely, though, that in this respect, too, the enforcement as well as the acceptance of the rules is somewhat weaker in the United States than in Germany.[59]

A final matter may further illustrate the consequences of the two systems of trial for professional obligations toward the administration of justice. In Germany, it is predominantly the judge who examines the witnesses, in the United States, witnesses are presented and examined mainly by the two sides. The American attorney may, and regularly does, interview witnesses prior to trial: "It is fair and right for an attorney to go over the testimony of a witness, to cross-examine in advance his own witness, and to point out to him traps and pitfalls into which he may be lured by opposing counsel."[60] The German *Anwalt* may interview witnesses out of court only when it is justified by special circumstances. He has to avoid even the appearance of influencing the witness and is, in principle, not allowed to take written statements. Kaplan, von Mehren, and Schaefer describe the average attorney's attitude: "In singluar cases he may and will talk with prospective witnesses; but by and large he will not feel free to do so. In the majority of cases he will prepare himself on the facts only by consulting with his client." In criminal cases his right to interview witnesses is somewhat broader, but he has to be careful to avoid the crime of illegally favoring a criminal, especially when he "knows" his client to be guilty.[61]

## CONCLUSION

This discussion has deliberately focused on the official norms of legal ethics. Although there are good reasons to assume that these are more similar from country to country than either typical attitudes and value orientations or patterns of actual behavior, this analysis corroborates a number of assertions about the contrasting subcultures of the two bars. Throughout the complex detail of technical rules reviewed there are consistent differences in major emphasis which occasionally also find expression in squarely contradictory regulations.

The American bar emphasizes loyalty to the client more than the German *Rechtsanwaltschaft,* and this emphasis goes beyond what can be explained by the difference in the systems of trial. While the status of the attorney as an officer of the court is, of course, not neglected in American legal ethics, it does not receive the same relative emphasis and is not reinforced as much by detailed regulations as in the German bar. In the same vein, German legal ethics stress more the obligation of the lawyer to maintain his independence and a certain distance toward the client, and here again specific regulations such as the freedom of the *Rechtsanwalt* to terminate the relation at any point underline what otherwise might be considered a vague difference in general principle. Related to the central contrast, but also resting on a different self-image of the *Rechtsanwaltschaft* as a distinct social group, are the differences in the obligations a lawyer owes to his colleagues and the profession as a whole. German legal ethics protect professional solidarity and the bar's reputation more than the

American norms, for instance in its rules about fee setting, advertising, and the handling of complaints against colleagues.

From the evidence available it appears that there is a greater cleavage in the American than in the German bar between official standards and the standards actually viewed as binding by the rank and file of the profession. This seems especially true in metropolitan centers but applies to smaller communities as well. Therefore, it cannot be exclusively explained by the differentiation and stratification of the bar in large cities which has been shown to be related to divergent attitudes toward legal ethics. On a broader scale, it is likely to be connected with value orientations predominant in the society and the different positions of the two bars in the wider social structure. At several points above, we have reached the conclusion that the informal ethos of the American bar is generally less distinct than that of the German bar from the routine morality of the wider community and especially the business community.

Finally, there is little doubt, although again systematic comparative evidence is lacking, that deviance from professional ethics, and especially structured and persistent deviance, is much more prevalent in the American than in the German profession. This is far less true, though, for the bar in smaller American communities. While certainly the conditions of legal practice and differences in enforcement are important for an explanation of this difference, it may be surmised that the apparently very strong influence of situational factors, social and economic, on the commitment of lawyers to professional norms, found in studies of legal ethics in America, reflects differences between the two bars in social background, socialization, and formal education as well as contrasts in the societal values in regard to law and order.

A final word of caution. I have used in the above the standards of legal ethics, and to some extent their observance, as evidence in a comparative analysis of the German and the American legal profession. My interest has been descriptive and analytic, rather than moral and evaluative. Yet, using the language of the bar and of legal ethics may easily give the impression that judgments of good and bad, moral and immoral are at stake. Thus, the reader may have gained the impression that American lawyers are to be considered less ethical than their German colleagues in a general sense of the term. Before drawing that conclusion, one should carefully separate offenses against rules of form and etiquette from those of a more consequential nature; and in considering the latter one has to go beyond the prescriptions of either code and include the various ways in which the bar's activities and orientations affect the integrity of individuals and the welfare of society as a whole. To raise but one point in this regard, one could argue that the American bar would have proved to be a stronger bulwark against the authoritarian lawlessness of the early Nazi regime than the German *Rechtsanwaltschaft* was. Since the facts in the case have by no means been clearly established and since all such hypothetical constructions founder against the incomparability of concrete historical constellations, this must remain an open question, but an open question it is indeed, and one crucial to the problem raised.

# 5

# THE LEGACY OF THE PAST

Differences in the historical past may be crucial in accounting for present contrasts since, first, sociocultural patterns, especially value orientations, have a great deal of stability once they are firmly "institutionalized"—anchored in the matrix of prevalent custom and up-bringing. As Schumpeter has said: "Social structures, types and attitudes are coins that do not readily melt. Once they are formed they persist, possibly for centuries."[1] Second, the future course of any new development is likely to be affected by the social context in which it begins—by the obstacles to be overcome, by the enemies to be subdued, and by the various supporting forces. Specifically, the relative timing of different aspects of modernization is of central importance for the development of the legal profession. The radical changes associated with full-scale industrialization during the nineteenth century took place in very different societal settings as far as the legal structure and the role of government were concerned, and in particular they impinged on patterns of legal practice which differed greatly in professional organization and public control. This impact at first widened the contrast between the two professions, but then we witness trends toward convergence which can be described as "reprofessionalization" in the American bar and as emancipation from government control in the German bar. Nevertheless, these developments stopped short of engendering the same conditions in both professions. A good many of the present contrasts reflect the different historical legacy and cannot be understood fully unless the tensions and development of the past are taken into account.

## LEGAL PRACTICE UNDER PRE-INDUSTRIAL CONDITIONS
## IN PRUSSIA

Throughout the eighteenth and nineteenth centuries, Prussia proved to be the state most important for the general political and legal development in Germany as well as for emergence of the modern bar.[2]

The eighteenth century saw the Prussian government bureaucracy attain a controlling position in political and social life, based on increasing organizational efficiency and technical competence. This process involved a protracted three-cornered struggle for pre-eminence, as well as repeated compromises, between the royal autocrats, their bureaucratic corps, and the landed nobility. The administration of justice, traditionally a major stronghold of the landed aristocracy, was a crucial arena of this fight for power between the central administration and its feudal opponents.[3] Mingled with this struggle for power were, increasingly, attempts of the bureaucracy to institute "enlightened reforms" in the administration of justice, to implement the ideals of rational procedure and impersonal evenhandedness.

The bar, in its great majority not an aristocratic group though frequently associated with aristocratic interests, was subjected repeatedly to drastic reform measures imposed by the central administration. The old order of a dual bar had provided for a limited number of *procurators* who were attached to a given court, while the frequently better educated *advocates*, who originally had no right to appear in court, were admitted without a *numerus clausus* if they could prove sufficient legal education and if they were able to pay the fairly high admission fee.[4] This system was not deemed to provide adequate controls when the distinction between procurator and advocate slowly disappeared and most advocates attained the rights of procurators, too. Around 1700, Prussia had a large number of attorneys, about 1200, or more than one for every 2,000 people, a ratio that the Prussian bar was never to reach again and that was approximated only in the twentieth century.[5] Many of these laywers were not full-time attorneys but acted as administrators for landed aristocrats, secretaries of cities, or members of patrimonial courts.

Several factors determined the character of the administration of justice in seventeenth and eighteenth century Germany; they set the conditions for legal practice and for the moral dilemmas of attorneys. Courts of law, with few exceptions, were not set apart as separate agencies with a specialized personnel; rather, the administration of justice was merged with other governmental functions, typically under the control of the nobility. This lack of organizational differentiation corresponded, furthermore, to a blurring of the lines between the private status of officials and their office in

147

court. The same held true for the separation of the role of litigants and their societal status. Generally, the differentiation of the administration of justice from the system of formal privileges and informal advantages of power and wealth was extremely tenuous.

Thus, both open bias and devious methods to fight bias were common. Proceedings were slow, complicated, and expensive. Frequently lawsuits were used to harass, intimidate, or spite the other party. In criminal justice, "arbitrary powers, ignorance and infamy" made it virtually impossible for the defense to succeed by regular procedures.[6] At the same time, as is to be expected in any authoritarian and traditional system, the notion of a clear-cut line between just and unjust causes was officially maintained even if the patterns of interests, power, and accommodation made a mockery of this command. The more sophisticated books on the ethics of advocates left the lawyer free to accept a case when in doubt; but this greater realism did not find much understanding with the wider public or with the authorities.

A last element shaping the situation was the very uneven distribution of professional competence among judges, procurators, and advocates. The old division between the learned bench and the noble bench was very slow to disappear; except for the higher courts, procurators often were completely dependent for their arguments on learned advocates; and finally, the group of people not affiliated with a court, but holding themselves out as legal experts, ranged from legal scholars whose opinions were famous and respected across state boundaries to the broad fringe of people from many trades who were versed in writing and impressed their clients with a few legal formulas and talk about technical tricks.

Considering this background, the typical forms of deviant bahavior in the bar seem but an outgrowth of the conditions under which legal practice took place. According to Weissler: "In the laws and ordinances are found countless exhortations and penal threats. Essentially they were directed against four points: accepting unjust cases, impeding the progress of a case, lengthy and misleading arguments, and greed for fees."[7] The bar, if this singular is appropriate, had to work for clients of very uneven power and influence in courts, which applied ancient and fragmented laws in any but an impartial manner. The notions of justice held by peasant and bourgeois, nobleman, royal officer, and monarch differed fundamentally in crucial respects. Small wonder that the reputation of the bar was extremely low with virtually all sides.[8] Widespread popular dissatisfaction with an incomprehensible and biased legal system, for which the attorneys served as the scapegoats, converged with the royal administration's attempts to curb the power of the aristocracy and to gain control over and reform the administration of justice.

The first striking measure taken by the royal bureaucracy was a purge of the bar in 1713. At least 60 percent of the attorneys lost their positions without compensation; the others had to pay high sums for a new patent issued by the king. The aim was to weed out the "incompetent and quarrelsome," although Weissler points out that inquiries into merit were impossible in the mass dismissal. Preference was given to the full-time lawyer—possibly a measure directed against the aristocracy, in whose employment many of the part-time attorneys were, certainly a policy which generally increased the differentiation of the attorney's role from other involvements. The requirement of paying high sums, finally, favored both those of great success and those of inherited wealth. The new admission requirements stress the same points explicitly; those of "too despicable and poor background" are excluded as well as those who do not show "reasonable and moral character"; university studies and articling with an attorney have to be documented and a court examination has to be passed.[9] With greatly reduced numbers of attorneys one should expect higher fees and an increased amount of legal work by outsiders. In characteristically "sovereign" fashion, however, fees were officially reduced by three-quarters and unauthorized practice threatened with severe penalties; one may have some doubts that the system worked.

This pattern of legislation continued throughout the century, with little regard for the vested interests of attorneys and for the practicalities of social life, but with the clear aim to simplify the administration of justice, to bring it under royal control and to improve the standards of competence and professional "honor." The policies were designed to reduce the number of attorneys, to control their admission by theoretically uniform standards, to suppress unauthorized practice of law, to insure supervision of the attorney's work, and to control the fees of the bar. Weissler says of Cocceji, the most important single man among the reformers in the middle of the eighteenth century, that he achieved "the abolishment of a court system debased by the sale of office and by income based on fees and the establishment of that system of work, order and rectitude which is the basis of the Prussian administration of justice until today" (that is, the first years of the twentieth century). This judgment accepts somewhat uncritically the aspirations of the day and the idealized self-image of the Prussian judicial service of a later period, but it indicates correctly the basic thrust of the reforms in the long run.[10]

From the middle of the century on, there were serious proposals to abolish private advocacy altogether. In 1781, the bar in private practice was indeed excluded from litigation and young members of the bench advised and represented the litigants in court. This remained, however, an episode of very short duration; it was an experiment which demonstrated

149

conclusively that the mediating position of the advocate was indispensable and that legal counsel and advice cannot effectively be put into the hands of government officials. To calm feelings of mistrust, parties were soon allowed to have their own advisers argue in certain phases of trial, and after several further concessions the figure of the *"Assistenzrath,"* the judge-counsel, had disappeared when in 1793 a new "General Constitution of the Courts" was issued.[11]

Ill-planned and arbitrary as many of the eighteenth-century reform measures seemed when taken singly, their outcome was a decisively modernized administration of justice, the principal features of which shaped German legal life until the last third of the nineteenth century. The courts, formerly instruments of aristocratic resistance to royal autocracy, had been reduced to the routine administration of a largely codified law. Increasingly, the judiciary was recruited from the ranks of commoners on the basis of prescribed legal studies and examinations. Gross inequalities before the law and arbitrary decisions were reduced. Bureaucratic rationality became now pervasive in the courts as well as in the royal administration.

Although its exclusion from litigation had failed, the legal and social status of the bar also had radically changed. The Prussian *Justizkommissare,* as attorneys were now called, were appointed by the Ministry of Justice. Appointments were made sparingly, with the consequence that an attorney's "position" was quite lucrative—so much so that judges frequently applied to become members of the bar, a development of great importance for the outlook of the German bar in private practice. The educational requirements became now the same for judges and attorneys, consisting of university studies and in-service training with comprehensive examinations at the end of each. If we add that supervision and discipline were in the hands of appellate courts with minor disciplinary powers vested in lower courts, too, we may virtually consider this bar a profession of civil servants—self-employed to be sure and free from the more direct forms of bureaucratic supervision, but in most other respects *preussische Beamte.* Weissler says: "Under this constitution the Prussian bar reached that high reputation which the courts testified to without exception."[12]

Bureaucratic reforms of the court system and strict regulations of admission and practice in the bar were, however, not the only developments which engendered a high level of competence and high standards of professional ethics. The increasing role of the urban bourgeoisie in economy and society, and therefore among the clients of the bar, had similar consequences. The rational ordering of contractual relations between equals, who share the same orientations, enter their legal relations voluntarily, and have a mutual interest in maintaining unambiguous, impersonal exchange relations over a long span of time, was not only a prominent element in the ideology of early liberalism; it represented also a good deal of the reality of the marketplace. Such patterns placed a premium on the work of the competent, reliable, and efficient attorney whose work guards smooth relations with customers and competitors rather than of the old-style advocate.[13]

Finally, there were forceful intellectual developments which contributed to a new ethos in the practice of law as well as in other professional fields. The philosophy of German idealism and the literary culture of Weimar exercised a strong influence on the educated strata. Rosenberg says: *"Bildung* as conceived by the German neohumanists in the age of Lessing, Herder, Winckelmann, Goethe, Schiller, Kant, Fichte, and Humboldt, meant more than advanced school training, general and vocational. Bildung, no doubt, called for trained minds and for more and better knowledge, but no less for character and personality development. Bildung implied supreme emphasis on inwardness and tenderness of the heart. It invited man to seek happiness within himself by orienting his total life toward the harmonious blending of spiritual elevation, emotional refinement, and individualized mental and moral perfection."[14] These ideals fostered a cultural self-confidence in the educated bourgeoisie, a strong desire to be treated with dignity, and a readiness to respond to grants of autonomy with self-disciplined morality. Certainly, the great majority of the members of the bar as well as of other university-educated professions were cultural "philistines," but the dominant tone was set by the new ideas, and their role in the change in professional attitudes can scarcely be doubted.

The influence of these ideals can only be understood if they are seen in the context of political developments. They played an especially crucial role in the transformation of the corps of higher civil servants and their emancipation from political control by the monarch. Hans Rosenberg has described how the ideas of German idealism became prevalent in the intellectual orientations of the Prussian bureaucracy through the stiffened requirements of university education, and he has pointed to the legitimating functions the new *Bildung* had for the status of commoners in the higher civil service and for the autonomy aspirations of the service as a whole.[15]

Autonomous rule by a bureaucracy of experts reached its classic form after the defeat of Prussia by the Napoleonic armies in 1806. Leading bureaucratic officers introduced decisive reforms under the slogan "revolution from above." The new order represented an authoritarian rule by professional, highly educated administrators which was based on compromises with the nobility and on concessions to the aspiring bourgeoisie, especially the educated bourgeoisie. It had profound consequences for the stabilization of the peculiar amalgam of modern and traditional feudal patterns which was characteristic of German society for more than a century to come. While traditional privileges were de facto retained, education became "now the official mainspring of privilege." Rosenberg says: "The removal of legal obstacles to individual advancement and, eventually, to the development of open classes was largely offset by the perpetuation of privileged professional status groups [*Berufsstände*] of high social rank which preserved or even fortified many of the persistent traditions and exclusive rights of the abolished First Estate."[16]

Education in particular became a point of crystallization for ascriptive privileges, and it is here that the peculiar combination of ascriptive and universalistic orientations, which we found characteristic of conservative circles in our analysis of the value system of German society, has its origin. In this new order we find also the modernized version of the old paternalistic conception of the "common good," defined and served by the ruler; it had now become wedded to the competence of experts who stood above the conflicting particular interests and pursued "objectively" the interest of the whole. Initially, the civil service elite understood their control of policy-making as the superior equivalent to popular control. During the first half of the nineteenth century, however, their rule came increasingly to conflict with democratic aspirations, and their dominant posture became defensive and extremely cautious wherever further developments of political emancipation and modernization seemed possible. A legacy of their ideology was that throughout the century the conception of the *Rechtsstaat,* government under the rule of law, was an ideal separate from, often in contrast to or a suitable substitute for, the democratic idea of popular control of political decision-making.[17]

This context explains the forceful influence in public life and professional mores of cultural developments apparently far removed from the practical affairs of government, business, and the practice of law. The ideas of neohumanism and German idealism were in one sense but the ideological complement of the developing bureaucratic order. These two factors, which contributed to a rise in "professionalism" of the German bar, largely reinforced each other. The implications of the new ideals of *Bildung* for self-determination and democracy were limited by their nonpolitical and strongly individual character and by the idealist orientation toward the "common good"; they were further contained by the overpowering position of dominance held by the central bureaucracies. The third development encouraging professionalism, orientations derived from the marketplace, is less obviously compatible with the other two. These contrasts and conflicts can, however, easily be exaggerated when the decades before and after 1800 are considered. There was a strong element in government policies that saw a liberal bourgeois society as its ultimate goal.[18] The incompatibilities became stronger with the later growth of commerce and industry and with the reactionary policies after 1815. Still, the Prussian bar, and with certain modifications also the bar in other German states, derived at the eve of industrialization its main features from government reforms which had turned it into a respected and privileged body of quasi-civil servants; and until the last two decades of the century this remained its decisive character, in spite of the fact that toward the end of the period "the immediately involved people saw only the negative aspects of the civil service status, its contradiction to the basic idea of advocacy, its diminution of independence."[19] New cultural ideals gave a deep foundation to the ethos of the bar, and even economic development engendered changes in the practice of law which contributed to the new elevated character of the bar.

## COLONIAL AND POST-COLONIAL AMERICA: CONTINUITY AND REVOLUTION

The American legal system and the American bar have multiple historical roots. The conditions for their initial development were on the one hand the simple social structure of the early settlements which made complicated legal disputes infrequent. On the other hand, there was the heritage of European and in particular British traditions. These traditions included the common law, although its substantive provisions and its procedures for the administration of justice were not simply and immediately transferred to the colonies; furthermore, basic ideas of constitutional law and political philosophy were retained from Tudor England. Among these traditions were also, however, the memories of feudal dominance and inequities with which a rigid law and its endless complications seemed bound up. Radical movements of strongly antilegal persuasion, which had been sectarian groups within the old structure of Britain, were stronger in the new land.[20]

In the early generations, the new settlements were thus characterized by little objective need for lawyers and widespread popular hostility toward them. It is the same antipathy toward the executioners of an incomprehensibly complex instrument of order, mostly benefiting the old hereditary upper classes, that we commonly find among the peasants and the urban lower classes in all of pre-modern Europe. But in the New World this sentiment was largely freed from the domination that had contained it in the old, freed from the at times conflicting, at time allied powers of local and regional nobility and monarchical centralism. Furthermore, the new "ruling class" in the developing societies of North America, "whether it was the clergy in New England, or the merchants as in New York, Maryland and Virginia, or the Quakers as in Pennsylvania, was extremely jealous'' of legal practitioners who might partially reestablish the old order under their own leadership.[21]

The level of competence among legal practitioners in the seventeenth and early eighteenth centuries was generally very low, and a sense of professional responsibilitiy was all but nonexistent. In part this was a consequence of legislation hostile to professional lawyers; yet it gave additional grounds for popular dissatisfaction with law and lawyers. Law in these early generations was rarely a full-time occupation; it was predominantly practiced by those types of people that constituted the fringe of the profession in Europe: "These 'attorneys' were largely traders, factors, land speculators and laymen of clever penmanship and easy volubility, whom parties employed to appear and talk for them in the courts. The few persons who acted as professional attorneys were at first mostly pettifoggers or minor court officers such as deputy sheriffs, clerks and justices, who stirred up litigation for the sake of the petty court fees.''[22]

In the English bar, both competence and professional orientation had been based on a corporate organization in the Inns of Court which formed the framework for the transmission of knowledge, legal ethics, and a sense of professional solidarity. The young aspirant entered into an apprenticeship with an established barrister in which—by practical experience supplemented by reading of treatises—he gained the technical knowledge for his work. In the early American settlements, there was no organization of the bar even remotely equivalent to the Inns. The apprenticeship system was the mode of learning the law in the colonies, too, and it remained prevalent in America until the end of the nineteenth century, but it functioned here in a far more decentralized setting.

In contrast to the continental system of university education followed by practical training—both subject to government supervision and in fact often established by modernizing bureaucratic rulers—the decentralized character of the apprenticeship system makes any change in competence and outlook a slow and variegated process, particularly if cohesion of the profession and social control through bar organizations are weak or absent. Planned change becomes virtually impossible. Whatever improvements come about are made in response to the actual needs of daily practice in the various parts of the profession.

Daily practice was thoroughly transformed during the eighteenth century, especially in the urban centers. While in frontier communities the old patterns may have persisted, the development of an urban economy with a great extension of commerce and the emergence of commercialized agriculture as well as the more complicated structure of government created legal disputes which were complex and frequent enough to sustain a body of professional practitioners in both bar and bench. The demand for adjudication of increasingly complex matters made for more frequent recourse to the common law instead of local regulation and custom. This led to a strengthening of the ties with the British legal system which was reflected in the patterns of recruitment and education. A period of "importing" English barristers was followed by a rise in the level of education and in the class background of those who would enter the profession. The new men "of family" frequently had a college education, and a large number went to London to study law at the Inns of Court.[23] There also developed a pattern of admission to practice controlled by the courts or by a centralized agency such as the highest court or the royal governor. Very high educational requirements were established in New York and Massachusetts, where the courts had delegated authority over admissions to the organized bar.[24]

The concentration of legal business in the urban centers and the growing homogeneity and respectability of lawyers by background and status laid the foundations for an organization of the bar as a professional group. The bar meetings in the New England colonies should not be mistaken for modern bar associations, although Warren speaks of "Bar Associations, designed to dignify the profession, excluding from practice pettifoggers and sharpers."[25] These were often rather informal organizations merging social and professional activities; however, they did foster a sense of professional identity and solidarity, they exercised effective control over the ways of practice, and they made the profession visible in public as a body of high standing and presumably responsible devotion. Considering technical competence as well as professional attitudes, collective organization, social reputation, and public leadership, in the critical opinion of Dean Pound, the bar in the colonies at the eve of the Revolution "had become a great body of lawyers," a judgment that does not deny great variations between different colonies and localities.[26]

If the eighteenth century in Prussia was the period during which the legal profession was disciplined by admission requirements, purges, regulations, and supervision imposed by the monarchical bureaucracy, the American legal profession in most colonies experienced during the same time a similar development of rising standards, but without the domineering impositions of a central government bureaucracy. In fact, the improvements in legal competence, professional responsibility, and professional solidarity were paralleled here by a process of collective advancement in which the bar attained a very high position of power, wealth, and reputation. Lawyers made up a good part of the political and social elite of the colonies at the eve of the Revolution, and in some places, such as Virginia,

Massachusetts, and New Jersey, "there were the roots of a self-perpetuating, more-or-less closed class of lawmen."[27]

The development of the bar in the two or three generations after the Revolution presents a paradox. On the one hand the period has been called the "golden age" of American law. "In seventy-five years at most, the English seventeenth century materials were made over into a common law for America . . . This was the work of great judges and great lawyers practicing before them."[28] On the other hand, the same author has described the development of the bar between the Revolution and the Civil War as a decline ending in an "era of decadence." The reference here is to the general level of competence, to professional organization, and collective self-control. The paradox is resolved when we separate the consideration of the elite of the bar from the legal profession as a whole. While an elite with very high technical standards was able to shape a legal system fit for the demands of a new age and accepted as legitimate by the majority of the people, the Revolution and subsequent developments broke up the professional structure of the bar and lowered general standards of competence as well as of professional ethics. Several factors can be isolated as crucial in this course of events.

Foremost among these factors is a change in personnel as a consequence of the Revolution which amounted to a "purge" of the bar similar in dimension to the purge of the Prussian bar at the beginning of the eighteenth century. But while in Prussia it was—at least by intention—the least competent, the least specialized in attorneys' work, the least loyal to monarchical rule, and the least wealthy who were thrown out, in short the bottom of the barrel as defined by the royal administration, the American bar lost a large part of its elite as defined by the standards of the legal profession itself. According to Warren, several hundred lawyers and "a large number of the most eminent and older members of the Bar, being Royalists, . . . either left the country or retired from practice." Of the lawyers who remained, Warren says, "many were either actively engaged in politics or in the army; while others had accepted positions on the bench. This left the practice of the law very largely in the hands of lawyers of a lower grade and inferior ability."[29]

In a certain sense, we may speak in both the Prussian and the American cases of a social revolution; in both there occurred a real shift in the power structure of society, and to the degree that lawyers are identified with or are even agents of a given pattern of power, such shifts result in the exclusion of a part of the profession from practice. In any event, the "purges" in both cases had consequences beyond the elimination of certain individuals. They disrupted the continuity and strength of group traditions and left the bar open to greater influence from its social environment. In Prussia, this influence led in the direction of increasing governmental regimentation. In the United States, it led to the breakdown of the instruments of professional collective self-control without establishing public control in their place.

The consequences of the "purge" in revolutionary America were particularly far-reaching because of the apprenticeship system of education, which relies so heavily on the continuity of high levels of everyday practice. Furthermore, the decades after the Revolution saw a considerable rise in numbers of lawyers. While in 1785 there were only 40 attorneys in New York City, one generation later, in 1818, the number was 290.[30] It is clear that such increases in absolute numbers would have placed great strains even on the late colonial organization of the bar. Together with the removal of a good deal of the old elite and a decline of the old professional institutions the fast growth combined to create virtually a new occupational group. Local bars with their sense of cohesion and their supervision of legal practice, standards of admission, fees set by courts or associations—all these institutions of the pre-Revolutionary bar declined rapidly under the impact of the Revolution and post-Revolutionary politics. The common law and the organized bar were identified with British rule and British institutions and rejected as such. It was not only revolutionary nationalism, however, that played a role. The old hostility toward lawyers, subdued for a few decades by the indigenous development of an urban establishment, broke out again. This hostility was now part of a more general antagonism between the propertied classes and aspiring lower and middle strata which had been partially mobilized during the Revolution.[31] The hostility toward the legal profession was aggravated by post-Revolutionary and post-war economic conditions which increased the amount of litigation and put lawyers into roles, such as that of debt collector, the incumbents of which are easily turned into scapegoats. During the whole nineteenth century, recurrent depressions intensified popular dissatisfaction with lawyers.[32]

These were not simply inarticulate and inconsequential swings in the popular esteem for the bar. They fed into and were embedded in political movements seeking to extend popular democratic control which drew policy conclusions from the popular distrust of the "pernicious order of lawyers."[33] True, the threat of a revolutionary upset of the establishment was followed by a constitutional convention preoccupied with balancing the interests of the propertied and privileged classes with democratic ideas; Jeffersonian Republicanism, which represented a more radical faith in democracy and expressed the interests and suspicions of farmers against the urban classes, was much less radical in practice than in the pamphlets of its promoters, and the same can be said of the later movement of

Jacksonian democracy. However, common to the latter two movements was a positive orientation toward the debtor class in a rapidly developing society with a chronic shortage of capital. Common to both, though stronger in the Jacksonian period, was also a rejection of special privileges for particular groups and a belief in the justice of the free play of economic forces.

It is in this context that we have to see the decline of the professional institutions of the pre-revolutionary bar. They were considered as privileges designed to give undue advantages and power to lawyers. There were demands to abolish the bar completely as well as other utopian reform proposals.[34] More successful were the efforts to fight admission practices of the courts with their educational requirements, grants of occupational monopoly to the bar, the setting of fees by courts or bar associations, and the very establishment and the influence of bar associations. As a consequence of changes in admission requirements the social composition of the bar changed. It became less exclusive and comprised more heterogeneous elements. This reinforced the consequences of organizational decline and of growing numbers; it lessened feelings of professional solidarity. The character of the bar as an organized profession virtually disappeared during the decades after the Revolution. If there was an English model for the American lawyer, it now became the solicitor, whose work, in contrast to that of the barrister, was much more comparable to that of a businessman.[35]

Although both Prussia and the American colonies at the end of the eighteenth century were predominantly agrarian societies, there were important differences between their social structures. That America does not have a feudal past has been observed often, and many differences between the two countries can be traced to this fact. Aside from slavery and temporary indentured servitude, there was much greater personal freedom in America. The distribution of power and wealth was more fluid, and, equally important, the latter was not as much as in Prussia, and in pre-revolutionary Europe generally, dependent on a hereditary position of power. Power was characteristically based on wealth rather than vice versa. In both societies prestige and honor were important to clothe naked power and riches, but in America they were faster acquired and far less significant in most contexts of social intercourse. Even people in high public office enjoyed far less respect and deference than was taken for granted in Europe.[36]

In the German territories of Central Europe, powerful vested interests had a stake in maintaining the traditional social order, the old modes of production and the *ancien régime* in politics. Certainly the bourgeoisie was neither independent nor strong and unified enough to challenge these forces effectively. It was the rationalization of royal government, the development of powerful public bureaucracies in the larger states like Prussia that constituted the most significant element of social change. This development did not completely subdue the position and the influence of the traditional nobility; in fact, the power of the king and his administration always rested in part on the support of the aristocracy gained in recurrent compromises. However, rationalization of the royal government did introduce a fairly high degree of centralization. It provided a strong leverage point for continued planned change. For the urban classes it replaced the arbitrary traditional authority of the nobility with a rational regimentation of many spheres of life and later conceded local self-government. Finally, it opened government career opportunities for commoners side by side with nobles based on education and bureaucratic achievement. The Prussian bar became in the course of the eighteenth century closely linked to this government service. The *Justizkommissare* were quasi-*Beamte*, educated at state universities and through in-service training. Their quasi-official status as well as their secure socioeconomic position made them relatively immune to demands of the clientele incompatible with their conceptions of duty and professional honor.

The American bar similarly reflects the developing structure of American society. Before the Revolution, the top of the bar had become part of the dominant groups—groups of a character very different from that of the social and political elites in Europe. This was a commercially oriented elite of merchants, plantation owners, successful artisans, and professionals, a bourgeois elite rather than a feudal-aristocratic one. This elite neither had the power nor did it face the problems that led the continental monarchies toward bureaucratic rationalization of government. Expansion into the continent and economic development could be achieved during most of the nineteenth century without a strong, rationally organized government apparatus. Not centralization and bureaucratic rationalization but rather extensions of democratic controls were the most characteristic developments in the American polity.[37]

The Revolution and subsequent political movements crucially diminished whatever growth there was of a closed quasi-aristocratic patriciate dominating politics. The same developments broke down the professional structure of the late colonial bar. The dominant temper was now hostile to corporate professional organization and especially to an "order of lawyers." Less unified by upbringing, education, and a sense of professional community and less subject to supervision than its Prussian counterpart, the American bar had to operate in a society in which social

159

distinction and public office counted far less in restraining people's demands and behavior. It was, in sum, more "vulnerable" to variegated influence from clients, politicians, and community opinion.

## THE IMPACT OF INDUSTRIALIZATION

Both America and Prussia/Germany were to experience during the following decades of the nineteenth century the drastic transformations associated with rapid economic development and industrialization. The task of mediating between the established legal order and the unprecedented demands and conflicts engendered by economic change fell on two very differently constituted legal professions in sharply contrasting social and political environments. To anticipate the result, the German bar was less exposed to pressures conflicting with its role as traditionally conceived, and its structure was more firmly set to resist such pressures.

It is patently impossible to analyze here in any detail the complex interrelations between industrialization, changes in the legal system, the role played by different parts of the legal profession, and internal developments in the two bars. The purpose of this section is simply to indicate major contrasts and thus to develop a link between conditions at the eve of industrialization, as just discussed, and certain developments which took place in the two bars toward the end of the nineteenth century and the beginning of the twentieth, developments which can be understood as trends toward convergence.

In both countries, large-scale industrialization developed fully during the last third of the nineteenth century—after the Civil War in America and after national unification in Germany. There are two broad conditions that made it a far less disturbing experience for the German than for the American bar in private practice. First, socioeconomic change itself was less tumultuous in Germany—because of more powerful institutional controls, because of the character of the societal elites, and because of related value traditions. Second, the German bar in private practice was less influential in the complex process of law-making, and this reduced the incentives for the new business interests to bring pressure on private practitioners.

The "great transformation" to an industrial society was initiated and presided over in Prussia/Germany by the old ruling elites, by a monarchical government run by career civil servants and supported by the aristocracy. This is not to say that government agencies operated most enterprises or that a planned economy was instituted. The techniques of economic development were those observed in the leading countries of the time; the government encouraged, at least in the early decades, free enterprise. However, the fact that political control remained largely in the hands of bureaucratic and pre-industrial agrarian elites had far-reaching consequences. Conservative value orientations, critical of the unfettered pursuit of private economic interests, remained strong. When in the last decades of the nineteenth century industrial leaders attained a strong and potentially dominant position, they were co-opted into the old ruling classes, which changed in the process, to be sure, but which retained enough of their distinctive character to transform the outlook and the allegiances of the new business leaders even more.[38]

Innovations in the legal framework were largely under the control of the bureaucracy. Many such innovations were consolidated in a general commercial code already in 1861. The early 1870's, following the victory over France and the unification of Germany, were the *Gründerjahre*, the period of greatest "Manchesterism," as conservative critics called the new economic order. Yet even at this point, the industrial and business development did not overflow the dams built by the law in ways comparable to the American case. For that, the regulating power of "the State" and the restraining weight of traditional notions of the right order of society were too great.[39] This result was probably also due to the fact that tendencies inherent in industrial development were tolerated and aided by legal policy. Thus, cartels and concentration were favored. The German economy was the first to see thorough and stable monopolization of markets through cartel contracts.[40]

On balance, then, Germany did not experience anything comparable to the "capitalist anarchy" of the American development. According to Cochran and Miller, "Traditional language had no words to describe the business activities of the new leaders after the Civil War, no words to define the functions of their institutions. Traditional politics could not cope with their demands, nor could traditional law harness them to social welfare."[41] There is little need to go into detailed examples of lawlessness, corruption, circumvention of legal regulation, and neglect of expressed public policy. It may be easy to exaggerate these aspects of capitalist development, but they were nevertheless real, and the temptation to overstatement may be indicative of important indirect consequences. This temptation seems to derive from the tremendous symbolic impact of such practices. They changed conceptions of the public interest and loosened the foundations of respect for the law and rectitude.

The ascent of American industrialists to a position of dominance in society was not unopposed. In the period before the Civil War, they "were hated by southern planters, vilified by New England radicals, despised by landed gentry and Quaker merchants."[42] However, in their outlook these groups were much more akin to the new elite than in the German case. Their opposition was the resistance of a bourgeois society based on commerce and agriculture rather than that of a quasi-feudal political class. Far less distinct from the new industrialists, they were furthermore not as entrenched in positions of power; and possibly most important, they could not rely on a government bureaucracy with a corps of civil servants highly trained, relatively autonomous, and committed to a vision of the future of society in which the "disinterested" expert is the guardian of the public interest. By the end of the Civil War the industrialists had overcome most of these resistances, and it was some time before their power was balanced to an extent by effective political forces, before their activities were regulated by restraining institutional controls. In the last decades of the nineteenth century, there was little interference with corporate interests by law or public policy. Hurst says: "The law provided an open field (assured broad markets), legal instruments (the corporation and manifold tools of contract, especially the devices of corporate finance), legal subsidies (grants of land and public credit, and currency inflation and deflation), and then substantially stood aside."[43]

The problem of restraints and controls is closely related to the role of different groups and institutions in law-making. In Germany, the central bureaucracies had the overriding influence. Even after popularly elected legislatures had become the channels for the enactment of statutes in the second half of the century, the administrative departments retained their dominant position through initiative, expertise, and efficient organization. The courts played a lesser role, although legal innovation can never completely be eliminated from adjudication. Least is known in detail about the part played by the bar in private practice, especially about its contribution to legal change through counseling and devising new legal instruments within the framework provided by statutes and prevailing legal doctrine. However, that the *Anwaltschaft,* too, played overall a lesser role than public administration is fairly certain. Finally, German law professors exerted a considerable influence on legal development in various ways—through their teaching as well as through treatises which were consulted by courts and the better attorneys, through highly reputed opinions as well as service on commissions preparing major pieces of legislation. It was the work of legal scholars that created and maintained whatever unity of law there was in Germany before the unification of the empire and its new codifications. These latter, too, were the work of administrators and scholars united through academic legal doctrines and shared policy orientations.[44]

By contrast, bureaucrats and law professors played a minor role in American legal development. In fact, there were no American equivalents

162

to the distinct corps of civil servants and to the relatively large group of professional law teachers in Germany who were clearly set off from the rest of the bar. The American courts were the guardians and the authoritative interpreters of the common law tradition. Major changes of the inherited body of law and adaptations to the new conditions were accomplished through creative argument of counsel and judicial decision, and the latter often relied on the former, giving the elite of the bar a tremendous chance of shaping the course of legal innovation. Legislatures played a competing role, a lesser one, it seems, as far as the basic legal framework rather than policy decisions were concerned.[45] In contrast to Germany, American legislatures were not steered and influenced by stable administrations and did not constitute a strong countervailing power in relation to the forces of change. Again the role of private practice out of court is most difficult to assess, but we should be on safe ground in assuming that American lawyers had more leeway for innovation and made more use of it than their German counterparts. If their greater role in court and the different place of case decisions in the two legal systems are taken into consideration, there is no doubt that the American bar in private practice was more involved in the complex process of law-making than the German profession.

These differences concern primarily the elite of the two bars, as the rank and file lawyer contributes in any system only in the most infinitesimal way to changes in the legal order, but the elites were crucial in shaping the outlook of the bar as a whole. This point is relevant not only for the relations between lawyers and their most powerful clients; it also should be of consequence for basic orientations regarding the nature of law and social order. German private practitioners, it appears, were led by experience as well as dominant legal doctrine to conceive of the law as an autonomous cultural system, logically closed and unfolded by scientific inquiry,[46] rather than as a system of man-made rules which are subject to change in the service of public policy or prevailing private interests. The open horizon of legal development, where decision is a matter of policy or value choice, was far more removed from the experience even of the elite of the German attorneys than in the American case.

How did these conditions and developments affect the law as a profession? In the earlier part of the nineteenth century, American lawyers had been the social and economic equals of merchants, plantation owners, and manufacturers. Their work, focusing largely on litigation, had been relatively separated from business, although the actual work patterns seem to have been always broader and less sharply defined as specialized legal work than in the German case. By virtue of their education, experience, and function, leading members of the bar had held important and largely autonomous roles of public leadership until the last third of the century. Professional distinction was often based on political achievement.[47]

The developments after the Civil War changed this pattern radically. The new industrial and financial leaders attained power unparalleled by any other group of men. The practice of lawyers concerned with problems of business shifted away from litigation toward legal and economic counseling, and lawyers often became directly concerned with business decision. The rewards, in both income and professional prestige, soon were highest in this new kind of work,[48] and the new elite of the bar responded to such inducements with highly efficient service: "Through most of the nineteenth century . . . entrepreneurs could legitimately complain of the clumsy and limited forms available to organize, control, and finance business. But for fifty years after the 1880's the tide of lawyers' inventiveness overflowed the levees that the law had so far erected to protect investors, consumers, labor, and everybody in the community who had reason to be concerned about the swings of the business cycle."[49]

At the same time, of course, older types of law practice continued, and in the rapidly growing cities with a population that contained large groups of recent immigrants new types of practice emerged. One major result of the impact of the industrial revolution on the American bar was a vastly increased heterogeneity of background, practice, and circumstance which further weakened the cohesion of the bar. In politics, we find lawyers both on the side of reformist movements and on the side of big business interests. While little evidence is available on the elusive subject of the "public influence of the bar," there is little doubt that the profession's elite working for the new industrial and financial interests had less autonomy in its exercise of power than the legal elite had during the first third of the century, whether its work was predominantly legal or political.

The German bar in private practice never had a similar position of public leadership.[50] In social prestige and income, German attorneys clearly belonged to the upper brackets of the bourgeoisie throughout the nineteenth century. In power and influence, they certainly were surpassed by the rising elite of business and finance, and that elite in turn did not achieve societal dominance. German law practice changed under the impact of economic developments, too; it became more differentiated and more concerned with legal problems of business. However, the heterogeneity and the strains on professional identification one would expect as a result were contained in several ways.

Aside from their closely regulated quasi-official status, which contrasted with the lowest level of professional self-regulation and public supervision in the history of the American bar, several factors shaped the German *An-*

*waltschaft* along the old lines. Perhaps most important was the recruitment of Prussian private practitioners from the career judiciary. From the end of the 1840's until the beginning of the 1870's virtually *all* positions in the bar were filled this way.[51] These lawyers brought with them judicial attitudes of rectitude and the civil servant's orientation toward the "common good." It was this generation of the bar that carried the main burden of legal practice in the years which were most crucial in the development of industrialism and during which the relations between the bar and its new clientele became established. Furthermore, German attorneys had a secure economic position. While access to legal practice was wide open in most American jurisdictions, it was closely regulated in most German states. Not only were the educational requirements high, but the number of attorneys admitted was, especially in Prussia, deliberately kept small. The consequent affluence gave the attorney in Prussia and a number of other German states a strong bargaining position even with wealthy clients.[52]

Finally, background and education also served to set the German bar somewhat apart from business. Judging from Prussian university statistics, it appears that in its recruitment the German *Anwaltschaft* was more exclusive than any other occupational group except the higher civil and military service. There was a fairly high level of self-recruitment and a strong influx from other university-trained professions and from government service. After 1870, the number of students increased rapidly, and increasingly men from business backgrounds joined the profession.[53] For some time to come, these were, however, probably assimilated into the prevailing subculture of the bar.

University education itself, required of all lawyers, was an alien element in the business world. Until well past the middle of the century, businessmen were consciously reluctant to send their sons to the university lest they were spoiled for business. When later in the century higher education became more popular in the entrepreneurial groups, it was often an education at one of the technical institutes rather than at a university, and university study was typically in scientific rather than in the traditional fields. This split in educational orientations was actually carried over into the field of high school education, where the *Realschule,* emphasizing modern languages and the sciences, rather than the *Gymnasium*, giving priority to Latin and Greek and opening access to the university, was the favorite school for the offspring of the business community.[54]

It appears, then, that *Akademiker* and businessmen belonged to two distinct subcultures dividing the bourgeoisie, but this statement has to be taken with a grain of salt, especially when used in an analysis of the bar in private practice. If any group provided a linking element, it was the bar in private practice, with its inevitable involvement in the affairs of their clients. However, the very fact that the cleavage existed must have exercised a subtle influence in the relations between lawyers and business clients, encouraging greater reserve on the part of the attorney.[55]

Relatively affluent and steeped in the culture of the civil service and the university-trained *Akademiker*, the German *Anwälte* were less easily drawn into business operations and into manipulations at or beyond the borderline of law, correctness, and dignity; and even if they became thus involved, their reputation was such as to create a presumption of rectitude—a circumstance which may be as important as the "actual" differences between developments in the two bars because it limited the symbolic significance of the changes in legal practice that did occur.

## LIMITED TRENDS TOWARD CONVERGENCE

The sharp contrasts between the two bars in the last decades of the nineteenth century were largely the result of divergent patterns of legal practice, as they had developed before the onset of industrialization, and of the different forms industrialization took in the context of the two societies. However, different professional traditions, different elites, and different societal values notwithstanding, one should expect that similar economic developments would also engender greater similarities in legal practice. To a certain extent, this expectation is confirmed. The following pages will be concerned with developments which began as early as in the 1870's and which can be characterized as trends toward convergence. Yet, as noted at the outset of this chapter, social patterns once set may not only prove resistant to change but define the context in which new developments take place. Furthermore, the dialectic between development and reaction may make the course of change erratic and unpredictable rather than a smooth evolution toward foreseeable ends. Some of these limitations of convergent tendencies will also be discussed.

The development of the bar in the United States since the 1870's and particularly since the early decades of the twentieth century has been described as a process of reprofessionalization.[56] The major elements in this development were an increase in the quality of legal education coupled with a rise in standards of admission, a greater concern with professional responsibility and professional discipline, and, as a basis for these two developments, a resurgence of bar associations at the local, state, and federal level. The German bar, in turn, achieved at the end of the 1870's greater autonomy from government control and a status more clearly distinct from that of the civil service. With the opening of the *Rechtsanwaltschaft* to all qualified persons, it increased considerably in size and

166

extended its services to a wider range of clients and legal problems; it also established a closer nexus with the business world. In Germany, too, the decisive changes had been discussed and demanded by state and national bar associations in the decades before, although the crucial step was taken by legislation; the change was not as much as in the United States an outgrowth of autonomous developments within the bar.

In both cases, changes in the demand for legal services and, generally, developments outside the profession may be said to be ultimately responsible for these convergent courses, but as far as the bar itself was concerned, voluntary associations were major instruments of change in Germany as well as in the United States. Before we turn to a discussion of each case, it may, therefore, be useful to consider some common aspects of this development of voluntary associations.

In both societies, certain conditions emerged in the course of the nineteenth century which were conducive to the formation of voluntary associations, increasingly formal in character. Actually, the emergence of such conditions is characteristic of all modernizing societies. What follows applies to other groups with common interests as well, although we will focus our attention on occupational, and especially professional groups. Improved communication and transportation facilities made organization on a regional and national level feasible. On the other hand, a host of interconnected developments tended to increase the utility of formal associations to their constituencies, both at the local and at the supra-local level. Chief among these developments were the following: First, the increasing size of the local occupational group in the larger communities made informal bonds and informal social control insufficient. Formal organization became imperative if any cohesion of the group was to be achieved or maintained. Second, the increasing size of communities also made the individual practitioner less visible. The "image" of the group increasingly took on the character of a stereotype—more influenced by notorious extreme cases than by the average individual performance and potentially subject to influence by organized effort. Third, increasing complexity of the division of labor introduced differentiation into local groups, while specialized interests became more homogeneous in different places; it thus made local and diffuse forms of organization which embraced various occupational groups such as all *Akademiker* less viable or at least insufficient and encouraged more specialized supra-local associations. Fourth, efforts to influence public policies affecting the occupation required legitimated representation and formal organization to be effective with an increasingly bureaucratized government, wider in its scope of operation and more relevant in its actions for many occupations. Fifth, changes in work and in recruitment required adaptations in education as

167

well as in the social control of occupational practice. The inadequacy of traditional arrangements called forth attempts to anticipate changes and to cope with problems in more rational forms. With increasing similarity of conditions in different localities, mobility of personnel, and statewide or nationwide scope of regulating and educating institutions, associations tended to be wider in scope, too, and more formal in organization.

While their relative importance varied from case to case, these conditions encouraged voluntary associations in many occupations and professions. Lawyers had typically certain advantages over other groups. Their profession and the literacy it required involved them in communications beyond the local level at an early stage. Their financial resources and their ability to be absent from the place of work and residence for limited periods of time eased problems of communication and transportation considerably.

These favorable circumstances were counteracted, however, during the first half of the nineteenth century by political constellations unfavorable to lawyers' associations. During this period, associations of lawyers met in both societies with political objections. These were based in both countries on similar considerations about the potentially influential role of lawyers as a group, although in the United States it was the ideal of popular democracy, while in Germany it was the stability of the monarchical regimes of the restoration period which was to be safeguarded.

In Germany after the failure of the revolution of 1848, in the United States at the latest after the Civil War, these objections lost force or simply died out. Large-scale associations organizing a wide variety of interests had grown up, and by the last quarter of the century, there was no important group which considered an organized bar as a real threat to its interests or ideals. Other groups and movements were now viewed this way in some quarters—political movements of the working class, unions, or big corporations, depending on the point of view. This change may be taken as another indication of the more limited actual or potential power of lawyers in this period, when compared to the early phases of modernization.

## DEVELOPMENTS OF REPROFESSIONALIZATION
### IN THE AMERICAN BAR

According to Pound, "although the organization of the American Bar Association in 1878 undoubtedly gave a decisive impetus to the movement for bar associations which has carried forward the reprofessionalization of American lawyers, the era of modern bar associations must be held to begin with the Association of the Bar of the City of New York in 1870."[57] After 1870 several local and state bar associations were founded, and the number increased rapidly after 1878. Still, many of these were unstable organizations, and "it was not till 1923 that there was an active state bar association in every state or territory of the Union."[58] Membership in all these associations was voluntary. Only after World War I began the drive for "integrated state bars" with compulsory membership.

New York City had in 1870 about 4,000 lawyers. The new association was founded by 235 men, and it remained an exclusive group in which membership was granted by vote on recommendation of an admissions committee. Dean Pound asserts that such selectiveness "indeed was necessary to its objectives after the breakdown of requirements of education, professional training, and admission."[59] The new association was to "maintain the honor and the dignity of the profession of the law, to cultivate social intercourse among its members, and to increase its usefulness in promoting the due administration of justice." The most immediate impetus for its establishment came from scandals in litigation and political corruption under the regime of the Tweed Ring. The event may thus be seen as part of the broader movement in the business community to free itself from costly corruption and blackmail by politicians.[60] Beyond this, the association concerned itself with amendments of laws, grievances against lawyers, and the improvement of legal education and admission standards.

Similar motivations led to the formation of other bar associations, although most were less active in these early years. The American Bar Association was founded in Saratoga Springs, New York, a fashionable summer resort. The location is symbolic of the great importance of convivial socializing in early bar association activities as well as of the fact that the seventy-five founders belonged to the affluent elite of the bar. The main expressed concern was again with restoring the dignity of the profession. Early discussions focused on reforms in education and admission, but little was accomplished in the first generation except in the formulation of uniform laws for adoption by the states, an activity supported by the association. Selective in membership and largely social in character, the American Bar Association in the first decades of its existence has been described as a "sort of juristic sewing circle for mutual education in the gospel of laissez-faire".[61]

Until the second decade of the twentieth century, most bar associations existed mostly for social reasons, were selective in membership, and comprised only a small fraction of the whole bar. The absence of any tradition of organized action for and in the name of the bar seems to be one cause for this long incubation time. Strong action was further impeded by the state of the bar in the "era of decadence". The heterogeneity especially of the urban bar "was the natural result of nearly a century in which admissions had been almost uncontrolled, standards undefined, discipline nonexistent, and the lawyer simply a runner in the nineteenth century race to get ahead."[62] Heterogeneity in competence, practice, professional orientation, and circumstance increased continuously with economic developments, urbanization, and the rapid influx of immigrants.[63]

This lack of cohesion and homogeneity was aggravated even by some of the reform responses as well as unplanned developments which appeared to be improvements of the state of the bar. Thus, while selective organization may have been inevitable under the circumstances, it also hardened lines of cleavage within the bar. A good deal of the growing concern with moral standards, with the improvement of legal education, and with raising the requirements for admission was against the interests of the less affluent members of the bar and of lower-middle class aspirants.

The canons of professional behavior which the American Bar Association adopted in 1908 were largely based on the conditions of work of the small-town lawyer, emphasizing devotion to the client and rules of etiquette between lawyers. They did little to accommodate the needs of moderately successful or desperately striving practitioners in the new metropolitan centers, for whom restrictions on advertising and soliciting were a heavier burden than for their small town brethren, a burden furthermore, which was not strongly legitimated by past tradition and practice; nor did the canons provide regulations that would have kept new patterns of practice within the bounds of professional dignity and the public interest, regulations about counseling in business matters in advance of action or about service to overpowering economic interests bent to evade the law. The new leaders of the bar who rose with corporate law practice largely sought after old style symbols of respectability. They joined others, law teachers, respectable men in public office and average middle class practitioners, who also were prominent in bar associations, in condemning bribery, ambulance chasing and soliciting in general, but the concern of these other groups with the public service character of the bar's function was not translated into specific regulations and policies. The philosophy of client-caretaking remained virtually unmodified. The canons could be seen primarily as an imposition of discipline on the lower ranks of the profession by bar leaders who frequently were associated with what middle class reformers considered the evils of "capitalist anarchy." This fact may have substantially contributed to the rather limited success bar associations had in changing the ways of the profession at large.[64]

The drive for raising the level of legal education met with more success but only after long delay and adverse unplanned developments. As noted before, apprenticeship had been the prevailing mode of legal education until the last decades of the nineteenth century. In the late eighteenth and the early nineteenth century, there already had existed a type of formal legal schooling in private institutions which constituted, however, but an extension of the apprenticeship system. Colleges, too, had provided some law instruction, but, says Hurst, "in terms of what was accomplished, until the 1870's legal education in the colleges and universities was part of the era of apprenticeship training and proprietory schools. And, taking the bar as a whole, all types of schools contributed but a trickle of men."[65]

While education at university law schools improved in the 1870's under the leadership of such men as Langdell at Harvard and broadened in scope, the old proprietary schools run by practitioners revived in the form of part-time and night schools. At first a supplement of office training, they grew in the metropolitan centers into schools which provided a less expensive law education to students who earned their living during the day. Frequently without adequate facilities, their instruction was oriented more toward practical problems and was typically inferior in quality. After the turn of the century, apprenticeship as the sole preparation for the bar died out, and for the lower ranks of the bar part-time law schools took its place. Between 1890 and 1916 the proportion of students in night schools increased from about one in ten to nearly 50 percent. This meant that during these transitional years a vast cleavage developed in the quality of legal education received by different strata of the bar. Although for some time many leading firms had graduates from night schools among their partners, the evolving typical career pattern was different. Lower-class and minority ethnic background led to study in part-time schools, and the graduates of these schools typically ended up in the lower ranks of the bar. Growing differences in the quality of legal education coalesced with the increasing differentiation of legal practice and made the stratification of the bar more rigid and more closely tied with the class and ethnic origin of lawyers.[66]

It was fateful, though not accidental, that during the same years after 1900 the modern large law firm developed. The same increase in the complexity of legal problems which encouraged formal education led to the growth of large firms which combined specialists of various sorts in one office. This development presents an interesting contrast to Germany, where large law firms still are rare. An explanation is probably found in the greater complexity of American law and in the larger part American lawyers take in ascertaining and evaluating the facts pertaining to a legal problem and in the development of new legal instruments and devices. Furthermore, it appears that the rapidly expanding American business corporations made less use of house counsel than their German counterparts, thus encouraging the expansion of private law offices. The evidence on these matters is insufficient, but this hypothesis fits with the greater readiness of American private practitioners to get involved in business affairs and with a higher valuation of self-employment in the American bar with its ethos of individualism than among German *Juristen*, many of whom had always worked in employed positions. In any event, American large law firms concerned with highly complex matters soon required the best education and tended to monopolize the most desirable areas of law practice. Their development thus narrowed the access to the top of the profession for lawyers with an inferior education and of lower social origin.

In the field of legal education, then, the larger pattern of the impact of industrialization was repeated. A system which had lacked unity before responded to divergent demands—for better and more systematic education as well as for opportunities for aspiring urban groups—without rational planning and control; in the process it became even more heterogeneous, and now in ways more sharply structured. The patterns that were established in this period provide the clue for several aspects of social stratification and professional orientation of the American bar today, which may only disappear in another generation.

A crucial point of leverage for change were the developing university law schools, through both the education they provided and the reform activity of their faculties. The impetus toward improvement "came consistently from teacher-members of the Association, supported by a handful of bar leaders."[67] When little tangible progress was made in the American Bar Association at large, a special section in legal education was formed in 1893, which in 1900 organized the Association of American Law Schools. In 1921, the American Bar Association adopted for the first time minimum standards for the operation of law schools. The system of approval of schools by the association brought improvements in the long run, but as late as 1936 there were as many unapproved as approved schools.[68]

Working for higher admissions standards was another route reformers took to raise the level of competence. However, the sudden spread of written bar examinations during the 1890's contributed to the rapid rise of the night schools, which had as their principal aim the preparation for such examinations, so that a move designed to improve the level of competence had in the short run rather ambiguous, if not clearly the opposite effects.[69] Educational requirements for admission to the examinations rose slowly and lagged behind prevailing practice. It was only in 1940 that all states demanded any definite period of professional study; most of them required three years. Requirements as to pre-legal education were typically weaker. Progress was made after 1921 when the American Bar Association had committed itself in favor of higher standards; in 1940 "over two-thirds of the states had adopted the requirement of at least two years of college preparation or its equivalent as a prerequisite for admission."[70]

172

Apart from inertia buttressed by tradition and the difficulties of establishing effective organizational patterns in a vast decentralized political system, the main obstacle to a more rapid improvement of educational levels and admission standards was the deeply ingrained notion that the bar as a quasi-political institution should be open to recruits from all social strata. Thus, the changes by and large paralleled the broadening of higher education in the society at large.

The emergence of the faculties of the better law schools as a highly competent subgroup of the legal profession was important far beyond legal education. Law professors became part of the leadership of the bar as a whole. This constitutes another convergence with the German pattern, where law professors had been a dominant group within the legal profession since the reception of the Roman law. However, while in Germany professorial influence was largely conservative and reinforced prevailing orientations, law professors in the United States often constituted a counterbalance to the outlook of leading business lawyers and to the laissez-faire ideology.[71] This new element in the American bar was instrumental in reviving ideals of public responsibility, and it was crucial in reconciling the bar to the strengthening of government intervention during the New Deal.

The stronger role assumed by the government in economy and society was of great importance for the position and the outlook of the bar. Hurst says: "In 1950 it appeared that if the bar was to be taken out of absorption in sheer technique or partisanship—whether these be regarded as naive or calculated attitudes—it would be mainly because of the simple pressure of government intervention in the economy."[72] After the middle of the century, legal regulation and governmental policy could not be ignored by any interest, and they could not any more as easily be challenged by private or court action as during the late nineteenth and the early twentieth century. Sound, if partisan advice to one's client was less often at odds with declared public policy, and the bar, mediating between private interests and the established legal order, found firmer support for public service ideals in the growing strength of the governmental system.

## EMANCIPATION OF THE RECHTSANWALTSCHAFT
### FROM GOVERNMENT CONTROL

There had been associations of advocates in a few German cities at the beginning of the nineteenth century. During the 1830's, a number of new associations were founded, and the 1840's, the decade of the bourgeois revolution, were a period of further growth of bar associations in a number of cities and in several states. Very little of such activity, however, was found in Prussia.[73]

These associations were viewed with suspicion by the territorial governments. Often, attempts at organization were ruled out or the stated aims
had to be modified. The associations were indeed frequently concerned
with political affairs, at least as these were defined in Restoration Germany; they aimed at reforms in the administration of justice and discussed
measures to introduce a unified German law. A typical demand regarding
the profession was the establishment of *Anwaltskammern*, institutions of
public law for the autonomous enforcement of discipline by the bar. Lacking these, many of the voluntary associations set up some disciplinary machinery by themselves.

Immediately before the revolution of 1848, there were three German
bar meetings, and in 1848 a German bar association was founded, which
disappeared, however, with the failure of the revolution. In the late 1840's
and during the 1850's most states followed Prussia in instituting elected
honors councils with limited jurisdiction over professional discipline. This
led in many places to a dissolution of previously organized associations,
while in other territories which did not introduce the new institution voluntary associations sprang up. Associations with wider aims, especially statewide associations, came to the fore again at the beginning of the 1860's,
when the Bavarian and the Prussian bar associations were founded. The
unification of the German empire, finally, brought the establishment of the
German bar association in 1871.

The development of bar associations in Germany thus follows a fairly
clear pattern. When facilities for their emergence became available and
when individual action as well as traditional forms of organization proved
ineffective, voluntary associations were formed for professional as well as
political reasons. These two concerns merged where the quasi-civil service
status of the bar was at stake, as it frequently was. The associations met
with governmental opposition wherever their goals questioned the status
quo. This status quo allowed for associations in some states, for instance
in southwest Germany or in Saxony, which were considered criminal con-
spiracies in others. When in the middle of the century the bourgeois revolution failed and when at about the same time many states gave to the bar
some autonomy in disciplinary matters, both sources of this drive for
organization weakened for a decade or two. The unification of Germany
and the related rapid changes of industrialization, urbanization, and legal
development called forth national as well as new regional and local
organizations.

The most far-reaching change in the German bar, the opening of access
to the profession for all qualified applicants and the emancipation from
control by the administrative and judicial bureaucracies, had been insisted
upon by the attorneys' associations since the 1840's. It was the politically

oriented organizations, which demanded this change, the German bar meeting of 1848 and—narrower in its political goals—the Prussian bar association in the 1860's, rather than an organization such as the Bavarian bar association which had been formed in response to public attacks on the integrity of the profession. The arguments put forth in favor of the *freie Advokatur*, the "free bar," were those of political liberalism; concern with legal etiquette and economic self-interest spoke more in favor of the status quo.

When these demands were fulfilled in 1879, the new *Rechtsanwaltsordnung* did not signal an unambiguous victory of the early liberal intentions. Greater autonomy was granted when a free bar was not any more considered a danger for the political regime. Moreover, this legislation was immediately followed by radical conservative policies regarding the personnel of courts and administrative bureaucracies. The newly constituted *Anwaltschaft*, which was not any more restricted in size, provided a convenient way to get rid of politically unwanted judges or government lawyers who were squeezed out of their positions by a reorganization of the courts and by political barriers to advancement in their careers.[74]

In the wake of the new legislation the *Anwaltschaft* changed in ways which seemed radical at the time, although in retrospect the basic continuity in spite of decisive changes is perhaps more noteworthy. Numbers rose rapidly, particularly in the centers of government and business. Before 1879, Berlin had 90 to 100 *Justizkommissare*; a generation later, in 1906, the number of *Rechtsanwälte* in Berlin was over 1,000. In Germany as a whole, lawyers in private practice tripled in absolute numbers and doubled in proportion to the population from 1880 to 1913. The long-run growth reflected the rapid development of commerce and industry as well as the growing size of the population, but the fast increase immediately after 1879 showed that there were large areas of legal needs which the old *Justizkommissare* had left unsatisfied.[75]

The increase in numbers brought more competition and a widening of the span of income differences, but the German bar maintained its place among the highest income groups until the end of Imperial Germany and in large part even later. Its economic situation, according to Feuchtwanger, "guaranteed at least a sufficient standard of living; for many it provided an income which exceeded by far the level of the middle classes."[76] All observers agree that the dire warnings about the decay of morals and competence in the bar which were to follow freedom of entry and emancipation from government control were mistaken. Max Jacobsohn could show in 1896 that there had been no relative increase in disciplinary actions in Berlin, although district attorneys, responsible then as now for the case of the prosecution in important matters, were certainly

175

not inclined toward leniency. What was lost were upper class glamour and the peculiar dignity of the higher *Beamter*, but there was no decline in legal ethics.[77] In Feuchtwanger's opinion, economic conditions made "an aristocratic outlook on life possible which takes money more or less for granted. One does not talk about it because one has it as inherited wealth or because, if its acquisition is after all linked to work, it accumulates in the form of sufficiently high salaries or fees, set by statute."[78] The bar gained considerably in intellectual stature. A number of the most important and influential commentaries on the new codifications were written by attorneys. The bar in Imperial Germany was "most decidedly a learned profession and very clearly distinguished from a mere business or occupation."[79]

The changes in legal practice regarding clientele and areas of work are difficult to assess. The range of clients definitely broadened to include more lower-middle- and lower-class persons. Where representation by attorney was compulsory, lawyers had to work for poor litigants without compensation; service to the poor was the *nobile officium* of a privileged profession. The number of such cases was large. For many attorneys they are said to have accounted for as much as one-third of their practice.[80] However, the *Anwälte* of Imperial Germany were part of the bourgeoisie, separated by a deep gulf from the lower strata. In part because of this social distance, most of the legal counseling of lower-class clients remained in the hands of union and party secretaries, charity organizations and "corner scribes." Class antagonism and a fundamental lack of trust in the *Anwaltschaft* found institutional expression when within a few years after World War I attorneys were excluded from representation in labor courts of the first instance.[81]

Whether business law became much more prominent in the work of the bar is unclear, although one should expect such a trend considering the rapid growth of industry and far-reaching changes in the organizational structure of the economy. The pressure of increased competition within the bar would also suggest that relief was sought in an expansion of areas of work. The corporation lawyer, both in private practice and in legal departments became the subject of concern and debate only after World War I, but house counsel developed almost certainly much earlier. As to the *Anwaltschaft* proper, one source states that in Berlin corporation law became concentrated in a few firms.[82] Continuous debates since the first decade of the twentieth century about a desirable extension of the bar's work into matters of business counseling, trust administration, and tax law suggest that traditional conceptions of the attorney's function as well as the competition of banks, accountants, and other new professions and institutions had limited such trends considerably. Certainly, nothing comparable to American conditions developed.[83]

Opening access to the bar had drastic consequences for the ethnic composition of the bar, a development of significance for the sense of professional community in the German bar during the next two generations. The relations between Jewish and non-Jewish lawyers assumed, of course, crucial importance with the rise of the Nazi regime in the early 1930's. Prior to 1870, practically no Jews had been admitted to judicial careers or to other positions of "public authority." Because of the peculiar recruitment practices, this meant that in Prussia Jews were also excluded from the bar in private practice. Some other German states, especially in the Southwest, admitted Jewish attorneys earlier. In the new German Empire, Jewish lawyers were appointed as judges, but were discriminated against in regard to promotion, and since the "conservative reaction" of the 1880's appointments were made only in exceptional cases. Thus, when in 1879 access to the bar was opened, many Jewish lawyers became attorneys and many attained an eminent position in the bar. By 1905, more than one-quarter of all Prussian attorneys and the majority of the bar in Berlin were Jewish.[84]

Previous public policy was indicative of an anti-Semitism which took discrimination for granted and was not strongly expressed in anti-Semitic agitation. It was found even among men who rejected prejudice and hostility against Jews when discussing high principles.[85] This changed during the last decades of the nineteenth century, when a rabid anti-Semitism became respectable in the urban middle classes and among university students. The anti-Semitic movement became influential in the legal profession, too. Complaints about "ruthless competition" in the bar and "commercialization of the profession" became associated with expressions of hostility toward the Jews. Feuchtwanger says, "Wherever personal selection of applicants occurred—in the civil service, in social life, in associations—Jews were discriminated against with the approval and even the cooperation of attorneys. The civil and military bureaucracy of Prussia with its spirit of Junkerdom and caste was the model for the other German states and also for the social and business practices of the bourgeoisie . . . The bar was in this period liberal against the wishes of its non-Jewish majority. Had it had the *numerus clausus* with personal selection of candidates, a quota system would certainly have developed."[86]

Even after the formal emancipation of private legal practice from government control, the dominant social groups retained many ways of indirectly influencing the bar in a conservative direction, by awarding of special honors and through patterns of privileged associations. These, too, reinforced the ethnic cleavage within the profession, in part because Jews were excluded from certain associations and privileged statuses, in part because Jewish lawyers had more often than others liberal political orientations. Exclusive student fraternities and the "connections" they established among alumni belong in this picture as well as the institution of the reserve officer. Reserve officers were chosen by the corps of regular officers of a regiment. Jews were typically not accepted, while for many upper middle-class Christians the pride in being a reserve officer overshadowed their commitment to other statuses, such as membership in a profession.[87] Finally, there were the honorific titles, sought after by many of the most respected lawyers and awarded according to professional accomplishments as well as political convictions. A later critic of conditions in Imperial Germany used strong words to characterize the effects of social control this seemingly innocent old-fashioned custom had, "the ministries of justice rewarded behavior favored by the state with titles such as *Justizrat, Geheimrat,* etc. while undesirable behavior was punished by withholding these honors. In effect this constituted an illegal system of discipline rivaling the disciplinary institutions set up by statute. The bar not only did not protest against this illegal practice, but participated eagerly in it."[88]

The *Rechtsanwaltschaft* of Imperial Germany was more differentiated than its predecessors. It became more autonomous, expanded rapidly, and changed in social and ethnic composition. Internally, increased competition, tensions between ethnic and political groups, and conflicts between conservative and more liberal interpretations of the attorney's obligations strained professional cohesion, but these strains were still relatively well contained. Politically more diverse, the bar remained isolated from working-class political movements, and if liberal orientations became more prevalent, conservative influence remained strong.

The elite of the profession consisted of highly competent lawyers steeped in an idealistic conception of their profession and, strange perhaps in a mundane occupation as the law, in ideals of *Bildung*, of literary culture, and a refined personality. Devotion to one's "calling" not infrequently had religious and quasi-religious overtones.[89] A deep belief in the law as an instrument of justice was often combined with a somewhat limited view of society and its development and with a retreat into the spheres of professional expertise and personal life. Abraham says: "Before the War, the *Anwaltschaft* represented a kind of intellectual professional elite of the bourgeoisie with all the virtues and flaws of the latter. In spite of great intellectual versatility it lacked political influence and power nearly completely. It provided competent experts, but only rarely leaders in the field of law; and this character it shared with lawyers in government

178

service. The prototype of the German lawyer found its ideal incarnation in a number of universally educated, harmonious, mature personalities."[90]

The defeat of Imperial Germany in World War I, the breakdown of the old order, and the establishment of the Weimar Republic in 1918-1919 initiated a period fateful for German society as well as for the *Rechts-anwaltschaft*. The latter reflected the tensions and conflicts of the wider society, which led in the early 1930's to the breakdown of democracy and the emergence of the totalitarian state; but perhaps these tensions and strains were more sharply experienced in the bar than in many other professions and strata.

For many lawyers, the end of the old order meant the end of a world of prosperity and of stability in moral and social relations. A privileged group in a society dominated by an authoritarian conservative elite, the bar had been protected against the full impact of industrialization and the emergence of a pluralistic society. The decade of the 1920's brought a sudden exposure to these forces and at the same time a decline of the authority of law and government as far as broad groups at the right and the left were concerned. Self-employed and in principle free in his choice of clients and causes, the individual *Rechtsanwalt* did not experience as sharp a conflict of sentiments and loyalties as lawyers in government service, but for the *Rechtsanwaltschaft* as a group, the new situation entailed deepening divisions; and the fragile legitimacy of the new political order weakened at the same time previously unquestioned beliefs in "the law."[91]

The differentiation of law practice increased further during these years. The number of business lawyers grew, both in private practice and in private employment. At the same time, most work still centered around the courts and related traditional fields of practice, and the old figure of the Prussian attorney with his attitudes of dignity and reserve had not disappeared. The run-away inflation of the early 1920's impoverished many members of the bar. Repeatedly observers spoke, with some exaggeration, of a "proletarization" of the *Anwaltschaft*.

It is against this background of changes in society as well as in the bar that we have to interpret the heightened concern with the fate of traditional professional ideals, which focused on the business lawyer. The issue divided the bar and its organizations. On the one side, employed syndic-attorneys were seen as an "alien body" in the *Anwaltschaft*, sharing little in its economic problems and not exposed to observation and control by colleagues while subject to other influences; and the development business practice took in general was viewed as undermining professional ethics. "We are becoming the shoe shiners of industry and commerce," was the drastic expression used to voice this opinion. On the other side, it was argued that the bar had to adapt to new conditions, that legal problems in

179

business constituted a challenge to the profession and an opportunity to find new areas of work. With many, it became a popular idea to separate the *Anwaltschaft* into two branches, a bar of business counsel and a bar of court advocates, with the latter carrying on the old traditions. If this idea never came close to being realized, it reveals the extent to which a large part of the bar was alienated from the problems of business.[92]

The tensions between "the starving gentleman and the sober businessman" within the bar[93] probably had some basis in a real divergence of professional orientations. It is very likely, however, that they were exacerbated by the strains arising out of a less secure economic situation and the possible threats to a stable moral and legal order. What is known about such strains suggests that anxieties engendered by these conditions were transformed into hostile suspicions about the developing new forms of law practice. These developments also made the integration of Jewish lawyers into the bar more precarious. At first glance, one might judge that not much had changed with the end of Imperial Germany, and if there was change it seemed to further the cause of equal rights and integration. While the proportion of Jewish lawyers in the *Anwaltschaft* increased moderately, many attained leading positions in legal scholarship, in practice, and in the organizations of the bar. Official discrimination had ceased with the new political order. However, anti-Semitic attitudes became much more pervasive and closely associated with political conservatism and radical nationalism. These movements were particularly strong among students and young *Akademiker*. They dominated the organizational life of German students from the late 1920's on, several years before the rapid rise of the Nazi Party in politics.[94] Competitive resentment merged in this growing anti-Semitism with irrational nationalism and romantic antagonism against central features of modernization—political democracy, increased salience of economic values and wide-ranging intellectual discussion. Anti-Semitic mythology saw Jewish influence behind the despised weak parliamentary democracy, the growing "materialism," and the "destruction of German culture" in literature and the arts.

Set apart to some extent from the beginning, Jewish lawyers were held responsible by many members of the *Anwaltschaft* for overcrowding and increased competitive pressures. Their political orientation was generally more liberal, and indirect evidence suggests that they were more than other lawyers able to gain a foothold in business law.[95] Thus, ethnic and political divisions, charged with hostility, coincided to a large extent with cleavages in type of practice. During the Weimar years, it was the influence of the elite of the *Rechtsanwaltschaft* that effectively restrained open anti-Semitism.

National Socialism, once in possession of governmental power, encountered little opposition from the *Anwaltschaft* in spite of the fact that it imposed swift and far-reaching changes on the profession. Up to 1933, the National Socialist lawyers' association had been a very small group, but by the end of that year it counted nearly all eligible German lawyers among its members. By 1936, more than one out of five *Rechtsanwälte* had joined the party itself, and further waves of joining occurred in 1937 and in 1940.[96] The public bar organizations, the *Anwaltskammern,* soon came under Nazi control, while the *Deutscher Anwaltverein,* the voluntary bar association, was absorbed into the Nazi organization. Even in the few months before that event, the *Anwaltverein* failed to react publicly and forcefully against the most drastic interference of the new government in professional matters, the exclusion of Jewish lawyers from public office and from the *Anwaltschaft.*[97]

The acquiescence of the bar in the anti-Semitic legislation affecting its own ranks grew in part out of fear and opportunism, but it would have been inconceivable without the strong, if largely latent, divisive hostilities in the *Anwaltschaft* of the Weimar period. The reaction of the legal profession to the new regime in general can be understood only if it is realized that the bar had long been divided along lines of ethnicity, ideology, and legal practice and had now been swept with enthusiasm for a regime believed to be able to take care of the troubles of the bar as well as of larger society. Many mistook Hitler's regime for conservative authoritarian regime rather than a revolutionary totalitarian force. Furthermore, many of those who despised the Nazi movement disdained its rabble-rousing style more than its presumed goals. This may have led them to dismiss openly announced illegal intentions as mere bad form while setting great store by the formally legal character of the Nazi takeover.

If this analysis seems to disregard the difficulties of public dissent even in the first years of the regime, it should be noted that at this early stage personal risks were high precisely because there was no widespread spontaneous opposition. Later, when the machinery of the totalitarian state was fully established, even pervasive private disagreement could not easily erupt into public dissent and had very little chance of affecting government policy.

Little is known in systematic detail about the development of the *Anwaltschaft* and the behavior of attorneys under the Nazi regime. Political considerations entered decisions concerning admission to practice and professional discipline,[98] and such politization reinforced in many ways the effects the exclusion of Jewish attorneys had on the character of the *Rechtsanwaltschaft.* Yet these developments in professional organization and

181

regulation were not the most important changes affecting legal practice; these are found rather in a thorough corruption of the administration of criminal justice and in less obvious developments in civil law.

In criminal and political justice one would, of course, expect the most drastic changes. Perhaps contrary to expectations, however, these were of a rather indirect nature. Innovations largely by-passed the regular court system. The creation of special courts for political crimes was combined with a terror system of political police and concentration camps that was not subject to judicial control. This "dual" arrangement left the regular administration of criminal justice relatively untouched. It thus avoided unnecessary opposition from bench and bar and gained a semblance of legality crucial for the stability of the regime without compromising the goal of eliminating political opposition.[99]

Fundamental, if less conspicuous, changes occurred in civil law, too. Government planning in economic matters made administrative decision-making increasingly more important than the market mechanism. The power of the party in various spheres of life—far less regularized by legal restraints than administrative action of government agencies—had parallel effects. By contrast, and probably as a consequence of these developments, the role of the courts was drastically diminished.[100] It appears that the *Anwaltschaft* did not succeed in making up losses in court work, traditionally the center of the *Anwalt*'s practice, by expanding into new areas of legal and quasi-legal work; rather it seems that the developments encouraged a further absorption of legal work into law departments of corporations and trade associations and that other professions such as accountants and tax advisors gained further ground at the expense of the bar. Ironically, the exclusion of Jewish colleagues, which many had hoped would ease the economic problems of the *Anwaltschaft*, was followed by a worsening of the situation.[101] In all probability, this exclusion actually aggravated the problems of the bar because it eliminated not only many of the most able lawyers but also a large number of those most suited to respond to the challenge of new types of work concerning business matters.

The Third Reich lasted a few months longer than twelve years. Despite this short duration it had profound effects on German society as well as on the German bar. The elimination of Nazi elements from the profession after 1945 was not very thorough.[102] Sentiments of professional solidarity, and perhaps feelings of national solidarity, too, obstructed such a development; furthermore, a pervasive redefinition of what happened took place so that all "decent colleagues" were seen as victims of deceit and coercion rather than convinced National Socialists or opportunistic careerists.

It would be unrealistic, however, to conclude from such continuity in personnel that the German *Anwaltschaft* of today essentially resembles that of the Nazi period. The experiences of total war, radical political suppression, and total defeat have established deep aversions against any political order resembling the Nazi regime, if not necessarily firm commitments to a democratic order. Still, there is far less open dissent and ambivalence about the basic tenets of democracy than there was in the Weimar period.

In the postwar years, the business community and its values have attained a prominence and autonomy they never had in Germany before. Fierce ideological arguments about the *Anwaltschaft*'s relations and orientations toward the business world are a matter of the past. However, it appears that the German bar in private practice is not more, and possibly less, involved in the business life of the country than it was during the Weimar years. The truncation of developments of the 1920's has perhaps permanently limited the involvement of the *Rechtsanwaltschaft* in business affairs.

## CONCLUSION

Perhaps a theoretical reflection on certain aspects of the development of the American and the German bar is more helpful in concluding this chapter than a summary of the arguments advanced. Attorneys mediate between the established normative order guaranteed by the state and diverse interests and developments in society. If one conceives of society as a system, the primary contribution of the bar to this system is in the area of "integration": it helps regulate the relations between differentiated social units, developing new forms for such relations, adapting old ones to new conditions, and channeling conflicts between organizations and individuals.[103]

Economic and political modernization entailed in both countries a vast increase in social differentiation. Severe problems of integration are inevitable in any such development. Specifically, the substance of the law as well as procedural forms change their meaning with changing socioeconomic conditions, especially with changes in the distribution of power and economic advantage. The implications of legal innovations are under such circumstances not easily assessed in advance. In time, such problems required of the legal profession in both countries an upgrading in the level of legal competence and a redefinition of its place in the changing context of society; in particular, the relations of the bar to government and corporate business were at issue in both countries.

The transformations of industrialization and modernization did not come smoothly in either country, but the deeper upheaval occurred in Germany, in part because the development had long been under the restraining control of traditional authorities which then broke down with the end of World War I. In an important sense, National Socialism was a revolt against the sudden full-scale emergence of modern patterns in society, culture, and economy. It constituted a search for a more primitive form of *Gemeinschaft*, of national solidarity and integration, in the face of rapid and open manifestations of socio-cultural differentiation. We have seen that these and similar sentiments were virulent in the bar of the Weimar period, too, a finding that does not come as a surprise if one looks at lawyers as primarily concerned with the integration problems of their society.

Prior to industrialization, Prussia/Germany and the United States had bars that came close to being as different from each other as any in the more developed countries of the time. Rapid economic growth and related developments in political and social life led in the long run to a convergence in the character of the two professions. Yet the forces that brought about these changes created tensions and strains which at least for some time aggravated the very conditions they set out to overcome. The form the reprofessionalization of the American bar took hardened divisions in the internal stratification of the bar; and these in turn impeded the development of professional cohesion and the implementation of renewed professional ideals. In Germany, the emancipation from government control led to grave tensions and divisions within the bar. In the long-term outcome, these subsided, but only after they had contributed to the moral and political catastrophe of the Nazi regime. The convergence of the two bars is not complete. Differences in pre-industrial conditions as well as the different paths social and economic modernization took in the two countries account in part for these contrasts, which were analyzed in detail in previous chapters.

# 6

# EPILOGUE

In spite of their basically similar social structures, the United States and Germany have legal professions which differ in important respects. In broad outline the differences concern, first, the relations of the profession to the system of government and the structure of power; second, its relations to the hierarchy of stratification and to status groups with a distinct subculture, and third, the internal structure of the bar, its norms, and its modal value orientations and patterns in its relations to clientele.

In all three dimensions, the contrasting patterns were much more clear cut in the first part of the nineteenth century than they are now. This may suggest that they are simply residues of earlier social structures, not yet eroded and washed out by the tides of change in a common direction, but doomed to disappear in another generation or two. We have observed important trends toward convergence, and they may continue, but it appears that the differences do not derive their staying power just from the inertia of social patterns once established. Industrialization and more generally modernization, the major forces behind the convergent developments, took a different course in the two cases owing in part to sharply different "starting" conditions, and they affected the legal profession as well as the wider society in far from identical ways. At present, furthermore, those aspects of the structure of each profession and its place in society which are different in the two cases are not unrelated to each other; rather they come close to forming a coherent system which is not without its tensions and contradictions but which is sufficiently cohesive to generate a considerable potential for resisting change.

The emergence of a system of generalized legal norms, relatively independent from both morals and religion, which legitimate these norms, and from political authority, which supplies the means of enforcement, constitutes a crucial phase in the development of specifically modern forms of social life. The groups primarily concerned with this system of norms, its systematization, and its application to diverse situations, took on a distinct occupational character with the emergence of the modern state. Since the monopolization of the use of force in the hands of the state became the foundation for enforcement of legal norms, there has always been some interpenetration of the legal profession, or of some of its branches, and agencies of government. However, as Parsons observed, "it is probably correct to say that from the beginning the lawyers maintained a certain independence of political authority as such."[1] The two broad circumstances which appear to provide an explanation for such a differentiation between political institutions and the legal profession are the need for legitimation of legal norms through moral beliefs transcending political authority as well as the very autonomy and diversity of the interests which require specifically legal forms of integration. Nevertheless, these conditions leave ample room for variations from society to society.

The differentiation between political authority and the legal profession is much weaker in Germany than it is in the United States. Roughly half of all German lawyers are career civil servants. Most of the positions in higher administration are in the hands of lawyers, a branch of the profession that is not closely related to the others except by a common education. Judges and prosecuting attorneys are in any system public officers and in some sense representatives of the government. In Germany, they are career civil servants; furthermore, the two groups are in the same career pattern under the supervision of the ministries of justice, if with different safeguards for the independence of their decision-making. It is in the various civil service groups that we find whatever continuity there is in the patterns of government throughout the last century. The traditions of the *Beamtentum*, diluted and differentiated by radical changes in political regimes and by a broadening of their social and political base but still alive, exert a subtle and pervasive influence on the bar in private practice, as one would expect in view of the large proportion of lawyers in government employment as well as the shared legal education. Studies at university law schools and the in-service training are primarily oriented toward the judicial branch of the profession.

The character of the *Rechtsanwalt*'s role as an officer of the court is strongly emphasized. He is self-employed and proud of his independence, a member of the *freie Berufe*, but many subtle restraints in his outlook and behavior can be traced to the strength of other branches of the profession, especially the judiciary, as reference groups. Professional ethics and discipline in the *Rechtsanwaltschaft* developed from an earlier pattern,

186

when the attorney was a quasi-*Beamter*. Home background and early up-bringing of many reinforce similar orientations.

In the United States, the bar in private practice is by far the dominant group within the legal profession as far as both numbers and the prevailing outlook of lawyers are concerned. Judges, of course, are public officials in America, too, but they remain more closely identified with the bar at large and have greater autonomy from the administrative bureaucracy. They very often come out of private practice, and they are not career civil servants but reach their positions through political competition, through "party appointment," as it were. Lawyers in government administration also often retain close links with the bar in private practice. They typically serve as legal experts and constitute a small proportion both of the bar and of higher civil servants.

These contrasting patterns find their main explanation in the relative timing of major aspects of the process of modernization—the bureaucratization of large-scale social organizations on the one hand and the spread of the rationality of the market on the other. In Prussia/Germany, bureaucratic rationalization of government preceded by a long time economic development and industrialization, imposing strong controls on all experts concerned with the legal order and absorbing many if by no means all functions of the legal profession into the orbit of administrative and judicial bureaucracies. Furthermore, law being in the pre-industrial period a less specialized discipline than it is today and one unrivaled by other fields in public affairs, lawyers came to dominate the higher civil service, shaping its ethos and outlook but also being themselves transformed into a body of officials, loyal to established authority and committed to "the public interest."

By contrast, public bureaucracies developed relatively late in the United States and thus were able to employ experts in a large variety of disciplines relevant to the operations of government. A weaker administrative branch of government left many fields which came under the control of government administration in Central Europe to more autonomous developments. If centralization and rationalization of government are characteristics of political modernization, America's polity remained relatively traditional. The primary advances in modernization came in America from entrepreneurial activity. The peculiar forms of interpenetration of the legal and the political realm, which contrast sharply with the German case, rest on older traditions, but were shaped decisively by developments of democratization during the nineteenth century. Egalitarianism and demands for popular control of the country's destiny undermined and broke down professional privileges and led from the 1830's on to popular election of judges. Judicial decision-making and its contribution to the development of law, then, is in neither case left within the autonomous province of the legal profession, although perhaps more so in the United States. However, in America it is linked to the political process in which varied interests and public opinion are integrated through parties and popular elections, while in Germany it is bound up with civil service administrations which represent more stable policy orientations. A related feature of the American case is that legal positions in public administration were largely kept in a separate category subject to political patronage when reforms instituted a civil service system in government employment.

The prominence of American lawyers in politics generally is strongly supported by such interconnections between party politics and recruitment patterns for judicial and administrative legal positions. It had its origins in the early phases of democratization when a less specialized elite of the bar had close relations with the dominant social classes and few competitors in knowledge of public affairs. The parallel to the German case is obvious. In this respect, law-trained civil servants in Germany were the equivalent of American lawyer politicians, though, of course, the societal context was sharply different. While the American bar today does not have the same position of relatively exclusive public leadership it had in the early nineteenth century, other conditions, such as the forms of judicial and administrative recruitment and the fact that American parties are less class-based than the German ones, maintain an unparalleled level of political participation in the American bar.

It we look at the role of members of the profession in the structure of power generally, disregarding the formal or informal character of power and influence exerted, it appears that German and American lawyers have about an equal share in such positions. It is a significant share, though lawyers do not dominate in either power structure. However, the prototypical lawyer of influence and power reaches his position in the United States through relatively open and frequently political competition while in Germany he achieves it by way of a bueaucratic career. Correspondingly, American private practitioners are more involved in grass roots politics and are more often found within the power elite than their German counterparts.

Any modern profession is to some extent embedded in the broader social context of the middle and upper middle classes. The prestige and income of the occupations which use a particular expertise in fields of knowledge central to society is such as to make them part of the middle and upper strata, and often their clientele is disproportionately made up of middle- and upper middle-class persons. The latter condition is in particular characteristic of the legal profession. These considerations suggest that the peculiar outlook of the professions, the conceptions of a special professional responsibility, and the legitimation of their prerogatives are grounded in upper middle-class culture and cannot adequately be understood simply in terms of the functions of highly trained experts in modern society.

We have analyzed a number of differences between the American and the German bar in relation to the system of stratification and subculturally differentiated groups. German lawyers in private practice, the branch of the profession of greatest interest in this analysis, enjoy relative to the national average a considerably higher income than their American counterparts. Furthermore, it appears that their social status, while not necessarily higher in a rank order of occupations according to their prestige, is more sharply distinct from other status groups, creating a greater social distance from people on lower standing. This status German *Rechtsanwälte* share with other *Akademiker*, a more homogeneous group than the American professions. In social background, German lawyers, like other university-trained professionals, are a more exclusive group than American attorneys. *Rechtsanwälte* of working class origin are extremely rare. Equally important, the dominant background groups even among the *Anwaltschaft*, not to speak of other branches of the profession, are lawyers from *Akademiker* and *Beamten* homes; together, these account for about three of every five private practitioners.

The American bar is far more heterogeneous in social origin. There is first the ethnic heterogeneity of American society which is reflected in the legal profession, although Blacks are only marginally represented. While this factor may be of declining importance if a likely future increase in the number of black attorneys is disregarded, the American bar is also more heterogeneous in terms of class backgrounds. Lawyers of working-class origin are underrepresented but form a sizeable minority. Sons of businessmen—proprietors and managers—constitute the largest single group but not a majority in the profession. If we disregard ethnic origins, none of the background groups are as sharply set off by a relatively distinct subculture as the sons of *Beamte* and *Akademiker* in the German case. And the same can be said about the bar itself. More heterogeneous in social backgrounds, it is not as insulated in its professional orientations from influence of the social environment as the German bar is.

The greater subcultural distinctiveness of the *Rechtsanwaltschaft*, evidenced for example in standards of mutual evaluation, is not peculiar to the bar as such but is shared with other traditional *akademische Berufe*. It is related to the peculiar place of these occupations in the status structure. I have argued that an "ascriptive" emphasis rather than an emphasis on individual success independent of one's profession, at least in more conservative German value orientations, makes membership in such groups an important criterion for social status and supports a tendency, on the part of members as well as of outsiders, to view status groups as a relatively homogeneous and distinct social entities. Historically, this pattern goes back to a traditional feudal order. As we have seen, it was transformed repeatedly and adapted to new constellations during the nineteenth century. Whether it is on its way out may be doubted even if the present broadening of the ranks of the professions is taken into consideration.

Businessmen form a major part of the clientele of private law practice in any modern society where the economy is relatively autonomous and market mechanisms play an important role in its functioning. The business world is thus an essential component of the subcultural environment in which the bar is embedded. We have seen, however, that the German private practitioners are less closely involved in business affairs proper as well as in the realm of business law. This can best be explained by the greater role of house counsel and other lawyers in business positions and by a greater share of competing counseling professions specializing in business matters. However, the pattern is supported by, and reinforces in turn, orientations in a part of the *Anwaltschaft* which derive from the bar's close relations to the subcultures of the *Akademiker* and the civil service and from pervasive conservative value orientations regarding the role of business. If syndic-attorneys are viewed in conjunction with the lawyers in private practice, we see today a bifurcation of the *Anwaltschaft* into a more conservative part, whose work centers around litigation and related matters and whose orientations are characterized by traditional reserve, and another part, which is rather closely integrated with the business world; even here, though, we may surmise that background and professional tradition often impose restraints less prevalent in the American bar.

The orientations of American private practitioners are less anchored in specific subcultures distinct from the business community. Business families provide the largest single group of lawyers as far as social origins are concerned, and furthermore, business and its values have a less contested place of primacy in American society. Thus, the impact of the most important client group on the bar's outlook and behavior is far stronger than in the German case.

It is a sociological commonplace that the internal structure of any modern occupation will be characterized by specialization, a variety of organizational settings for work, and, accompanying such differentiation, by the development of stratification in regard to prestige and control over valued resources. These tendencies are at odds with traditional notions of professional solidarity and professional ethics, since these rely strongly on individual and collective self-control of equals who are relatively autonomous and have insight into each other's work and situation.

Specialization is not highly developed in either bar, but far more so in the large cities of America. In conjunction with the large number of practitioners in the American metropolitan bar and their consequent anonymity, with the growth of large law firms, which can be interpreted as the functional equivalent of a more widespread use of house counsel in Germany, and with the circumstances of the relatively recent transition in professional training from apprenticeship to law schools of highly varied quality, this higher level of differentiation of law practice has engendered in the metropolitan bar of the United States a steep and rigid system of stratification, unparalleled in Germany. The differences in income found in the German *Anwaltschaft* actually come close to those of the American profession, but a stronger sense of professional community is engendered by more homogeneous recruitment and education and by the peculiar character of the status of *Akademiker* in society. Financial success is not to the same extent equated with professional accomplishment as in the United States. Generally, the internal stratification of the German *Rechtsanwaltschaft* is more set apart from the stratification system of the wider society, while the American bar reflects in a far less "filtered" way the divisions and the criteria of evaluation and discrimination of American society. This difference would be misunderstood, of course, unless it is seen together with the fact that the German legal profession is more exclusive and privileged as a group.

Less divided by internal cleavages and more deeply embedded in wider supportive subcultures, the German *Rechtsanwaltschaft* differs systematically from the American bar in regard to professional ethics. These rules of conduct may be considered as largely concerned with trivial matters of etiquette and with technicalities of legal practice rather than with the broader questions about the impact of the bar's work on society. They should not be dismissed as irrelevant, however, since they are important in shaping the attorney's relations with his immediate role partners and since both their content and the degree of acceptance and conformity are indicative of broader orientations prevalent in the profession.

In analyzing these matters we again found evidence that the American bar is less insulated from the attitudes and pressures of its environment and especially the business community; there also was evidence for the generally more "official" character of the *Rechtsanwaltschaft*. Loyalty to the client and efficiency in serving the client are dominant themes in the formal and informal norms of the American bar, while they are more strongly counterbalanced in the German case by emphasis on the role of officer of the court and on the independence and dignity of a learned profession. What evidence there is on the actual acceptance of official standards and their violation suggests that in large groups of the American bar, especially in metropolitan areas, accepted standards and actual practices differ little from what is acceptable in the business community and occasionally fall below that level. In contrast to its American counterpart, the German *Anwaltschaft* does not even in its lower strata in large cities appear to have comparable "pockets" of structured deviance, defined by field of practice, status of practitioners, and type of clientele and/or public agencies involved. This contrast in particular seems closely related to the greater homogeneity of German private practitioners in background and education and to the fact that internal stratification has induced less deep cleavages in the German bar. These conditions are also reflected in associational organization. German bar associations are more inclusive than their American counterparts and less differentiated by status and specialization of lawyers. The *Rechtsanwaltskammern* are institutions of public law and constitute a compromise between the principles of professional autonomy and government supervision.

The two professions have, in the last two or three generations, moved closer to each other in functions, professional organization, and outlook, but important contrasts remain. The areas of work as well as the extraprofessional roles of German *Rechtsanwälte* are still more sharply circumscribed than the fields of activity of American attorneys. In particular, German private law practice has not branched out as much into business matters and is unlikely to do so in the future, since competing professions have become firmly established in this area. At the same time, the *Anwaltschaft* has retained much of the traditional character of an *akademischer Beruf*, a university-trained profession, privileged by conservative notions about the proper status structure of society; and it has also retained close, albeit mostly indirect, relations to the subculture of government officialdom.

The American bar has become more circumscribed in its role in society than it was in the first part of the nineteenth century and has assumed more specialized functions. Reprofessionalization improved, and continues to improve, technical legal education, and attempts are made to instill a stronger sense of professional responsibility. However, if more circumscribed social roles mean, among other things, a decline in the "public influence of the bar," American lawyers are still more involved in community affairs and politics than any other occupation in any other society. The American bar in private practice also continues to be the recruitment ground for the judiciary. Finally, and perhaps most important for its outlook and value orientations, it has retained a broad involvement in business affairs.

The value orientations of the profession and the ways in which lawyers define the situation and the problems of law practice appear to be shaped

192

by these differences in work and extraprofessional activities and by the ties with various more or less distinct and influential groups outside the profession that arise from characteristic patterns of work as well as of social background and legal education. The effects of these conditions may be modified by general value orientations prevalent in the wider society, especially by the value orientations of the middle and upper strata to which both lawyers and their clients belong. Such value orientations, while similar in many respects in the two countries, show subtle contrasts which are relevant for law practice and the legal profession and which tend to reinforce differences in the outlook of the two bars. These contrasts in values concern the moral attitude toward competitive pursuit of gain and the relative evaluation of the business world. Another dimension of contrast is found in the area of tolerance for social conflict, particularly conflict about issues which involve the integrity of the moral and social order. There are, furthermore, differences in respect for the law and in conceptions of the functions of law in society—whether emphasis is on the resolution of conflicts, with the definition of substantive ideals largely left to other institutions and agencies, or whether law is seen as an instrument for the realization of substantive justice and the common good. Finally, the two value systems differ in the relative strength of egalitarian and elitist orientations. Important changes have occurred in these value orientations but they are often not yet firmly established, and the old orientations still lock up with each other so as to generate an effect of mutual reinforcement. Where confusion and ambiguity ensue as a consequence of rapid change, the old system of interrelated attitudes offers one way of gaining firm ground again; and even if it is not fully re-established it colors and shapes the new patterns.

This study has focused on the social conditions that shape the work and outlook of lawyers in Germany and America. It has not primarily analyzed the contribution the two legal professions make to their societies, and I have refrained from evaluating their contribution in relation to the needs for legal services in each country. The partial emancipation of the Blacks and the poor during the 1960's have substantially increased legal demands in America. These developments can be seen as part of epochal trends in both countries, in fact in all modern societies. Extending realistic equality and protecting civil liberties are in my judgment the most important long-run tasks for lawyers in both Germany and America aside from the "routine" tasks of operating and developing institutional frameworks for socioeconomic cooperation and conflict mediation. How this challenge will be met depends to a large extent on other, political forces but the legal profession makes a difference, too. Both bars studied seem less than ideally suited for these tasks as they are closely linked to the more conservative positions in each society. On balance, however, the American bar is likely to have an important advantage through its very diversity and flexibility. One may take the movement of public interest law and the new radical idealism of a minority of law students as recent responses to these challenges.[2]

In conclusion, certain implications emerge from this study for the sociology of law and especially for the sociological analysis of the professions. I have argued in the first chapter that the bar differs in essential respects from other professions, in particular from the modern ones whose work is based on scientific knowledge. In contrast to the medical profession, the study of which has dominated sociological thinking in this area and has provided the materials for the current theoretical model of a profession, the bar does not apply a body of scientific knowledge; its expert knowledge rather concerns man-made standards and rules, grounded in values and power constellations and subject to change. This difference affects the character of the lawyer's authority vis-à-vis his client, which is either weaker than the doctor's or based on institutionalized power and shared values rather than predictive science. Furthermore, and again in contrast to the medical profession, the values served by lawyers—order and justice—are, although of intense concern for many, open to divergent interpretation, which in turn is shaped by dissension about societal values. Closely related is the crucial fact that law practice is concerned with the accommodation and alignment of divergent interests, with actual and potential conflict. Finally, attorneys more often than most other professionals branch out in their work beyond the specific area of legal competence; this narrows the gap in expertise between lawyer and client and further reduces the specifically professional authority of the lawyer.

All these contrasts concern the core of the theoretical model used most often for the sociological analysis of the professions. In the preceding chapters we have encountered many of the ramifications of these peculiar characteristics of the practice of law—for example, the alternative patterns of dependency on government supervision and one-sided client caretaking or the interrelations between the type of the lawyer's work, the character of his expertness, and his authority and independence vis-à-vis the clientele. I believe it would be fruitful to reverse the predominant perspective and to look at other professions with the legal profession serving as a model. This changed perspective would sensitize research to variations in the character of the "knowledge" base of different professions and to the consequences of such variations. It would focus attention on the elements of conflict and dissension regarding the ultimate goals served by professional work, even in fields like medicine. Lastly, it would suggest not only looking for variations in the gap of knowledge and skill in different professions and subfields of practice, but searching for other bases of professional privileges than the "bargain" between the professional community and the public, designed to protect the vulnerable and to ensure trust in the expert as well as high status and autonomy for the professional group and its members.

The series of alternative institutional arrangements for the dispensation of expert services as discussed theoretically in the first chapter as well as the review of the historical development of the two bars suggest that the societal structure of power and the patterns of prestige, income, and subculturally differentiated status groups are of extraordinary importance for professional practice, for the relations to clients and other role partners, the conceptions about special professional responsibilities, and the justification of professional privileges.

This is not the place for an assessment of the state of the sociology of law. I will therefore confine myself to the suggestion that major advances could be accomplished along lines explored half a century ago by Max Weber, that is, by emphasizing historical and comparative analysis and by integrating studies in comparative law with sociological analyses of the legal profession, the organizations it is involved in, and its place in the wider societal context. This approach would combine the analysis of systems of legal standards with the study of legal institutions and the legal profession and insist in both respects on a consideration of the societal context. The framework provided by such research would also give perspective and added significance to more narrowly defined studies on specific aspects of the law, its institutions, and its personnel in individual countries.

# NOTES

1. Richard D. Schwartz and James C. Miller, "Legal Evolution and Societal Complexity," *American Journal of Sociology*, 70:159-169 (September 1964). Evidence on the comparative incidence of substantial division of labor, writing, and counsel is found on p. 167.

2. Ibid. The evolutionary interpretation was challenged by Stanley Udy, Jr., "Dynamic Inferences from Static Data," *American Journal of Sociology*, 70:625-627 (March 1965); cf. Richard D. Schwartz', "Reply," ibid., pp. 627-628. However, with regard to the emergence of the institution of counsel, I know of no account from legal history where the development of the role of attorney preceded the institutions of "mediation" and "police" or even the more specific one of adjudication.

3. See, for example, Max Gluckman, *The Judicial Process among the Barotse of Northern Rhodesia* (Manchester, Manchester University Press, 1955).

4. See Max Rheinstein, ed., *Max Weber on Law in Economy and Society* (Cambridge, Mass., Harvard University Press, 1954), p. 199, and Adolf Weissler, *Geschichte der Rechtsanwaltschaft* (Leipzig, C. E. M. Pfeffer, 1905), pp. 25-91. Paul Koschaker, *Europa und das römische Recht* (Munich and Berlin, Biederstein, 1947), p. 165, discusses the role of magical formalism in the emergence of legal experts in general.

5. The conditions and consequences of bureaucratization have been a major concern of Max Weber; see his *Economy and Society*, ed. by Guenther Roth and Claus Wittich, 3 vols. (New York, Bedminster Press, 1968), and, for the effects on the law, the selections in Rheinstein, ed., *Weber on Law*. The most comprehensive study of historical bureaucratic systems is S. N. Eisenstadt, *The Political Systems of Empires* (New York, Free Press, 1963). The following analysis is greatly indebted to this work. However, since legal developments and especially the emergence of different kinds of legal specialists were not the main problem of Eisenstadt's study, his text as well as his tabulations had to be used as springboards for inferences the responsibility for which I have to assume.

6. On the marginal role of private legal counseling in pre-modern China see John H. Wigmore, *A Panorama of the World's Legal Systems* (St. Paul, Minn., West Publishing Co., 1928), p. 178; and T'ung-tsu Ch'ü, *Law and Society in Traditional China* (The Hague, Mouton, 1965; Chinese ed. 1947), p. 284f. Among the bureaucratic empires analyzed by Eisenstadt, Chinese regimes from the seventh to the nineteenth century received the highest ratings on bureaucratic involvement in the legal sphere, with the exception of two relatively short periods. At the local level, this was paralleled only in two instances, the Inca empire at the eve of the Spanish conquest and absolutist Austria; see Eisenstadt, *Empires*, appendix, table 1, pp. 404-411.

7. See Fritz Schulz, *History of Roman Legal Science*, 2d ed. (Oxford, Clarendon Press, 1953); on the conservation and the later diffusion of the heritage of the Roman law see

Koschaker, *Europa und das römische Recht*, and Max Weber, *General Economic History* (New York, 1927), p. 340f., as well as Rheinstein, ed., *Weber on Law*, p. 210f.

8. In the technical language of recent social theory, these particular aspects of contractual relations have been called "performance orientation" in contrast to "ascription" or "quality orientation," "universalism" in contrast to "particularism," and "specificity" in contrast to "diffuseness." See Talcott Parsons and Edward A. Shils, "Values, Motives and Systems of Action," T. Parsons and E. A. Shils, eds., *Toward a General Theory of Action* (Cambridge, Mass., Harvard University Press, 1951), esp. pp. 80-88.

9. Rheinstein, ed., *Weber on Law*, p. 96; the preceding quote is from p. 72; for nonlegal guarantees of contractual relations see p. 68f.

10. Eisenstadt, *Empires*, p. 137f. The main thesis of Eisenstadt's work is concerned with the dilemmas of early bureaucratic rule sketched above.

11. On the role of merchants in Imperial China see Eisenstadt, *Empires*, p. 43. On the role of lawyers in the English case see J. D. Eusden, *Puritans, Lawyers and Politics in Seventeenth Century Politics* (New Haven, Conn., Yale University Press, 1958).

12. Rheinstein, ed., *Weber on Law*, pp. 122f., 199; and Roscoe Pound, *The Lawyer from Antiquity to Modern Times* (St. Paul, Minn., West Publishing Co., 1953). e.g., p. 70.

13. For a general discussion of structural problems of this kind, see my "Partial Modernization," J. J. Loubser et al., eds., *Explorations in General Theory in the Social Sciences* (New York, Free Press, forthcoming).

14. Weber expresses the latter poignantly: "The maxim *caveat emptor* obtains, as experience shows, mostly in transactions involving feudal strata or, as every cavalry officer knows, in horse trading among comrades. The specific ethics of the market place is alien to them. Once and for all they conceive of commerce, as does any rural community of neighbors, as an activity in which the sole question is: who will cheat whom." Rheinstein, ed., *Weber on Law*, p. 194.

15. See, for other than pre-modern European conditions, Bernard S. Cohen, "Notes on Disputes and Law in India," in L. Nader, ed., *The Ethnography of Law*, Special Publication of *American Anthropologist*, 67(6), Part II: 82-122 (December 1965); also Bernard S. Cohen, "Some Notes on Law and Change in North India," *Economic Development and Cultural Change*, 7(1): 79-93 (October 1959). It is interesting that the late medieval and post-medieval imagery concerning the attorney is full of military metaphors. The language of combat was apparently for many groups in these societies as appropriate as the language of justice and morals to deal with legal matters.

16. See Weissler, *Geschichte*, pp. 229-235, chapter xxx, and many other passages; also Erich Döhring, *Geschichte der deutschen Rechtspflege seit 1500* (Berlin, Duncker und Humblot, 1953), p. 138f.

17. Vilhelm Aubert sees the disappearance of such divisions as one of the major conditions for the development of a modern profession. "The Legal Profession in Norwegian Social Structure," unpublished MS, University of Oslo.

18. Philipp Melanchthon, the close associate of Martin Luther, dealt with this problem in one of his writings. His answer was positive, but he wrote "as an ecclesiastical statesman intent on serving civil government, rather than as an overwrought religious leader of turbulent masses." Benjamin Nelson, *The Idea of Usury* (Princeton, N.J., Princeton University Press, 1949), p. 40. The concepts used in the above argument refer to Max Weber's distinction between substantive and formal orientations of legal systems which is cut across by the other distinction between systems guided by general rules and those guided by reaction to individual cases and by tests beyond the control of reason; Rheinstein, ed., *Weber on Law*, pp. xlviii-lviii passim.

19. On the Russian revolution see Boris Gerschun, "Russland," in Julius Magnus, ed., *Die Rechtsanwaltschaft* (Leipzig, W. Moeser, 1929), pp. 216-250, esp. pp. 228-231; also Harold J. Berman, *Justice in Russia* (Cambridge, Mass., Harvard University Press, 1950), p. 23, and John N. Hazard, *The Soviet System of Government*, 4th ed. (Chicago, University of Chicago Press, 1968), p. 182. On the French Revolution see Weissler, *Geschichte*, p. 396f. Hitler and other leading National Socialists were extremely hostile toward the legal profession and by-passed regular procedure in many respects, but they did not attempt to do away with

an autonomous bar. On the American revolution and enlightenment-inspired policies in eighteenth-century Prussia see Chapter 5 below.

20. A sampling of the literature is found in Howard M. Vollmer and Donald L. Mills, eds., *Professionalization* (Englewood Cliffs, N.J., Prentice-Hall, 1966). Various statements of the theory sketched above are given by Talcott Parsons, William J. Goode, Robert K. Merton, and others in several essays, of which one may be cited as representative: William J. Goode, "Community within a Community: The Professions," *American Sociological Review*, 22:194-200 (April 1957). For one critical evaluation of the model see Dietrich Rueschemeyer, "Doctors and Lawyers: A Comment on the Theory of the Professions," *Canadian Review of Sociology and Anthropology*, 1:17-30 (1964). The discussion least vulnerable to the criticisms advanced is William J. Goode, "The Theoretical Limits of Professionalization," A. Etzioni, ed., *The Semi-Professions and Their Organization* (New York, Free Press, 1969), pp. 266-313. An important recent critique which is similar to my own position in some respects, yet differs in important others, is Eliot Freidson's *Profession of Medicine. A Study of the Sociology of Applied Knowledge* (New York, Dodd, Mead, 1970).

21. N. S. Timasheff has pointed out that in fascist Italy and Germany as well as in communist Russia public bureaucratic controls have been the predominant pattern of control of professional work. Timasheff, "Business and the Professions in Liberal, Fascist, and Communist Society," *American Journal of Sociology*, 45, 6:863-869 (1940). He does not mention that the absolutist regimes of continental Europe had a long tradition of such public service ideals and governmental controls regarding the classical professions. These traditions never completely lost their force during the liberalizing developments of the nineteenth century, as we will see in detail when comparing the history of the bar in Germany and the United States.

22. "There is no doubt that the Anglo-American variety of modern Western society gave rise to the highest 'rugged individualism' in business and to the greatest freedom of professions." Timasheff, "Business and the Professions," p. 863. He might have added the absence of strong centralized government as a further condition. It is noteworthy that it was a scholar who took his understanding of English institutions as one of the main guides for his policy recommendations who was most influential in freeing the German bar from a quasi-civil service status: Rudolf Gneist, *Freie Advokatur. Die erste Forderung aller Justizreform in Preussen* (Berlin, 1867). Still, the formula he used for the desirable role of the bar was couched in terms of the contrast between civil service and business, rather than referring to an ideal of professional autonomy and self-control.

23. A. M. Carr-Saunders and P. A. Wilson, *The Professions* (Oxford, Clarendon Press, 1933), p. 300.

24. See, for instance, William Kornhauser, *Scientists in Industry: Conflict and Accommodation* (Berkeley, University of California Press, 1962), and W. Richard Scott, "Professionals in Bureaucracies—Areas of Conflict," Vollmer and Mills, eds., *Professionalization*, pp. 266-275.

25. See, for instance, Herbert H. Hyman, "The Value Systems of Different Classes," Reinhard Bendix and Seymour M. Lipset, eds., *Class, Status and Power*, 2d ed. (New York, Free Press, 1966), pp. 488-499.

26. William Duran, *The Lawyer, Our Old-Man-of-the-Sea* (London, 1913), p. 50, quoted in T. H. Marshall, "The Recent History of Professionalism in Relation to Social Structure and Social Policy," *Canadian Journal of Economics and Political Science*, 5:330. Benjamin Twiss, *Lawyers and the Constitution. How Laissez Faire Came to the Supreme Court* (Princeton, N.J., Princeton University Press, 1942), documents and analyzes the drastic influences of this sort in the development of American constitutional law from 1875 to 1935.

27. The following material is based on ideas first developed in Rueschemeyer, "Doctors and Lawyers."

28. Weber, *Economy and Society*, esp. vol. I, pp. 212-301.

29. The emphasis on procedural law at the operative level that is characteristic of a developed legal profession may be interpreted as a defense against involvement in the various substantive notions of justice, which are charged with strong emotions, as well as against the biases, passions, and outbursts of violence that may grow out of the clash of conflicting interests. However, this formalism is at the same time a further source of alienation between

the ways and ideals of the legal profession and substantively defined orientations of various publics.

30. Talcott Parsons, "A Sociologist Looks at the Legal Profession," *Essays in Sociological Theory*, rev. ed. (Glencoe, Ill. Free Press, 1954), p. 376.

## NOTES TO CHAPTER 2

1. I refer here and in the following to the Federal Republic in West Germany only. The German Democratic Republic in East Germany exhibits radically different patterns in regard both to the general societal structure and to the place and function of the legal profession.

2. See Benjamin Kaplan, Arthur T. von Mehren, and Rudolf Schaefer, "Phases of German Civil Procedure," *Harvard Law Review*, 71:1461 (1958).

3. Aside from the different role in shaping the development of the law, German judges in all except the lowest courts work in a collegiate pattern. Anonymity of individual opinions is regarded essential for the court's and the law's authority. Recently, however, the federal constitutional court has adopted signed opinions, including dissenting ones.

4. E. J. Cohn, "The German Attorney—Experiences with a Unified Profession (I)," *International and Comparative Law Quarterly*, 9:587 (1960). Cohn, who practiced both in Germany and England, explains: "Commentaries vary in size from a little one-volume pocket edition to huge standard works approximating in size our 'Halsbury.' But it is believed that a good selection of pocket commentaries together with a more elaborate edition of one or two codes, plus the last fifteen years of the leading legal periodical, *Neue Juristische Wochenschrift*, and the current official Statute Book will do for the needs of a large percentage of attorneys in all but a fairly small number of cases, in particular if this 'library' is supplemented by some of the better-class students' textbooks from his university days" (p. 586).

5. The regular German courts of first and second instance, for example, are courts of the *Länder*; "but they are national courts in the sense . . . that their jurisdiction and procedure are established almost exclusively by national law just as the substantive law which they apply is predominantly national law." Kaplan, et al., "German Civil Procedure," p. 1195f. (footnotes omitted).

6. See Chapter 3, below.

7. "The judicial career and that of the public prosecutor are distinguished in theory rather than in practice. Judges are appointed to positions in the prosecutor's career and prosecutors have as much expectation of attaining high judicial office as judges." Cohn, "German Attorney, I", p. 590, note 21. They also share a common association, the *Deutscher Richterbund*.

8. Even the "syndic-attorney," primarily working in private employment, but also admitted to work at court, is felt to be an alien element in the Rechtsanwaltschaft by many attorneys. "Whether admitted to practice or not, [business employed lawyers] are at best merely nominally members of the legal profession," asserts Cohn, "German Attorney, I," p. 586, identifying "legal profession" and *Anwaltschaft*.

9. See J. Willard Hurst, *The Growth of American Law. The Law Makers* (Boston, Little, Brown, 1950), chapter vii.

10. See Peyton Ford, David Reich, and Clive W. Palmer, *The Government Lawyer. A Survey and Analysis in the Executive Branch of the United States Government* (Englewood Cliffs, N.J. Prentice-Hall, 1952), p. 11, note 5, and pp. 19 ff. On lawyers in the federal government in the perspective of private practitioners dealing with federal agencies see Charles A. Horsky, *The Washington Lawyer* (Boston, Little, Brown, 1952).

11. This judgment is based on considerations stated below. On house counsel in the United States see Charles S. Maddock, "The Corporation Law Department," *Harvard Business Review*, 30:119-136 (1952); and the excellent chapter in Quintin Johnstone and Dan Hopson, Jr., *Lawyers and Their Work* (Indianapolis, Bobbs-Merrill, 1967), pp. 199-242.

12. See Albert P. Blaustein and Charles O. Porter, *The American Lawyer. A Summary of the Survey of the Legal Profession* (Chicago, University of Chicago Press, 1954); and Glenn Greenwood, *The 1961 Lawyer Statistical Report* (Chicago, American Bar Foundation, 1961).

13. See Wolfgang Kaupen, *Die Hüter von Recht und Ordnung* (Neuwied and Berlin, Luchterhand, 1969), pp. 35-38.

14. The *Martindale-Hubbell Law Directory*.

15. In 1960 and 1961, respectively, there were 540 and 560 people for each law school graduate active in the labor force in the United States and 680 in 1961 in Germany. The figures for every member of the bar, as defined in Table 1, are 710 and 950 to 990, respectively. For data on the population of the United States and Germany see U.S. Bureau of the Census, *Statistical Abstract of the United States: 1964* (Washington, D.C., 1964), p. 5, and *Statistisches Jahrbuch für die Bundesrepublik Deutschland 1963* (Stuttgart and Mainz, 1963), p. 34.

16. A comparison of these figures for 1960 with data for 1951 and 1966 reveals interesting trends. While the proportion of lawyers in private legal practice declined steadily, though not dramatically (1966: 74 percent), the percentage of lawyers in private employment roughly doubled in the fifteen-year period (1966: nearly 12 percent). The proportion of lawyers in judicial office and in government employment remained more or less stable. See U.S. Bureau of the Census, *Statistical Abstract of the United States: 1968* (Washington, D.C., 1968), p. 154 (based on American Bar Foundation, *The 1967 Lawyer Statistical Report*, Chicago, 1967). Exact proportions cannot be determined meaningfully because the data contain varying amounts of double entries. Table 1 makes use of the 1960 figures only, since they are most directly comparable to the only data available on the German legal profession.

17. It should be noted that for purposes of comparison I have classified in Table 1 two groups of lawyers differently than is customary in Germany. Prosecuting attorneys are usually grouped with the judiciary, and all lawyers admitted to practice at court, whether privately employed or not, are usually treated as one group, the *Rechtsanwaltschaft*.

18. Reinhard Bendix collected information on higher civil servants in federal employment in 1940; *Higher Civil Servants in American Society* (Boulder, Colo., University of Colorado Press, 1949). Of the top civil servants in his sample, which excluded political appointees and officials whose work was primarily technical in character, 29 percent had law degrees, p. 59. W. Lloyd Warner, Paul van Riper, Norman H. Martin, and Orvis F. Collins, *The American Federal Executive* (New Haven, Conn., Yale University Press, 1963), took in 1959 a broader sample of 11,000 civilian federal executives, also excluding "professional, scientific and technical personnel serving primarily in individual capacities as specialists," p. 302 and p. 11. Of these federal officials, 14.4 percent had law degrees. Politically appointed executives—18 percent of the whole group—had, with 39.9 percent, the highest share of lawyers, while among career civil service executives the proportion was just below 10 percent, pp. 357, 129.

19. Although Bendix considered only relatively high positions relevant for policy-making—of the legal departments only the "principal legal advisor of department or agency" (p.15)—and although the Department of Justice was strongly underrepresented in his sample (p. 18), nearly one-third of those with a law degree actually worked as lawyers. The job and career descriptions in recent more inclusive, if also more superficial analyses focusing on the government lawyer very clearly bear out the technical legal character of the work of most attorneys in government service; see Blaustein and Porter, *American Lawyer*, pp. 58-63 and 97-107; and Ford, Palmer, and Reich, *Government Lawyer*.

20. For a higher estimate (at 85 percent in selected departments) see Wolfgang Zapf, ed., *Beiträge zur Analyse der deutschen Oberschicht* (Munich, Piper, 1965), p. 18. Zapf included in this estimate those lawyers who did not pass the second state examination. For details see his "Die Verwalter der Macht," in *Beiträge*, pp. 77-94.

21. This parallel was suggested to me by the late Daniel Lewin, who did research for his doctoral thesis on the recruitment of the German foreign office. Ralf Dahrendorf developed a similar idea in his "Ausbildung einer Elite. Die deutsche Oberschicht und die juristischen Fakultäten," *Der Monat*, 14:15-26 (1962).

22. Until the beginning of the Roosevelt administration, and to some extent even now, federal agencies had great difficulty in attracting and retaining lawyers of good quality. See Ford et al., *Government Lawyer*, p. 5 passim; Edwin S. Rockefeller, "The Status of the

Federal Government Lawyer Is Important to the Legal Profession," *American Bar Association Journal*, 47:350-352 (1961); and Blaustein and Porter, *American Lawyer*, p. 62f.

23. Wolfgang Kaupen, "Zur Soziologie der deutschen Juristen," in: *Recht und Politik. Mitteilungen der Arbeitsgemeinschaften Sozialdemokratischer Juristen. Berlin - Hessen - Niederrhein*, 44:22 (1966). These were not necessarily fully qualified lawyers, though. On the work of house counsel in the United States see Maddock, "Corporation Law Department," and Johnstone and Hopson, *Lawyers*, chap. vi.

24. W. Lloyd Warner and James C. Abegglen, *Occupational Mobility in American Business and Industry, 1928-1952* (Minneapolis, University of Minnesota Press, 1955), found in a sample of 7,500 business leaders that 6 percent were lawyers; p. 122. Heinz Hartmann, "Der zahlenmässige Beitrag der Hochschulen zur Gruppe der industriellen Führungskräfte," *Zeitschrift für die gesamte Staatswissenschaft*, 112:144-163 (1956), ascertained from an analysis of directories of "leading men in German business" that 19 percent of executives with academic titles had a training in law; this would be 6 percent of the total, although a good number may not have indicated their degrees. Warner and Abegglen included selected members of the board as well as top executives, while Hartmann excluded members of the supervisory *Aufsichtsrat*, in which lawyers are more frequently represented. Both these qualifications suggest that the proportion of lawyers among business leaders is somewhat higher in Germany. Wolfgang Kaupen found in a replication of Hartmann's study for both 1953 and 1963 that the proportion of business leaders—top executives as well as members of the *Aufsichtsrat*—who listed a law degree was 9.2 percent in 1953; by 1963 it had declined to 7.8 percent, a decline mainly accounted for by changed proportions among the executives, while the share of lawyers among the members of the *Aufsichtsrat* remained stable; recalculated from Kaupen, *Die Hüter von Recht und Ordnung*, table 98, p. 211.

25. See Kaplan et al., "German Civil Procedure," pp. 1467-1470. "Legal aid is granted in perhaps twenty percent of all civil litigation (excluding dunning process) in the regular courts." P. 1469. Cohn points out a consequence of the rule that the loser pays all costs: "No German attorney can ever tell his client that a law suit would be unprofitable even in case of success." "German Attorney, II," p. 114. On p. 120, he remarks that the German population is specially litigious.

26. For instance, keeping of the land registry is in the jurisdiction of the lowest courts, the *Amtsgerichte*. The strict German system of land registration accounts for major differences in the field of real estate law. Title examination and title insurance that the American system makes necessary have, however, been taken over to a large extent by title guaranty companies. See Hurst, *American Law*, p. 319; and Quintin Johnstone, "Title Insurance," *Yale Law Journal*, 66:492-524 (February 1957).

27. In the following material I rely mostly on the excellent account of Kaplan et al., "German Civil Procedure." Cohn, "German Attorney, II," p. 120f., goes so far as to suggest that the German judiciary does the work of the English bench and bar combined, equating the work of the German *Anwalt* approximately with that of the English solicitor.

28. Kaplan et al., "German Civil Procedure," p. 1224f. The section of the code of civil procedure stating the duty of clarification (ZPO, 139) has been called by one commentator the "Magna Charta of German civil procedure." Neglect of section 139 is "a usual claimed error" in appeals for revision at the highest regular court, and the Bundesgerichtshof "seems rather strongly to enforce section 139" p. 1229.

29. Kaplan et al., "German Civil Procedure," pp. 1222, 1225, and 1235, respectively. It should be noted that in many cases oral argument is perfunctory only and preparatory writings and documents are decisive.

30. Kaplan et al., "German Civil Procedure," p. 1452.

31. Letter of the *Deutscher Anwaltverein* (German Bar Association) to the author. A partner of one large firm with many and important foreign clients estimated in an interview that "more than fifty percent" of the firm's business is other than litigation. Exclusive counseling is extremely rare. "The backbone of their practice is for most lawyers litigation work in civil cases," Arthur Müller, "Sozietäten von Rechtsanwälten ein Vorbild für Arzte?", *Arztliche Mitteilungen*, April 21, 1962, p. 866.

32. Committee on Legal Education of the Harvard Law School, *"Preliminary Statement"* (MS), Harvard Law School, 1947, p. 15. See also Hurst, *American Law,* pp. 295-305.

33. On New York see Jerome E. Carlin, *Lawyers' Ethics. A Survey of the New York City Bar* (New York, Russell Sage Foundation, 1966), pp. 16, 26, and 190. For one large firm in Milwaukee Emily P. Dodge gave the following percentages for 1950, which of course would be misleading if generalized:

| | |
|---|---|
| Litigation | 8.1 |
| Counseling | |
| advice | 47.1 |
| drafting | 11.1 |
| appraising advice or | |
| papers from others | 1.5 |
| Negotiation | 31.6 |
| Involvement in clients' | |
| organization | 0.6 |

"Evolution of a City Law Office, Part II. Office Flow of Business," *Wisconsin Law Review,* January 1956, p. 48. Erwin O. Smigel considers the basic pattern as not untypical of large firms with more than fifty lawyers in New York; see his *The Wallstreet Lawyer* (New York, Free Press, 1964), p. 165.

34. Hurst, *American Law,* p. 300f., sketches the business of two leading law firms in "a moderate-sized Illinois city" in 1874, around 1900, and in 1934 showing, among other things a decline in court work. One can also infer a rather moderate proportion of litigation in the practice of firms in small and medium-sized cities from the following rank order of fields of practice in 101 counties of Illinois, excluding Cook county: estates and wills, land titles and sales, mortgages, personal injuries, collections, commercial practice, and criminal law. *Opportunities for Young Lawyers of Illinois,* Rochester, N.Y., Lawyers Cooperative Publishing Co., 1940; related in Erwin O. Smigel, *Wall Street Lawyer,* p. 168, n. 4. See also the description by Joel F. Handler, *The Lawyer and His Community. The Practicing Bar in a Middle-Sized City* (Madison, Wis., University of Wisconsin Press, 1967), p. 16f.

35. Fritz Ostler, *Der deutsche Rechtsanwalt. Das Werden des Standes seit der Reichsgründung* (Karlsruhe, C. F. Müller, 1963), p. 45f., speaks of the danger that "nearly all economically interesting matters, particularly in legal consulting (contracts!), will be handled by the tax consulting professions" and that "the genuine type of attorney of the past completely disappears"—the "genuine type," presumably in contrast to the syndic-attorney on the one hand and the *Rechtsanwalt* without any business work on the other.

36. This judgment is based on evidence that is not directly comparable. Roughly a third of a sample of 240 German attorneys, lawyers fully in private practice as well as syndic-attorneys, spent in 1965 most of their time in business-related fields of legal work—including labor law and tax matters as well as the fields more obviously to be classified as business and commercial law; "Ergebnisse der Befragung deutscher Juristen 1965," (MS), Forschungsinstitut für Soziologie of Cologne University, a collection of data gathered by Wolfgang Kaupen, p. 3. About 40 percent of a random sample of *Rechtsanwälte* answered the mail questionnaire (Kaupen, "Zur Soziologie der deutschen Juristen," p. 22). Similar conditions were found by Wolfgang Kaupen in a city with 100,000 to 200,000 inhabitants in Southwestern Germany: 35 percent of the attorneys spent more than 30 percent of their time in such work (according to preliminary data made available to the author). For the United States I do not know of any national data. In Carlin's New York City sample nearly half of all lawyers received most of their income from work in similar fields (*Lawyers' Ethics,* p. 12). Of the 67 individual practitioners Carlin studied in Chicago about 40 percent spent a third of their time or more in business-related fields—including individual income tax and collections, but not including real estate work, which is to a large extent business work. See Jerome E. Carlin, *Lawyers on Their Own. A Study of Individual Practitioners in Chicago* (New Brunswick, Rutgers University Press, 1962), p. 118, note 5. In the Midwestern city bar studied by Handler, 57 percent of the lawyers derived most of their income from work on business matters, *The Lawyer,* p. 14.

37. One lawyer informant compared Cologne and Dusseldorf, two neighboring cities in the range of 500,000 to 1,000,000 inhabitants, relating the relatively good situation of the bar in the former city to the predominance of middle-sized business firms and the economic problems of the bar in the latter to the large number of big corporations. That the small law firm with a business practice has declined in number because of an increase in the use of house counsel was the observation of other informants. That in the nonmetropolitan city in Southwestern Germany referred to above the number of attorneys specializing in business law approached the same proportion as in the national sample, although syndic-attorneys were relatively few in number there, can be interpreted in the same sense.

38. In the Southwestern German city about half of the lawyers found business and tax law the "most interesting fields." Of those attorneys in the national sample who spent most of their time in a business-related specialty 69 percent had an income of more than DM 3,000 per month, while the figure for all lawyers was 46 percent, "Ergebnisse der Befragung deutscher Juristen 1965," p. 3.

39. On the rising proportion of house counsel in the American bar see note 16 above. For descriptions of the work done by large law firms see Smigel, *Wall Street Lawyer*, chap. vi, and such historical accounts as Robert T. Swaine, *The Cravath Firm and Its Predecessors*, 3 vols. (New York, Ad Press, 1946-1948); Dodge, "City Law Office," or Arthur H. Dean, *William Nelson Cromwell 1854-1948* (New York, Ad Press, 1957). For a detailed description of business work at the lower level of the metropolitan bar see Carlin, *Lawyers on Their Own*, chap. ii.

40. Committee on Legal Education of the Harvard Law School, *Preliminary Statement*, p. 107, and Carlin, *Lawyers' Ethics*, p. 8. Carlin found similar conditions in his study of individual practitioners in Chicago; see his *Lawyers on Their Own*, p. 114f. It appears, from a table dealing with related matters, that in "Prairie City" more than half of the lawyers were officers or members of the board of client corporations; Handler, *The Lawyer*, p. 190.

41. In Southern Germany an attorney is not allowed to join the executive board of a corporation, although a nonprofessional employee may substitute for him. In the Rhineland and Northern Germany executive work is not frowned upon but appears limited to middle-sized firms. No such limitation exists for the supervisory board of corporations. Cohn estimates that "the number of German public companies whose board includes an attorney in actual practice is in excess of 30 percent" ("German Attorney, I,'', p. 592, for the whole argument see pp. 591-596). However, since the number of *Aktiengesellschaften* is rather small—2,560 in 1962—this estimate would concern only 800 to 900 attorneys out of a total of 13,000 (Statistisches Bundesamt [federal office of statistics] *Statistisches Jahrbuch für die Bundesrepublik Deutschland 1963*, p. 208).

42. Cohn, "German Attorney, I,'', p. 591.

43. "Every purchase or transfer of land or mortgages, every general meeting of a company, every sale or a participation in private limited company—to mention only a few examples—requires notarial collaboration." Cohn, "German Attorney, I,'', p. 581.

44. See Statistisches Bundesamt, *Jahrbuch*, 1969, p. 100.

45. Blaustein and Porter, *American Lawyer*, pp. 210 and 235. Richard Hammer reports of Alabama, Louisiana, and Mississippi that this right of outside counsel to appear in local courts has been severely curtailed by determined efforts of judges and bar associations. The reason for and the importance of this development appears in the following statement: "In the Deep South, it has always been, and still is, extremely difficult, if not impossible, for defendants in civil rights cases to find local counsel . . . Even when a Southern lawyer does take a civil rights case, his advocacy almost invariably is less than adequate." See his "Yankee Lawyer Go Home," *New York Times*, March 12, 1967, p. 8E.

46. See Cohn, "German Attorney, I,'', p. 582, n. 6. For the whole pattern of admission see pp. 581-584. It should be noted that the local courts, the *Amtsgerichte*, have jurisdiction over a wide variety of matters not involving litigation that provide grist for the mill for many practices. This softens considerably the constraints imposed by admission to one *Landgericht* or one *Oberlandesgericht* only. Furthermore, lawyers admitted to different courts may associate in one firm thus circumventing the second rationale mentioned.

47. In 1967, 26.5 percent of all German *Anwälte* were partners of firms; see "An-

waltssozietäten," *Anwaltsblatt,* 18:109 (1968). This figure is not directly comparable with that of 37 percent for the proportion of partners among all lawyers in private practice in 1966 (see U.S. Bureau of the Census, *Statistical Abstract of the United States: 1968,* p. 154), because the German total does not include associates, legally trained employees of law firms, unless they are admitted to court as *Rechtsanwälte.* On the other hand, the German percent base does include a large proportion—between a quarter and a third—of syndic-attorneys, most of whom are formally solo practitioners. Matters are complicated by the fact that we do not have comparable time series of data on partnerships and firm size. We do know that the proportion of individual practitioners has steadily declined in the Unites States (from 68 percent of all lawyers in private practice in 1951 to 53 percent in 1966; see *Statistical Abstract of the United States: 1968,* p. 154), and Table 2 shows that there has been a parallel increase in firm size. In Germany, the average size of partnerships remained, with 2.3 partners per firm, stable from 1959 to 1967, while there may have been a moderate decline in the proportion of individual practitioners; this is based on recalculations from the *Kostenstrukturstatistik* (cost and operations analysis) of the federal office of statistics for 1959 and 1963; see "Die Anwaltspraxis in der Statistik," *Anwaltsblatt,* 12:210-214 (1962), and "Die Anwaltschaft in der Statistik," ibid., 16:58-63 (1966); data for 1967 are found in "Anwaltssozietäten," ibid., 18:109 (1968).

48. For "Prairie City" see Handler, *The Lawyer,* p. 8. By checking one volume of the Martindale-Hubbell directory, Carlin found similar conditions in all cities of less than 200,000 population, *Lawyers on Their Own,* p. 39, n. 30. On the size of the largest American firms see "Why the Law Is a Growth Industry," *Business Week,* January 13, 1968, p. 78f; and Smigel, *Wall Street Lawyer,* pp. 32, 34, n. 9; on firms outside New York, see pp. 178-180. Firm size is ideally measured by number of all lawyers rather than of partners alone. On the former, I have for Germany only estimates of my informants and indirect statistical evidence. The question is whether the larger German firms compensate for a smaller number of partners by employing lawyers. Recalculations from the *Kostenstrukturstatistik (Anwaltsblatt,* 16:58-63 [1966], and 12:210-214 [1962]), compared to data on the largest American firms as well as on a random sample of Manhattan firms reported by Smigel, *Wall Street Lawyer,* pp. 183, 190, and 203, n. 13, suggest that, to the contrary, German associates are somewhat more evenly distributed among firms of different size than their American counterparts. A few German firms, typically built around the success of the principal(s) in one field, had in the recent past a very high ratio of associates to partners; for a polemic of a partner of a more balanced large firm against these "factories" see Walter Oppenhoff, "Anwaltsgemeinschaften, ihr Sinn und Zweck," *Anwaltsblatt,* 17:270 (1967). One German firm was mentioned by informants as having had at one time about one hundred lawyers. However, this firm specialized in matters of restitution to victims of the Nazi regime, a field in which referral from foreign lawyers and other factors are likely to have resulted in a concentration of matters in a few hands; if the transitory character of this law business is taken into account, the statement in the text holds true as far as stable firm size is concerned.

49. Cohn asserts: "Even in large practices there is not a very great deal of specialization." He argues that Continental codified law "leaves more room for the all-around man"; "German Attorney, I,'', p. 598. For a contrary opinion on this see Karl N. Llewellyn, "The Bar's Troubles and Poultices—and Cures?", *Law and Contemporary Problems,* 5:104 and 118 (1938). According to my informants Cohn exaggerates in saying that "partnerships are hardly ever formed with a view to offering clients a more all-round service" (p. 585), but he points correctly to parallel specialization of partners in the same field as the prevailing pattern of association of specialists. Significantly, Müller, "Sozietäten von Rechtsanwälten," pp. 865-868, fails to include complementary specialization in his discussion of the advantages of partnership and even argues that such specialization would work against association because it is an obstacle to substituting for each other during sickness and vacations and to other traditional advantages of partnership. On the division of labor in the largest and most specialized firms in the United States see Smigel, *Wall Street Lawyer,* chap. vi.

50. Partnership agreements include not infrequently provisions for the widow and children of the senior partner; see Arthur Müller, "Sozietäten von Rechtsanwälten," p. 866. The great concern with retirement problems is evident from other sources, too. In 1958-1959 the bar

associations prepared proposals for the establishment of a compulsory pension plan for the profession and held a referendum in which nearly 60 percent of all attorneys participated; nearly three-quarters voted favorably. Bundesminister für Wirtschaft, (federal minister of economic affairs) *Bericht über die Lage der Mittelschichten,* Deutscher Bundestag, 3. Wahlperiode, Drucksache 2012, 1960, p. 154. .

51. Twenty percent of the firms listed in the *Anwalt- und Notarverzeichnis 1963* (Munich, F. Fackler, 1963), for cities with a population of more than 500,000 had partners with identical names.

52. Hurst, *American Law,* p. 306; see p. 306f. for later developments.

53. This is the opinion of Johnstone and Hopson, *Lawyers,* p. 240f. "The nature of big-firm clients and practice is changing too, as a result of law department encroachment. There are more small corporations among their clients, usually those without law departments, and greater emphasis is being placed on such fields as litigation, antitrust and securities' regulation—specialities that law departments still refer to private firms." (Reprinted from *Lawyers and Their Work,* copyright 1967, by the Bobbs-Merrill Company, Inc. Reprinted by permission. All rights reserved.) These changes would go in the direction of the German pattern.

54. On the whole complex of specialization see Johnstone and Hopson, *Lawyers,* chap. iv.

55. See Johnstone and Hopson, *Lawyers,* p. 137f. The German admission pattern was discussed above.

56. The *Notariat* is not very frequently the main field of a lawyer's practice. See "Ergebnisse der Befragung deutscher Juristen 1965," p. 3, for details on this and other aspects of specialization in Germany that are, however, not directly comparable to American data and that do not permit a clear differentiation between true specialization and major emphases; see Table 5 below.

57. See Smigel, *Wall Street Lawyer,* pp. 192-195, on such "satellite firms."

58. The German bar has lost a good deal of this business to other professions, such as tax consultants, and to labor representatives. Kaplan et al., "German Civil Procedure," p. 1202, assert that a "specialized 'plaintiff's bar' in accident cases is growing up in Germany," although it is certainly less developed than in the United States. A good deal of such work brings lawyers into contact with insurance companies rather than regular courts. Specialization in immigration matters is a further example of specialization by agency in the United States, while tax law combines in various degrees the two bases of technical complexity and particular agency.

59. Arthur L. Wood found in a sample of 93 lawyers with more than 10 percent of their work in criminal law that less than one out of seven chose this work by preference; see his *Criminal Lawyer* (New Haven, Conn., College and University Press, 1967), p. 54. Carlin, *Lawyers' Ethics,* p. 76, reports that in New York lawyers working in the fields indicated in the text have high rates of violation of legal ethics. It should be noted that the violations involved were neither trivial nor few in number nor confined to advertising and solicitation. Classification as "violator" involved typically norms designed to protect the client or the integrity of the administration of justice. That in some communities illegal solicitation effectively protects these fields against competitors not engaging in such promotion is discussed by Johnstone and Hopson, *Lawyers,* pp. 122 and 125.

60. See Müller, "Sozietäten von Rechtsanwälten," p. 865. A frequent comment of my German informants about the practice of criminal law was: "It is different in character, but not inferior in standing." See also note 87 below.

61. In two Northwestern German cities with a population between 100,000 and 200,000, one of every six *Rechtsanwälte* had the additional title "Fachanwalt für Steuerrecht" (according to the *Anwalts- und Notarverzeichnis 1963).* My informants agreed that a good number of attorneys with the title were not really specialists in tax law, while some actual tax specialists did not care to adopt the title. It seems that one major intention of this exception to the rule that specialties cannot be announced in public is to fight the competition of accountants and tax consultants and to regain "lost territory."

62. Carlin, *Lawyers' Ethics,* p. 13. "New York City" refers here to Manhattan and the Bronx. To which degree specialization is associated with large firms can be seen from the

fact that 77 percent of lawyers in firms with fifteen or more partners and associates spend three-quarters or more of their time in a single area, while the corresponding figure for individual practitioners is 27 percent.

63. Wood, *Criminal Lawyer*; the cities were: New London, Conn. (population 31,000), the Borough of Brooklyn, New York (3,000,000), Jersey City, N.J. (300,000), Birmingham, Ala. (330,000), and Madison, Wis. (100,000); p. 28f. The data on specialization of civil lawyers are found on p. 42. Handler, *The Lawyer*, p. 15f., found less specialization in "Prairie City"; only five percent of the lawyers spent three-quarters or more of their time in one field.

64. Johnstone and Hopson, *Lawyers*, p. 37, n. 61. "For instance, the Real Property, Probate and Trust Law Section has a separate Real Property Division with, among others, committees on Condemnation Law, Leases, Mortgage Law and Practice, Public Regulation of Land Use, Tax Aspects of Real Estate Transactions, and Title Aspects of Real Estate Transactions." The fifteen sections are: Administrative Law; Corporation, Banking and Business Law; Criminal Law; Family Law; General Practice; Insurance, Negligence and Compensation Law; International and Comparative Law; Labor Relations Law; Local Government Law; Mineral and Natural Resources Law; Patent, Trademark and Copyright Law; Public Utility Law; Real Property, Probate and Trust Law; Taxation. Four sections deal with matters cutting across fields of specialization: Bar Activities; Judicial Administration; Junior Bar Conference; and Legal Education and Admissions to the Bar; see p. 37.

65. Johnstone and Hopson, *Lawyers*, pp. 43 and 136.

66. This becomes clear if the sections, committees, and subcommittees of the American Bar Association are compared to the following list of committees of the *Deutscher Anwaltverein*, listed in the *Anwaltsblatt* in the years 1963-1967 as active in one way or another. Constitutional Law; International Law; Commercial Law; Tax Law; Real Estate Matters; Tenant Landlord Matters; "Civil Law"; Traffic Matters; Administrative Law; Restitution Matters; Labor Law; Social Security Matters; Criminal Law; Criminal Law of the Armed Forces; Nuclear Energy Matters; Civil Procedure and Administration of Justice; Notariat; Statutory Regulation of Legal Practice; Statutory Regulation of Fees; Insurance for Legal Costs; Office Rationalization. A similar indirect—and similarly exaggerating—indication of patterns of specialization is found in the list of seminars organized by the *Deutscher Anwaltverein* in its program of continuing legal education: Construction Matters; Law of Cartels in the Federal Republic and the European Economic Community; Commercial Law in the European Economic Community; Legal Problems of the European Economic Community; Trademarks and Unfair Competition; Insurance Law; Traffic Law I and II; Family and Estate Matters; Administrative Law; Tax Law; Fees of the Notar; Fees of the Rechtsanwalt.

67. Johnstone and Hopson, *Lawyers*, pp. 145 and 146f. Some twenty to thirty further types of specialization in the area of real estate law were also mentioned. They were not included in the major list because they were named less frequently or because they were not peculiar to real property work.

68. Johnstone and Hopson, *Lawyers*, p. 146, report one vivid example: "Most of the lawyers interviewed showed very limited familiarity with specialized practices unrelated to their own, even if those other practices were centered on real property. For instance, an operator's lawyer was not likely to know much about the specialists in Title I or syndication, even their names. Nor would a zoning lawyer be likely to know much about specialists in tenant relocation. There are so many lawyers in a large city and the practice is so diverse that professional visibility is extremely limited. Except for lawyers in his own fields of expertise, those he has referred to, and those in his firm, the big city lawyer generally knows little about the lawyer specialists in his city, and even his knowledge of other fields of specialization is likely to be sketchy."

69. This was true from 1951 through 1966; see U.S. Bureau of the Census, *Statistical Abstract 1968*, p. 154. The proportion of German *Anwälte* in cities with a population of 500,000 or more, 43-45 percent, was calculated from the *Anwalts- und Notarverzeichnis 1963*. For the concentration of the population in cities of more than 500,000 inhabitants in 1963 see U.S. Bureau of the Census, *Statistical Abstract of the United States 1964*, p. 17, and Statistisches Bundesamt, *Jahrbuch 1963*, p. 36 ff.

70. In 1960, there were about 17,000 lawyers in private practice in Manhattan and the

Bronx alone, Carlin, *Lawyers' Ethics*, p. 11. For the German bar as a whole see Table 1. The figures for German local bars, which include syndic-attorneys, were derived from the *Anwalts- und Notarverzeichnis 1963*. For the American figures see American Bar Foundation, *The 1961 Lawyer Statistical Report* (Chicago, 1961), pp. 112-119.

71. See Carlin, *Lawyers' Ethics*; Smigel, *Wall Street Lawyer*; Carlin, *Lawyers on Their Own*; Dan C. Lortie, "Laymen to Lawmen: Law School, Careers, and Professional Socialization," *Harvard Educational Review*, 29:352-369 (1959); Jack Ladinsky, "Careers of Lawyers, Law Practice, and Legal Institutions," *American Sociological Review*, 28:47-54(1963); Wood's study of the *Criminal Lawyer* included practitioners from cities under 100,000 population as well as larger metropolitan areas.

72. In New York City, 21 percent of all lawyers in private practice worked in 1960 in large firms (15 or more lawyers), 15 percent in medium-sized firms (5 to 14 lawyers), 17 percent in small firms (2 to 4 lawyers), and 47 percent in individual practice. Carlin, *Lawyers' Ethics*, p. 18.

73. In Chicago, their "practice consists largely of a bookkeeping operation, seldom going beyond the filing of a standard form or a routine appearance before a court or agency." Carlin, *Lawyers on Their Own*, p. 42; see also pp. 42-122.

74. Carlin, *Lawyers' Ethics*, p. 25f.

75. On a national scale, partners in firms with nine or more principals earned nearly five times as much as individual practitioners; see Liebenberg, "Income of Lawyers," table 10.

76. Carlin, *Lawyers' Ethics*, chaps. iv and v. Firm size is "related to ethical behavior . . . primarily because [it affects] the process by which lawyers become exposed to situational pressures to violate norms." P. 130.

77. On contacts between lawyers and membership bar associations see Carlin, *Lawyers' Ethics*, pp. 34-36. A solo practitioner describes the situation in Chicago: "We (the Jewish lawyers) have the Decalogue; the Colored, the Cook County; the Slavs and the Poles have their associations. The reason for this is that there is something missing in the social life of the Chicago Bar Association. The whole setup is wrong, too many snobs in the higher echelons who don't mix." Carlin, *Lawyers on Their Own*, p. 177; see also pp. 175-182.

78. See Carlin, *Lawyers' Ethics*, pp. 32-34, on mobility within the bar and its relation to education and social background. That large firms tend to discriminate in terms of religion is no doubt a reflection of the discrimination prevalent in corporate business; on the latter see E. Digby Baltzell, *The Protestant Establishment: Aristocracy and Caste in America* (New York, Random House, 1964).

79. Smigel, *Wall Street Lawyer*, p. 173.

80. Carlin, *Lawyers on Their Own*, pp. 186f., 188f.

81. Smigel, *Wall Street Lawyer*, p. 173

82. Carlin, *Lawyers' Ethics*, p. 35.

83. Handler, *The Lawyer*, pp. 15f. and 58-64. On stratification in this bar see chap. iii.

84. Tax statistics use a special definition of income and are subject to various manners of "understatement" in the reporting of income. Recalculations from two later German surveys yield lower ratios between the ninth and first decile, 7.1 to 8.5 (1959) and 6 to 7.7 (1965). They were not used in Table 4 because of their dates and because the first required complicated recalculations and the second covered a relatively small sample. See the cost and operations analysis of the federal office of statistics in *Anwaltsblatt*, 12:210-214 (1962), and "Ergebnisse der Befragung deutscher Juristen 1965," p. 7.

85. For the two bars as a whole, income differences between partners and individual practitioners are actually quite similar. Precise and comparable data are not available. I estimate from crude recalculations of the data given by Liebenberg, "Income of Lawyers," and from the cost and operations analysis of German law firms referred to in the previous note that in both countries the median income of solo practitioners is less than half that of partners. Wolfgang Kaupen's survey of 1965 yielded this contrast in the incomes of partners and individual practitioners (personal communication):

| Income | Individual practitioners (percent) | Partners (percent) |
|---|---|---|
| Less than DM 36,000 annually | 63 | 34 |
| More than DM 36,000 annually | 37 | 66 |
| | 100 | 100 |
| | (183) | (77) |

Here one has to remember that a large proportion of individual practitioners are syndic-attorneys with a fairly stable but often relatively low income who are not considered full members of the bar in private practice. Their proportion is particularly high in cities with populations over 500,000, and yet it is a reasonable estimate from data provided by Kaupen that, with syndic-attorneys included, 40 percent of individual practitioners in large cities earn more than DM 36,000 annually compared to 85 percent of partners.

86. Cohn, "German Attorney, I,", p. 598.

87. In addition to the judgment of several informants, the above is supported by the answers lawyers in one local bar gave to the question which fields of practice they found "most interesting" and which "least interesting." The results are from the same survey in a southwestern German city with a population of about 150,000 and a highly dynamic economy, which was used already in other contexts (personal communication from Wolfgang Kaupen).

*Fields of Practice Judged Most and Least Interesting*

| Field of Practice | Percentage of attorneys expressing | | |
|---|---|---|---|
| | (1) highest interest | (2) least interest | (1) minus (2) |
| Business law including several specialities | 40 | 3 | 37 |
| General civil law including family and estate matters | 13 | 5.5 | 6.5 |
| Matrimonial matters | 9 | 6.5 | 2.5 |
| Criminal law | 12 | 11 | 1 |
| Tax law | 7.5 | 10 | − 2.5 |
| Traffic matters | 1 | 7.5 | − 6.5 |
| Public Administration | 4.5 | 11 | − 6.5 |
| Labor relations, social security | — | 11 | −11 |
| Tenant-landlord matters | — | 24 | −24 |
| Other fields | 1 | 3 | |
| All equal, none | 1 | 2 | |
| No answer | 10 | 5.5 | |
| | 99 | 100 | |
| | (92) | (92) | |

No doubt, other factors than professional prestige determine the judgment of a field as interesting, but a rough indication of the standing of the field can be gained from these data. What stands out are the fairly even evaluation of most types of practice and the high ranking of business law (the extent of the latter may well be a local phenomenon, according to the judgment of W. Kaupen).

88. This judgment is based on varied qualitative evidence and inferences from other research results. Informants who worked in both systems tended to corroborate it. Walter O. Weyrauch, an American law professor who previously has been an attorney in post-war Germany intensively interviewed about 100 German lawyers. He stated: "It was surprising to the visitor from the United States in talking for hours with successful lawyers, some of whom specialized in problems of business, to find apparent indifference to wealth . . . The phenomenon . . . became even more puzzling when contrasted with the economics of contemporary Germany." *The Personality of Lawyers* (New Haven, Conn., Yale University Press, 1964), p. 187. One officer of the organized bar asserted: "I am quite certain that lawyers here are not classified according to the net worth of their clientele. Many lawyers of low income are highly regarded" p. 139. Income and wealth are not likely to take first rank among the criteria for professional standing in the American bar either, especially if the question is which things *should* be more important. They do seem, however, to play a significantly more salient role in the evaluations of American lawyers.

89. Weyrauch, *Personality of Lawyers,* p. 145; cf. also pp. 140 and 143f.

90. That there is no general association for all lawyers is symptomatic for the fact, noted at the beginning of this chapter, that lawyers in Germany do constitute not one but several professional groups. Such a common association existed only during the Nazi regime, *Der Bund Nationalsozialistischer Deutscher Juristen.* It was used as an instrument of totalitarian control. That it was an inclusive association is partially explained—aside from the obvious advantages of control—by its history before the take-over. Founded in 1928, it remained relatively small until 1933. Like other political and religious associations of lawyers or other professionals it was not primarily concerned with occupational differentiations, which in addition create organizational difficulties for any group of limited appeal. In the *Deutscher Juristentag* the elite of the various branches of the profession have created a forum for the discussion of problems of legal development and reform.

91. See Werner Kalsbach, *Bundesrechtsanwaltsordnung und Richtlinien für die Ausübung des Rechtsanwaltsberufs. Kommentar* (Cologne, O. Schmidt, 1960), pp. 488-682.

92. Personal communication from Wolfgang Kaupen, based on the survey referred to before.

93. See Kalsbach, *BRAO*, p. 489f. For the actual size see *Anwaltsblatt,* 10:70 (1960).

94. More detailed information on bar associations in America is found in the following books: Glenn R. Winters, *Bar Association Organization and Activities,* (Chicago, American Judicature Society, 1954); Edson R. Sunderland, *History of the American Bar Association and Its Work* (Boston, Lord Baltimore Press, 1953); Roscoe Pound, *The Lawyer from Antiquity to Modern Times* (St. Paul, Minn., West Publishing Co., 1953); M. L. Rutherford, *The Influence of the American Bar Association on Public Opinion and Legislation* (Philadelphia, 1937); Blaustein and Porter, *American Lawyer*; Corinne Lathrop Gilb, *Self Regulating Professions and the Public Welfare. A Case Study of the California State Bar,* unpub. Ph.D. diss., Radcliffe College, 1956; and C. L. Gilb, *Hidden Hierarchies. The Professions and Government,* (New York, Harper and Row, 1966).

95. For the quoted overall rate of membership see American Bar Foundation, *The Legal Profession in the United States* (Chicago, 1965), p. 14. Carlin, *Lawyers on Their Own,* p. 202, n. 2, and Wood, *Criminal Lawyer,* p. 129, report evidence on lower and more differentiated membership in larger cities.

96. Blaustein and Porter, *American Lawyer,* p. 340.

97. *Self Regulating Professions,* p. 32.

98. In a few jurisdictions "disbarment cases must be either filed and conducted by the attorney general of the state, or it is made his duty, after a case has been filed by someone else, to appear on behalf of the bar association or other complainant." Charles S. Pott, "Disbarment Procedure," *Texas Law Review,* vol. 24, 1946, quoted in Elliott E. Cheatham, *Cases and Materials on the Legal Profession,* 2d ed. (Brooklyn, Foundation Press, 1955), p. 84. Other materials on the subject of discipline are found on pp. 79-114. See also Henry S. Drinker, *Legal Ethics* (New York, Columbia University Press, 1953), chap. iii, and Blaustein and Porter, *American Lawyer,* pp. 252-263.

99. American Bar Foundation, *Legal Profession in the United States,* p. 18. "The public has had good cause for dissatisfaction with the profession's . . . laxity in many places—Bench

and Bar alike—in enforcing the Canons of Judicial or of Professional Ethics." Bernard G. Segal, "President's Page," *American Bar Association Journal,* 56:199 (March 1970).

## NOTES TO CHAPTER 3

1. On "reference group theory" see Robert K. Merton, *Social Theory and Social Structure* (Glencoe, Ill., Free Press, 1957, chaps. viii and ix, and Herbert H. Hyman and Eleanor Singer, eds., *Readings in Reference Group Theory and Research* (New York, Free Press, 1968). I focus here on so-called normative reference groups. The crucial problems of which groups are points of such reference and why they are so "chosen" are far from solved, but a number of hypotheses are available to guide our analysis which follow largely accepted principles of social psychology. Although a systematic and approximately complete codification is still lacking, I refrain from undertaking such a task here, because it would lead too far from the problems at hand.

2. German figures for professionals give the income earned from independent work of those who derived most of their income from nonsalaried practice. The equivalent American figures give the income of nonsalaried practitioners. While this difference raises some problems of comparability, a more important difference is that the German figures derive from income tax statistics while the American data were gathered by the U.S. Department of Commerce. This latter difference is likely to make the major contrast noted in the text even greater, since professionals have opportunities to reduce their income for tax purposes. Because of greater investment expenditures, physicians may have such possibilities to a greater extent than lawyers, but this is not likely to wipe out the contrast in the differences between lawyers' and physicians' incomes noted in the text. The figures for workers' incomes, finally differ in definition: the U.S. data are for production workers in manufacturing only, while the German figures are for all workers in industry, including mining and construction. Since miners' and construction workers' wages are characteristically higher, this difference, too, results in an understatement of the contrast noted in the text. The inclusion of mining and construction also compensates for the higher proportion of women among the workers in German manufacturing. Annual income figures for workers were calculated from statistics on weekly earnings.

3. For the United States, see National Opinion Research Center, "Jobs and Occupations: A Popular Evaluation," *Opinion News,* 9:3-13 (Sept. 1, 1947); Albert J. Reiss, Jr., *Occupations and Social Status* (New York, Free Press, 1961), p. 54f., and, for a comparison over time, Robert W. Hodge, Paul M. Siegel, and Peter M. Rossi, "Occupational Prestige in the United States 1925-1963," *American Journal of Sociology,* 7:286-302 (1964-1965). For Germany, there is evidence on the prestige standing of a *Regierungsrat,* the lowest position in the higher civil service which requires university training. It resembles that of American lawyers. See Karl Martin Bolte, *Sozialer Aufstieg und Abstieg* (Stuttgart, Enke, 1959), p. 42; and, for a local study, Gerhard Wurzbacher, *Das Dorf im Spannungsfeld industrieller Entwicklung* (Stuttgart, Enke, 1954), p. 33. For some evidence on professional status in general as a determinant of prestige standing, see Louis Kriesberg, "The Basis of Professional Prestige: The Case of the Dentist," *American Sociological Review,* 27:238-244 (1962), and also Bolte, *Aufstieg und Abstieg,* p. 92.

4. The concept of "ascription" in contrast to "achievement orientation" refers to a special emphasis—in interaction, role expectations, value orientations, and perception of others—on what an actor *is* rather than on what he *does* and how he has succeeded in the past. See Chap. 1, n. 8.

5. See Talcott Parsons, *The Social System* (Glencoe, Ill., Free Press, 1951), pp. 192 and 191-194. Parsons refers to pre-Nazi Germany. Ralf Dahrendorf has discussed the role of ascription in present-day German social structure in his *Society and Democracy in Germany* (Garden City, N.Y., Doubleday, 1967) pp. 105-132. See also Erwin K. Scheuch, "Continuity and Change in German Social Structure" (MS), University of Cologne, October 1965, p. 22 ff. On the basis of as yet unpublished survey findings, Scheuch points out that the *respect* a person gets from his immediate environment, in contrast to the prestige accorded to his position in wider society, is very much contingent on competence and accomplishment (*Tüchtigkeit*).

A man can be *tüchtig* or not in virtually any position with a given societal prestige. This emphasis on personalized respect and the self-respect derived from accomplishment may be seen as fulfilling two functions: (1) it motivates performance in a relatively ascriptive status system, and (2) it provides a compensating dimension of evaluation which makes ideals of equality more compatible with accentuated and ascriptive divisions in the hierarchy of societal prestige.

6. In 1962, 82 percent of the West German population had only eight years of elementary schooling, 13 percent graduated from "middle-school" (a total of ten years of schooling), and 5 percent graduated from high school (a total of twelve to thirteen years). Cf. Institut für Demoskopie, *Jahrbuch der öffentlichen Meinung, 1958-1964* (Allensbach, 1965), p. 4. It is estimated that less than half of these high school graduates went on to graduate from university studies. By contrast, in 1960, 37.6 percent of the American population over 25 had eight years of schooling or less, 19.2 percent had one to three years of high school, 25.8 percent graduated from high school, another 9.3 percent went to college for a period of one to three years, and another 7.7 percent had four or more years of higher education. Cf. U.S. Bureau of the Census, *Statistical Abstract of the United States: 1964* (Washington, D.C., 1964), p. 113.

7. Joseph A. Kahl, *The American Class Structure* (New York, Holt, Rinehart and Winston, 1957), p. 281. This judgment excludes the discrimination against the black population from consideration by limiting itself to "social-class differences."

8. "In Germany occupational association and friendship are specifically segregated." "In a sense the German system is more favorable to strict impartiality and less open to nepotism and other clique-like disturbances, but at the same time probably involves other elements of instability." Talcott Parsons, "Democracy and Social Structure in Pre-Nazi Germany," *Essays in Sociological Theory,* 2d ed. (Glencoe, Ill., Free Press, 1954), pp. 112 and 113, n. 3. Erwin K. Scheuch stresses in a different context similar patterns in his discussion of empirical findings about value orientations and communication patterns among members of the German elite, "German Social Structure," pp. 42ff. Kurt Lewin's comparative observations about America fit with Parsons' about Germany; in "Some Social-Psychological Differences between the United States and Germany," *Resolving Social Conflicts* (New York, Harper, 1948), pp. 3-33, he distinguished "central" and "peripheral" regions of a person's life and argued that in American society the central regions are more narrowly defined than in Germany, leaving a wider range of concerns open to influence from others. He concluded that in the United States "there are less differences . . . between sub-groups . . . the behavior of the same sub-group or the same individual will be less constant in different situations than in Germany and social life will therefore be more 'fluid' in the United States;" p. 32. Finally, David C. McClelland concludes from a variety of evidence that establishing and maintaining friendly interpersonal relations ranks lower in German than in American culture, and he suggests that this is related to an emphasis on living up. to an "idealistic" code of social obligations; see his *The Roots of Consciousness* (Princeton, N.J., Van Nostrand, 1964), chap. iv.

9. See for the United States: C. Wright Mills, *The Power Elite* (New York, Oxford University Press, 1956); Talcott Parsons, "The Distribution of Power in American Society," *World Politics,* 10:123-143 (October, 1957); Floyd Hunter, *Top Leadership, USA* (Chapel Hill, N.C., North Carolina University Press, 1959); Suzanne Keller, *Beyond the Ruling Class: Strategic Elites in Modern Society* (New York, Random House, 1963); Arnold M. Rose, *The Power Structure: Political Process in American Society* (New York, Oxford University Press, 1967); and G. William Domhoff, *Who Rules America?* (Englewood Cliffs, N.J., Prentice-Hall, 1967). See for Germany: Wolfgang Zapf, *Wandlungen der deutschen Elite: Ein Zirkulationsmodell deutscher Führungsgruppen, 1919-1961* (Munich, Piper, 1965); Wolfgang Zapf, ed., *Beiträge zur Analyse der deutschen Oberschicht* (Munich, Piper, 1965); Dahrendorf, *Society and Democracy*, chaps. 14-18; Scheuch, "German Social Structure." A much more extensive literature deals with power on the community level.

10. It is clear that this assertion would have to be modified considerably to fit modern dictatorial or totalitarian systems. Without going into any detail, it is suggested, however, that pragmatic predictability will be a concern here, too; that interference tends to be camouflaged because of the moral implications it has; that open curtailment of professional judicial

autonomy will be elaborately justified by populistic appeals to widespread value orientations and dissatisfactions with the professional court system, and that interference contravening popular attitudes will be selectively used as an instrument of terror.

11. It is significant that popular election of state and local judges became general in the decades after 1830, in a period of the greatest distrust for professionalism. "Jacksonian Democracy inaugurated in the 1830's a resistless demand for the popular election of public officials, great and small." J. Willard Hurst, *The Growth of American Law* (Boston, Little Brown, 1950), p. 97, and chaps. i, v, and vii. Hurst considers it "one of the paradoxes of our legal growth that this most basic assertion of the people's control of the courts came at the threshold of the greatest period of judicial power in our history" (p. 87), but the paradox resolves itself when the underlying attitudes are considered together with the fact that rapid social, political, and economic change, characteristic of the period, opens greater opportunities for judicial decision-making.

In line with much of past argument, the above does not distinguish between elite justifications and popular attitudes and implicitly focuses on the former. For a very interesting analysis of both in interrelation, see Jack Ladinsky and Allan Silver, "Popular Democracy and Judicial Independence: Electorate and Elite Reactions to Two Wisconsin Supreme Court Elections," *Wisconsin Law Review* (Winter 1967), pp. 128-169. Acquiescence and ignorance as well as respect for a high government office and men of distinguished achievement seem to be the most important foundations of judicial independence in popular attitudes.

12. A symptomatic institutional difference is that dissenting opinions in German courts are not published. The different practice of the Federal constitutional court is a recent innovation. For comments of German lawyers see Walter O. Weyrauch, *The Personality of Lawyers* (New Haven, Conn., Yale University Press, 1964), pp. 219-221. Weyrauch also reports qualitative evidence about other attitudes of German lawyers fitting the above description; see especially chaps. vi, x, and xii. For a more general discussion see Dahrendorf, *Society and Democracy*, chap. xiv.

13. See Xaver Berra (pseudonym for Theo Rasehorn), *Im Paragraphenturm: Eine Streitschrift zur Entideologisierung der Justiz* (Neuwied, Luchterhand, 1966), p. 36. Further documentation on the bureaucratic control which this polemic attacked was brought out in a constitutional complaint of five German judges; see *Der Spiegel*, Aug. 14, 1967, p. 44. "Political" appointments are of some significance, but—excepting the federal constitutional court—their importance is likely to be exaggerated precisely because they contravene major tenets of German legal culture. For a variety of comments of German lawyers see Weyrauch, *Personality of Lawyers*, pp. 135 and 227-230. The special courts for labor, social security, public administration, and fiscal matters have each more or less strong ties to the respective ministerial departments. On the recruitment of judges for the highest federal court in fiscal matters see Johannes Feest, "Die Bundesrichter," Zapf, ed., *Beiträge*, pp. 95-113.

14. Friedrich Karl Kübler, "Der deutsche Richter und das demokratische Gesetz: Versuch einer Deutung aus richterlichen Selbstzeugnissen," *Archiv für die civilistische Praxis*, 162:106 (1963). For the Nazi period, fear and opportunism responding to much more ruthless techniques of influence were also a major factor, particularly in the later years.

15. Heinz Eulau and John D. Sprague, *Lawyers in Politics: A Study in Professional Convergence* (Indianapolis, Bobbs-Merrill, 1964), p. 11, give a survey of such statistics (p. 11f.) as does Donald R. Matthews, *The Social Background of Political Decision Makers* (Garden City, N.Y., Doubleday, 1954). Mapheus Smith and Marian L. Brockway, "Mobility of American Congressmen," *Sociology and Social Research*, 24:511-525 (1939-1940), found similar percentages for all decades between 1800 and 1919. The averages for the whole period were 60 percent lawyers in the House of Representatives and 67.5 percent in the Senate.

16. See Zapf, ed., *Beiträge*, p. 18, and Zapf, *Deutsche Elite*, p. 178. These figures may, of course, be subject to substantial fluctuations, though similar percentages for 1925 suggest a long-run stability of sorts.

17. 22 percent of the members of the fourth Bundestag had studied law at a university; see Zapf, ed., *Beiträge*, p. 18; details are given by Wolf Mersch, "Volksvertreter in Ost und West," in the same volume, pp. 30-54, esp. p. 35f. If only fully qualified lawyers are counted the figure is reduced to 15 to 16 percent, estimated on the basis of information from

*Taschenbuch des öffentlichen Lebens 1962,* vol. 12 (Bonn, 1962) and consistent with Mersch's information on types of academic and professional degrees. A similar figure is given for the previous Bundestag by Adolf Arndt, "Der Jurist im Parlament," *Juristenjahrbuch,* 1:82 (1960), who also provides the data for state legislators in 1960; here percentages varied from 4 to 22.5. See also Gerhard Loewenberg, *Parliament in the German Political System* (Ithaca, N.Y., Cornell University Press, 1966), pp. 103-128; this is the best study of the Bundestag.

18. Jerome E. Carlin reports of Chicago: "Close to half of the respondents strongly emphasized the importance of political connections . . . and the necessity, especially for the young lawyer, for being active in politics." *Lawyers on Their Own* (New Brunswick, N.J., Rutgers University Press, 1962), p. 133. On findings in New York City, see Carlin, *Lawyers' Ethics* (New York, Russell Sage Foundation, 1966), chap. v. For comparable findings in a smaller city see Joel F. Handler, *The Lawyer and His Community* (Madison, Wis., University of Wisconsin Press, 1967), p. 53.

19. For a small-scale documentation of the view that lawyers are particularly suited for political office, see John Thomas Doby, "The Lawyer as a Political Leader," *Wisconsin Law Review,* 1950, pp. 308-315. In a small town in Kentucky, over 80 percent of clerical, business, and professional respondents preferred a lawyer over a nonlawyer for legislative office if equal in other respects. The percentage for working class respondents was nearly 60.

20. Joseph A. Schlesinger, "Lawyers and American Politics: A Clarified View," *Midwest Journal of Political Science,* 1:32 (May 1957). For U.S. Senators, members of the House of Representatives, and legislators in four states, see Madge M. McKinney, "The Personnel of the 77th Congress," *American Political Science Review,* 36, pp. 71, 72 (1942); Donald R. Matthews, *U.S. Senators and Their World* (Chapel Hill, N.C., University of North Carolina Press, 1960), p. 35; and Eulau and Sprague, *Lawyers in Politics,* p. 52. Eulau and Sprague advance an argument against the crucial importance of this factor which is not convincing. Referring to data which show that a larger proportion of nonlawyers than lawyers have held public offices outside of law enforcement before they entered the legislature, they conclude: "The advantage lawyers have that stems from their monopoly of legal offices is clearly offset by the advantage non-lawyers have in holding legislative and executive offices" (p. 52). This assertion is clearly at odds with logic. Obviously, "non-lawyers" constitute a much larger group outside of politics than lawyers. Therefore, if nonlawyers who did become state legislators have more often held public office other than law enforcement positions than lawyers, this does not at all show that they had an "advantage . . . in holding legislative and executive positions." On the contrary, the data show that lawyers had an "advantage" here, too, though not a monopoly as in the case of law enforcement positions.

21. For the share of the judiciary in the federal parliament see Arndt, "Jurist im Parlament," p. 82. Arndt gives as a major reason that judges have to retire from their posts if they assume legislative office. In the questionnaire survey of Wolfgang Kaupen, 14 percent of all lawyers in private practice and 10 percent of members of the *Justizdienst* were members of political parties. The higher proportion of Social Democrats among the latter (5 percent in contrast to 4 percent CDU members, while the respective figures for attorneys were 2 percent and 10 percent) may be interpreted as a reflection of political influences in judicial appointments, but the dominant affiliation of lawyers in private practice with upper middle-class and business interests has to be taken into account, too.

22. Appointment to the bench and the handling of the government's law business are subject to political patronage in Canada, too. However, appointment is for life, and it seems that informal restraints built into the process of appointment keep the aspirants from too intense involvement in party politics; "a fanatical loyalty may weaken their prospects of appointment to the bench," as Harold A. Innis put it; *Essays in Canadian Economic History* (Toronto, University of Toronto Press, 1956), p. 400.

23. Of course, more is involved than value orientations alone. W. L. Guttsman, "Changes in British Labour Leadership," in Dwaine Marvick, ed., *Political Decision-Makers.* International Yearbook of Political Behavior Research, vol. 2 (New York, Free Press of Glencoe, 1961), pp. 91-137, concludes that centralization in London and professionalism have become characteristic of Labour's leadership. Such developments may provide a partial explanation for the rise of the proportion of lawyers in Labour's parliamentary delegation which has

increased from zero in 1918 to 7 to 9 percent in the 1920's to 13 to 15 percent in the 1930's; (Guttsman, ibid., p. 101). In 1945 the percentage was 12 according to J. F. S. Ross, *Parliamentary Representation,* p. 271.

24. The labor parties in both countries have proportionately about half as many lawyer legislators as their "center-right" opposites, according to the sources used in Table 8 and note 17. The share of labor legislators in Germany is somewhat lower, reflecting the looser relation of the Social Democratic Party to the labor unions and the fact that lawyers in Germany include a smaller percentage involved in private practice. The policy character of the SPD is roughly equivalent to that of the British Labour Party. Tendencies to vote along class lines are of similar strength. While I know of no information directly comparable to Alford's, a comparison of stable party preferences shows a contrast between Germany and the United States similar to what Alford found between Great Britain and America; see Werner Zohlnhöfer, "Parteiidentifizierung in der Bundesrepublik und in den Vereinigten Staaten," E. K. Scheuch and R. Wildenmann, eds., *Zur Soziologie der Wahl,* special issue no. 9 of the *Kölner Zeitschrift für Soziologie und Sozialpsychologie* (Cologne and Opladen, 1965), p. 153. Finally, Lipset assesses the strength of elitist value orientations in contemporary Germany as similar to British patterns; Seymour M. Lipset, *The First New Nation,* (New York, Basic Books, 1963), p. 238f.

25. See Adolf Arndt, "Jurist im Parlament," p. 82, and Heinz Brangsch, "Rechtsanwälte in den Parlamenten des In- und Auslandes", *Anwaltsblatt,* 7:64-65, 1957.

26. See Brangsch, "Rechtsanwälte in den Parlamenten."

27. Walter I. Wardwell and Arthur L. Wood, "The Extra-Professional Role of the Lawyer," *American Journal of Sociology,* 61:304-307 (January 1956).

28. "Our data suggest that in smaller communities practically all lawyers are at some time active office holders or are otherwise active in politics and that even in large cities there are social pressures, although somewhat attenuated, encouraging lawyers to be active in politics." Wardwell and Wood, "The Extra-Professional Role," p. 305. Michael Cohen found a similar pattern in New York State; see his "Law and Public Office Holding: A Study Comparing Political and Non-Political Lawyers," unpub. Ph. D. diss., Cornell University, 1966. Another Ph.D. dissertation of Cornell University brings forth confirming detail for the bar in Elmira, N.Y.: Thomas James Matthews, "The Lawyer as a Community Leader: One Dimension of a Professional Role," 1952. Handler found a lower rate of political participation in a middle-sized community in the Midwest, which he tentatively relates to the city-manager form of local government; *The Lawyer,* pp. 20-22; 49-52; 151f. That participation in politics as well as in nonpolitical voluntary associations is still substantial in large metropolitan areas is also suggested by the findings of Carlin, *Lawyers on Their Own,* pp. 150 and 152. In his sample of 67 individual practitioners in Chicago two-thirds were members of voluntary associations and one-quarter were active in local politics.

29. Wardwell and Wood, "The Extra-Professional Role," p. 306. In one large Southern city 56 percent of the individual practitioners, 40 percent of the partners, and 28 percent of the associates were or had been active in politics. The respective percentages for participation in nonpolitical associations were 36, 48, and 23, ibid. For similar differences between criminal and civil lawyers in five cities see Arthur L. Wood, "Informal Relations in the Practice of Criminal Law," *American Journal of Sociology,* 62:52 (July 1956).

30. See Erwin O. Smigel, *The Wall Street Lawyer* (New York, Free Press, 1964), pp. 8-10, on the political and quasipolitical activities of members of very large law firms. "Few . . . are active in grass-roots politics." "The list of those who have been appointed to high public office is almost endless" (p. 9).

31. In Kaupen's sample, 14 percent of all *Rechtsanwälte* were members of a political party (see n. 21). Comparing this with estimates of the number of party members in the population at large (see Wolfgang Hartenstein and Klaus Liepelt, "Party Members and Party Voters in West Germany," *Acta Sociologica,* 6:44, 1962), I estimate that the percentage of political participants in the *Anwaltschaft* is not more than five times as high as that of the male population of voting age. If local party office, volunteer campaigning, and similar work are taken as comparable indicators of political participation in the United States, I estimate that the ratio of political participation of American lawyers is at least 10 to 15 times as high as that of

the average citizen: this is based on the studies of the bar quoted above and Robert E. Lane's estimates for the adult population in the United States in *Political Life: Why and How People Get Involved in Politics* (New York, Free Press, 1959), p. 56.

32. 38 percent of the *Anwälte* in the Southwestern German city with a population of 100-200,000 were members of one or more nonpolitical associations, and 21 percent were office holders in such associations (information of W. Kaupen). In the bar of the five cities studied by Wood and his associates about three-quarters of the civil lawyers had been officers in voluntary associations during their careers (Wood, "Informal Relation," p. 52). The high level of participation in voluntary associations among individual practitioners in Chicago was noted previously. In the smaller city of Elmira (population in 1950: 50,000), nearly all lawyers belonged to voluntary associations, 85 percent belonged to more than three associations, and more than half were office-holders at the time of the survey. See Thomas James Matthews, "The Lawyer as Community Leader," p. 60. For similar, if less detailed findings on associational memberships of the bar in a middle-sized city (population of the metropolitan area: 120,000) see Handler, *The Lawyer*, p. 48. Service organizations concerned with government, health, youth, and welfare are far more prominent among the associations in which American lawyers participate than among the associations to which the *Rechtsanwälte* in this German city belonged.

33. "Our government is permeated with politics . . . there is virtually no sphere of 'administration' apart from politics." Edward C. Banfield and James Q. Wilson, *City Politics* (Cambridge, Mass., Harvard University Press, 1963), p. 1. For an analysis of the German civil service along the lines indicated, see Karl W. Deutsch and Lewis J. Edinger, *Germany Rejoins the Powers* (Stanford, Cal., Stanford University Press, 1959), p. 81-83.

34. Deutsch and Edinger, *Germany*, p. 81.

35. On political influences in the appointment of government lawyers, see Peyton Ford, David Reich, and Clive W. Palmer, *The Government Lawyer* (Englewood Cliffs, N.J., Prentice-Hall, 1952), pp. 10 and 21. "Among the 10,851 civilian federal employees in this study 1,865, or about 18 percent, are political appointees. They hold one-half of all law degrees reported by civilian executives." W. Lloyd Warner et al., *The American Federal Executive* (New Haven, Conn., Yale University Press, 1963), p. 129. The Federal Bar Association, which comprises both federal employees and lawyers appearing before federal agencies, has been listed among the twenty most influential associations in America; see Floyd Hunter, *Top Leadership, U.S.A.*, pp. 13-15.

36. Karl Siegfried Bader, *Die deutschen Juristen* (Tübingen, J.C.B. Mohr, 1947), p. 19. The author continues, writing under the immediate impressions of the Nazi time: "Their opportunities to support by their action, as members of the legal profession, the *Rechtsstaat* and to stand up in political life for the idea of law were in principle greater than those of their colleagues in the judiciary. Of this chance of 'closeness to the government' the administrative lawyers did not make use . . ."

37. See Suzanne Keller, "The Social Origins and Career Lines of Three Generations of American Business Leaders," unpub. Ph.D. diss., Columbia University, 1953 (the data refer to 1950), reported in Keller, *Beyond the Ruling Class*, p. 294. Information on chief executives of the fifty largest German corporations in 1964 is reported in Wolfgang Zapf, "Die deutschen Manager," Zapf, ed., *Beiträge*, pp. 136-149, esp. p. 139. Wolfgang Kaupen also found evidence that the proportion of lawyers increases with the importance of the positions examined. Among business leaders who are members of executive boards in one firm *and* members of supervisory boards in others, the proportion of law-trained people was 12.0 percent in 1963 and 15.8 percent in 1953. *Hüter* . . . , p. 211. On the proportion of lawyers in a more broadly defined business elite see Chap. 2, n. 24 above.

38. Heinz Hartmann, *Authority and Organization in German Management* (Princeton, N.J., Princeton University Press, 1959), p. 163, argues convincingly that lawyers have been most prominent among German business leaders when "National Socialism was replacing Weimar's relatively liberal economy with a tight net of economic rules and regulations and legal counsel was needed to keep the firm running and to press for some elbow room". Mabel Newcomer, *The Big Business Executive* (New York, Columbia University Press, 1955), pp. 90 and 92, presents data on the share of lawyers among executives in different industries in 1900, 1925,

and 1950. The most conspicuous development is the decline of lawyers in the top management of railroad corporations since the turn of the century when their legal and political know-how was at a premium in the context of vast land acquisition, complex and highly speculative financing, graft, and the merger of companies; see on these conditions Thomas C. Cochran and William Miller, *The Age of Enterprise* (New York, MacMillan, 1942, and Harper, 1961), chaps. vii and ix.

39. All German studies referred to use professional degrees as an indicator of profession, while the American studies use professional experience.

40. Wolfgang Zapf analyzed the career patterns of those of 221 top executives in the 50 largest corporations for whom the appropriate information was available (41 percent) and found that 4 percent made their way to the top as independent professionals, "Die deutschen Manager," p. 144. Mabel Newcomer reports that in 1950, 10 to 12 percent of the presidents and board chairmen studied had been in independent professional practice before, *The Big Business Executive,* p. 93. Although it is possible that the difference is solely due to the inclusion of supervisory officers, the facts that many large American corporations rely on outside legal counsel and that the top legal advisors have special chances for reaching presidential or vice-presidential positions make this interpretation unlikely.

41. Ten percent of all executive officers studied by Wolfgang Zapf had been high administrative civil servants and another 6 percent had been politicians, "Die deutschen Manager," p. 144.

42. For a short analysis of German business associations and their development, see Hartmann, *German Management,* chap. vii. Gabriel Almond states: "If one compares the BDI (Federation of German Industry) with the NAM, it is quite apparent that the German organization is far more inclusive and centralized." "The Politics of German Business," research memorandum of the Rand Corporation, Santa Monica, Cal., 1955, p. 39f., quoted in Hartmann, *German Management,* p. 223f. Gilbert Burck asserts—probably with some exaggeration—that the BDI is ten times as influential as the NAM: "The German Business Mind," *Fortune,* 49:114 (May 1954). See also Deutsch and Edinger, *Germany,* p. 89: "German interest groups are more inclusive, more tightly organized, and occupy a more privileged position in public life than do their American counterparts." It seems important to keep the question of the strength of business associations distinct from the question of the influence of big business in political life. For the latter question the existence of a large social democratic party in Germany is a decisive factor, even if the SPD has not reached a majority or plurality of the seats in parliament. By contrast, both major parties in the United States are open to business influence, if differentially so.

43. In one sample of 100 American lobbyists, three-quarters had been trained as lawyers; see Lester Mulbrath, "Lobbyists and Campaign Politics," paper read at the 53rd Annual Meeting of the American Political Science Association, 1957, quoted in Samuel J. Eldersveld, "American Interest Groups: A Survey of Research and Some Implications for Theory and Method," in Henry W. Ehrmann, ed., *Interest Groups on Four Continents* (Pittsburgh, Pittsburgh University Press, 1958), p. 193, n. 51.

44. In view of the complexity of the subject matter, I can do no more than state this opinion without discussing objections that have been raised against it. See the literature quoted above, n. 9.

45. Dahrendorf, *Society and Democracy,* chap. xvii; for the quotes see pp. 269 and 270.

46. For an analysis of "McCarthyism" in these terms see Talcott Parsons, "Social Strains in America," *Structure and Process in Modern Societies* (Glencoe, Ill., Free Press, 1960), chap. vii; see also chap. vi, "The Distribution of Power in American Society." Dissatisfaction with the rise of big business and with the loss of "true" authority was one factor contributing to the rise of National Socialism in Germany and is also discernible in the recent development of a nationalist and conservative radical right. The coexistence, within the German business community, of rather extravagant claims to societal leadership and widespread abstention from political life can be interpreted along similar lines; see Hartmann, *German Management,* pp. 30-33, 228-234, for some documentation.

47. In the Bundestag of 1961 to 1965 they accounted for 25 to 33 percent of all lawyers, depending on whether all members with a legal education or only those qualified by a second

state examination are counted as lawyers. In 1962, civil servants of all ranks accounted for 23 percent of members in the federal parliament, and their share varied from 17 percent to 51 percent in the state legislatures; *Der Spiegel,* 1962, no. 35, p. 24.

48. An example may illustrate this. In the *Anwaltsblatt* of 1955 there was an extended debate when in an article on the professional code the phrase, "the judge stands above the attorney," was used; see Werner Kalsbach, *Standesrecht des Rechtsanwalts* (Cologne, O. Schmidt, 1956), pp. 148-151.

49. This hypothesis is analogous to the "breakage effect" found in voting studies. The political orientation dominant in the community often tips the balance where the immediate environment subjects a person to cross-pressures. This was the interpretation of empirical findings by Bernard R. Berelson, Paul F. Lazarsfeld, and William N. McPhee, *Voting: A Study of Opinion Formation in a Presidential Campaign* (Chicago, University of Chicago Press, 1954), p. 100.

50. Justice Henry B. Brown of the U.S. Supreme Court said in a speech to the American Bar Association in 1893, when business dominance over American society was perhaps strongest: "It is the desire to earn money which lies at the bottom of the greatest efforts of genius. The man who writes books, paints pictures, moulds statues, builds houses, pleads causes, preaches sermons or heals the sick, does it for the money there is in it . . . the motive which prompted Angelo to paint . . . the frescoes of the Sistine Chapel was essentially the same as that which induces a common laborer to lay bricks or dig sewers." Quoted by Benjamin Twiss, *Lawyers and the Constitution* (Princeton, N.J., Princeton University Press, 1942), p. 163f. With such ideas, a man would have made himself an outcast even in most German business circles. René König says of the image of culture and society which derives from pre-industrial German idealism and which dominated, and in part still dominates, the cultured bourgeoisie in Germany: "everything that is related to applied science and the economy is not only pushed to the margin of this image of the world, but is completely severed from the idea man has of himself." "Der Ingenieur und seine Stellung in der Gesellschaft," *VDI-Nachrichten,* Nov. 23, 1960, p. 2.

51. The quote, referring to Laski and others, is from Robin M. Williams, *American Society, A Sociological Interpretation,* 2d ed. (New York, Knopf, 1960), p. 418. A study of responses of German and American high school boys preparing for college, one of the few empirical studies comparing value orientations in the two countries, comes to conclusions consonant with this interpretation: "in Germany . . . conscientious striving is included in a network of idealistic sentiments relating to decent social behavior. In the United States, rational striving is part of no such framework." "In the United States a high spontaneous interest in achievement is counterbalanced by much experience in group activities in which the individual learns to channel his achievement needs according to the opinions of others. In Germany a strong sense of self as a striving, controlling entity is offset by an equally strong sense of obligation to a *code* of decency. Interestingly enough, the American 'value formula' appears to be largely unconscious or informally understood . . . For the Germans, on the other hand, the whole matter seems to be much more consciously worked out." David G. McClelland, J. F. Sturr, R. H. Knapp, and H. W. Wendt, "Obligations to Self and Society in the United States and Germany," *Journal of Abnormal and Social Psychology,* 56:249 and 252 (1958); see also the extended interpretation by McClelland, *Roots of Consciousness,* chap. iv.

52. See, for example, Parsons, "Power in American Society," p. 213, who uses the phrase quoted in a sketch of the historical developments referred to; and Dahrendorf, *Society and Democracy,* pp. 261, 242, and 244, for some of the observations mentioned. Scheuch reached from several survey studies the conclusion that "the single most resented group are businessmen, and the most resented activity is accumulating money by selling." *German Social Structure,* p. 39a, n. 140.

53. Scheuch refers to unpublished survey results showing a high incidence of such views both in the population at large and in the elite; *German Social Structure,* pp. 74ff., 95ff. At the lower levels of the organizational structure this emphasis has, of course, the reverse effect—as the proverb has it: "Cobbler stick to your last." The latest treatment of the often noted aversion against open conflict in German culture is Dahrendorf's *Society and Democracy,* especially "Conflict or the Nostalgia for Synthesis," pp. 135-213. Conjectures on the related

faith in objective solutions for social and political problems were confirmed by survey research: "we found amongst the elite a majority for the belief that there are always 'true' solutions, provided one is only qualified to find them." Scheuch, *German Social Structure*, p. 98.

54. The stereotype is strikingly expressed in the joke attributed to Stalin that the Germans will never have a revolution because they are not allowed to walk on public lawns. Wolfgang Kaupen and Raymund Werle, "Public Opinion about Law and Legal Reforms," paper presented to the Research Committee on Sociology of Law, Seventh World Congress of Sociology, Varna, 1970, p. 4, report that two-thirds of a sample of the German population agreed that one should obey the laws even if one does not think that they are just; this contrasts with less than half of the respondents in Polish and Dutch surveys.

55. Hurst, *American Law*, p. 249f.

56. Max Rheinstein, Review of F. von Hippel, "Rechtstheorie und Rechtsdogmatik," *American Journal of Comparative Law*, 13:324 (Spring 1964). Rheinstein phrases his statement cautiously as a "suspicion" rather than as a definitive assertion. See also his comparison of von Hippel's and the prevalent German view of procedure with the American one, p. 325.

57. Weyrauch, *Personality of Lawyers*, p. 249f. Weyrauch reports opinions of German lawyers about American law and jurisprudence which show awareness of the differences discussed here, often expressed in critical terms: "many subjects felt [American law] to be different from the way law ought to be." (p. 169) In a discussion of legal scholarship and education in America, a German judge ponders: "I wonder whether it is wise to put so much emphasis on problems instead of results. I feel that the underlying skepticism may lead to pessimistic outlooks on the part of the American people. Doubts will invade every sphere of life" (p. 77). And an old member of the German legal elite relates this encounter with Chief Justice Charles Evans Hughes: "Hughes asked, 'What are you doing in the United States?' I answered, 'I am studying the American system of law.' Whereupon he replied, 'The American system of law? How interesting. We don't have any!' Little incidents like this . . . illustrate attitudes, . . . When Americans write about the law it always looks to me like one of our popular works on zoology. They describe the law as if it were some animal—the way it barks and sneezes, its mating and breeding habits, and whatever else it does" (p. 181).

58. Lipset, *First New Nation*, pp. 1-2 *passim*. The same assessment was, of course, made already by nineteenth-century observers like de Tocqueville.

59. See William J. Goode, "The Protection of the Inept," *American Sociological Review*, 32:5-19 (February 1967). Goode advances the hypothesis that the modern industrial system may be "more productive because its social structures *utilize the inept more efficiently,* rather than because it gives greater opportunity and reward to the more able," p. 17. The antinomies of a society in which rewards are based purely on achievement are exposed in Michael Young's satire *The Rise of the Meritocracy* (London, Thames and Hudson, 1958).

60. See S. M. Miller, "Comparative Social Mobility," *Current Sociology*, 9, 1:56 (1960).

61. See Scheuch, *German Social Structure*, p. 22f., who refers to survey data published in DIVO, *Umfragen 1958* (Frankfurt, 1959), p. 124 *passim*.

62. It was noted earlier that relations between professional and client in Germany tend to be more specific, more limited to the business at hand. Though superficially in contrast to the noted tendency toward status generalization, this pattern of specificity is actually supported by the generalization of occupational prestige into the area of informal interaction. The latter introduces an element of mutual reserve into the professional-client relationship whenever status differences separate the interaction partners.

63. For an analysis along these lines see Talcott Parsons and Winston White, "The Link Between Character and Society," T. Parsons, *Social Structure and Personality* (New York, Free Press, 1964), pp. 195-198.

64. Many observers, foreign and American, past and present, have noted the strong moral orientation characteristic of Americans as well as the sensitivity to the opinions of others in a variety of groups which Riesman has called "other-directedness"; see Williams, *American Society*, pp. 424-426, and Seymour M. Lipset, "A Changing American Character?" S. M. Lipset and L. Lowenthal, eds., *Culture and Social Character* (New York, Free Press, 1961), pp. 136-171. These patterns are quite consistent with each other, since the moral orientations do not approach a systematic canon of shared values but are typically more implicit and open

ended. Such an interpretation is congruent with the conclusions McClelland and others reached from their empirical findings; see n. 51. On the relation of law to moral convictions as well as diverse group traditions and collective interests see the characterizations of Hurst and Rheinstein quoted above.

65. Helmuth Plessner, *Die verspätete Nation* (Stuttgart, W. Kohlhammer, 1959; first published in 1935), and Hans Weil, *Die Entstehung des deutschen Bildungsprinzips* (Bonn, F. Cohen, 1930), trace this value orientation to its historical roots in secularized Lutheranism, idealist neo-humanism and in the political conditions in the fragmented absolutist states of pre-Imperial Germany.

66. For instance, René König has shown how German sociology in the 1920's and 1930's was pervasively related to Hegelian traditions; see R. König, "Germany," J. S. Roucek, ed., *Contemporary Sociology* (New York, Philosophical Library, 1958), pp. 779-806.

67. Empirical evidence about the stability of some of the German and American orientations discussed is presented by Lipset, "A Changing American Character?" and by McClelland, *Roots of Consciousness,* pp. 88-90.

68. See Hansjürgen Daheim, "Die Vorstellungen vom Mittelstand," *Kölner Zeitschrift für Soziologie und Sozialpsychologie,* 12:241 (1960). Civil servants constitute only 8 to 9 percent of the male labor force or 6 percent of the total labor force; *Statistisches Jahrbuch für die Bundesrepublik Deutschland, 1963* (Stuttgart and Mainz, Kohlhammer, 1963), p. 141.

69. Peter R. Hofstätter, "Eliten und Minoritäten," *Kölner Zeitschrift für Soziologie und Sozialpsychologie,* 14:59-86 (1962). Hofstätter refers to widespread pessimistic opinions of civil servants about their standing in society as reported in Arthur Rathke, *Wie leben die Beamten?* (Bad Godesberg, Deutscher Beamtenbund, 1958), and presents findings of a study of student attitudes which used associations of occupational and national labels to sketched portraits together with the semantic differential technique. The civil servant was characterized by greater discipline and rigidity, social reserve, and a lack of emotion and vitality, while being serious, orderly, and thrifty he shared with "the German." Slavery and death were concepts associated with the image of the civil servant, while merriment, love, and tenderness were antithetically related. University students, relatively free from family and career obigations, are particularly unlikely to have warm feelings for such a figure. That many may have taken the label *Beamter* as referring to a minor official is suggested by data on the prestige standing of various occupations and of the portrayed faces (p. 80). Semantic differential characterizations of several portrait sketches said to resemble civil servants suggest the existence of different subimages.

70. Thirty-seven percent of all professionals and 22 percent of self-employed professionals in the United States had fathers in blue collar occupations; see Peter M. Blau and Otis D. Duncan, *The American Occupational Structure* (New York, Wiley, 1967), pp. 39 and 496. For German *Akademiker,* I estimate that 3 to 5 percent come from working-class families; this is based on evidence for all German students in 1928-1929 (2.2 percent) and in 1958-1959 (5.3 percent); see Walter Richter, "Die Richter der Oberlandesgerichte der Bundesrepublik," *Hamburger Jahrbuch für Wirtschafts- und Gesellschaftspolitik,* 5:248 (1960), for the 1928-1929 data, and Statistisches Bundesamt, *Statistische Berichte,* VII/4/40:24-29 (1960). The contrast remains considerable even if the wider definition of "professional" in the United States is taken into account. This section draws on ideas and materials first published in Dietrich Rueschemeyer, "Rekrutierung, Ausbildung und Berufsstruktur," *Kölner Zeitschrift für Soziologie und Sozialpsychologie,* special issue no. 5:122-144 (1962).

71. Louis A. Toepfer, Dean of Harvard Law School, in his introduction to Seymour Warkov, *Lawyers in the Making* (Chicago, Aldine, 1965), p. xviii.

72. For the German estimate see the statistics on student backgrounds referred to in note 70. The American estimate is based on a variety of sources. Nearly one out of five students graduating from college in 1961 who intended to go to law school had working class fathers; Warkov, *Lawyers in the Making,* p. 4. Not all of them may have actually entered the profession; on the other hand, college graduation is not universally required for legal studies or admission to the bar. Widely varying proportions of lawyers with blue collar backgrounds were found in six cities in Massachusetts (34 percent), Ohio (12 percent), and Texas (5 percent); see Stuart Adams, "Regional Differences in Vertical Mobility in a High-Status Occupa-

tion," *American Sociological Review,* 15:231 (1950). In New York City, nearly a quarter of all lawyers are from lower-class backgrounds, Carlin, *Lawyers' Ethics,* p. 201.

73. Cf. J. Conrad, "Allgemeine Statistik der deutschen Universitäten," W. Lexis, ed., *Die deutschen Universitäten,* vol. 1 (Berlin, 1893), p. 140f., for parental occupations of students before the turn of the century.

74. Some *Akademiker* fathers are or were also proprietors or managers of business firms, and some fathers classified as "employees with management status" are in the employment of government rather than of business firms, although they are not members of the career civil service. While the latter cases are not included in the categories of civil servants, an estimated number of the former was counted both as *Akademiker* and as businessmen. The interpretation of the high percentage of law students from independent business backgrounds in 1928-1929 must take into account that Jewish students came disproportionately often from such origins; while in 1933 28.5 percent of the Prussian lawyers in private practice were of Jewish ethnic origin (Horst Göppinger, *Der Nationalsozialismus und die jüdischen Juristen,* Villingen, Ring-Verlag, 1963, p. 38), very few Jewish members of the German bar stayed in Germany and survived the Nazi regime or returned after 1945. Equally important for the comparison of the figures in 1928-1929 and 1958-1959 are, of course, the decline of the proportion of self-employed persons in the labor force and the increased access to the universities for people from lower white collar origins.

75. In 1960, one percent of the lawyers in New York City were Blacks; "slightly over 60 percent are Jewish; 18 percent are Catholic; 18 percent are Protestant," Carlin, *Lawyers' Ethics,* pp. 19 and 21. James A. Davis reports of the senior class of 1961 that compared to other students those choosing law had a specially high proportion of Jews and Catholics. Nationwide the percentages were: Protestant—45, Catholic—36, Jewish—19; *Undergraduate Career Decisions* (Chicago, Aldine, 1965), pp. 71 and 72.

76. Carlin, *Lawyers' Ethics,* p. 147.

77. In fact, most of the sources used above—aside from the student data—referred to private practitioners only.

78. According to Zapf, "Verwalter der Macht," p. 19, 46 percent of the higher civil servants in state and federal *Innenministerien* (general administrative departments) had fathers who were *Beamte.* Administrative lawyers seem to come more often than both judges and attorneys in private practice from lower-class and lower middle-class families; thus, 4 percent of the higher administrators studied by Zapf came from working class homes, ibid.

79. Five percent of all West Germans graduated from high school, but more than four times as many, 22 percent, had some high school training; Institut für Demoskopie, *Jahrbuch der öffentlichen Meinung, 1958-1964,* p. 357. Limited admission based on grades was introduced only very recently.

80. See Hasso von Recum, "Soziale Strukturwandlungen des Volksschullehrerberufs," *Kölner Zeitschrift für Soziologie und Sozialpsychologie,* 7:574-579 (1955), for one regional study of elementary school teachers. The estimate for high school teachers is based on the same student statistics in 1928-1929 and 1958-1959 which were used above in the discussion of social origins of lawyers.

81. The quote is from an official publication of teachers' associations in response to reform proposals, as quoted by Dahrendorf, *Society and Democracy,* p. 325f. The invidious contrasts between "civilization" and "culture," and of mere training versus personal and cultural formation (*"Ausbildung"* und *"Bildung"*) correspond to those between a spiritually impoverished modern society and a more traditional order which was the bearer of classical culture; these dichotomies have a venerable tradition in German philosophical and political thought.

82. See Kaupen, *Hüter . . . ,* pp. 142-154, and Erika Spiegel, *Elternhaus und Schule,* part 1 (Frankfurt, 1962), p. 157.

83. Dahrendorf, *Society and Democracy,* p. 237. For the quote of Justice Frankfurter, Warkov, *Lawyers in the Making,* p. xv. A committee of German lawyers concerned with problems of legal education came to a similar conclusion; see Arbeitskreis für Fragen der Juristenausbildung, *Die Ausbildung der deutschen Juristen* (Tübingen, J. C. B. Mohr, 1960), p. 202. *Der Spiegel,* Dec. 14, 1960, p. 43f., reported in 1960 a striking development. While from

1954 to 1959 the number of law students had nearly doubled, the number of first year law students decreased within one year by 69 percent, apparently in response to a leaflet campaign of the German bar association addressed to all high school graduates which described in drastic and exaggerated terms the overcrowding and the low income level of the *Rechtsanwaltschaft*.

84. See Christian von Ferber, "The Social Background of German University and College Professors since 1864," *Transactions of the Third World Congress of Sociology*, vol. III (London, 1956), pp. 239-244. Ferber reports data for all German university teachers in 1951 which show that the proportion of sons of *Beamte* was 42.5 percent; the proportion for law professors is likely to be higher. Generally, professors come from higher social backgrounds, but aside from that their recruitment field resembles that of students in 1928-1929.

85. For the character and problems of German legal education see Arbeitskreis für Fragen der Juristenausbildung, *Ausbildung*, pp. 195-225 *passim*. No data are available on the first two options—change of field and leaving the university, although there is a consensus that they are of considerable quantitative importance. As to the use of commercial complements to university studies, the committee on problems of legal education estimates that only an insignificantly small percentage of students dares to do without them altogether; nearly half of the respondents in a survey of young lawyers in Southwestern Germany gave the *Repetitor* (commercial law teacher) the highest rating in educational efficiency, *Ausbildung*, p. 196.

86. Heidrun Haas found in a small survey in Cologne that nearly half of the law students in contrast to less than a third of other students were members of student fraternities; "Die Kölner Studenten," diploma thesis, University of Cologne, 1961, p. 119. The survey of the committee on problems of legal education in Southwestern Germany revealed that 85 percent of the young lawyers had attended courses in other fields; Arbeitskreis für Fragen der Juristenausbildung, *Ausbildung*, p. 201. W. Kaupen relates results of a study of the Institut für Sexualforschung at the University of Hamburg which showed that 52 percent of the law students indicated a leisure time interest in theater and literature in contrast to 42 percent of all students; the respective percentages for interest in politics were 78 and 56; *Hüter. . . ,* p. 159. The greater involvement of law students in extracurricular activities and interests is also reflected in the fact that they have more often than other students social contacts with students in other fields than their own; see Haas, "Kölner Studenten," p. 117f. This should effectively support their diffuse socialization as Akademiker.

87. Table 14 does not directly say anything about changes over time, giving data for students of different seniority at one point of time only. Statistics for earlier years show, however, a similar pattern, so that the interpretation seems justified.

88. These are the old time requirements. The shortening by more than one year does not affect this analysis. See Arbeitskreis für Fragen der Juristenausbildung, *Ausbildung*, pp. 114-123. E. J. Cohn comments on this and related aspects of legal education: "Thus a man may become an attorney after several years of academic study, a number of years in preparation for the judicial career and only a few months of training as an attorney. It is significant that the German legal profession has never made any determined effort to change this curious position. On the contrary: it derives satisfaction from the fact that its members share their training with future magistrates and judges. All textbooks, in particular those on procedure, are in fact written from the point of view of the judge or court rather than from that of the attorney. Some quite large books on German legal history make very few references to attorneys. Their interest circles around the law and the court. Both academic theory and legal training treat the attorney's branch of activity as a quantité négligeable." "German Attorney, II,'', p. 105.

89. By 1966, the proportion of those who never attended college or who did not receive a law degree had declined to 8 percent, but there were still 31 percent who did not graduate from college; all percentages are calculated on the basis of the number of lawyers for whom there is information; see U.S. Bureau of the Census, *Statistical Abstract of the United States: 1968* (Washington, D.C., 1968), p. 154. See Blaustein and Porter, *American Lawyer*, chaps. vi and vii, and Albert J. Harno, *Legal Education in the United States* (San Francisco, Bancroft-Whitney, 1953)) for details on the changes in requirements.

90. For this and the following assertion see Williams, *American Society* p. 296; see also p. 310.

91. A recent comparative analysis of educational systems classified them in terms of four

dimensions that pertain to the selection of students for advanced study. It tentatively characterizes several national systems, including the German and American ones, as follows: (1) centralization and standardization of selection: United States and Canada low; West Germany, England, and Australia medium; France, Sweden, and U.S.S.R. high. (2) Early differentiation and specialization of educational routes: United States, Canada, and Sweden low; U.S.S.R. and Australia medium; West Germamy, England, and France high. The third and fourth dimensions concern ideologies defining: (3) who should be selected, and (4) why. The third dimension is conceived as a continuum ranging from particularistic orientations, stressing ascribed characteristics and diffuse skills which are typically learned early and in class-specific ways, to universalistic orientations, stressing specific technical skills and deemphasizing diffuse skills. Both particularistic and universalistic criteria of who should be selected can be justified—the fourth dimension of the typology—in terms of individual rights and needs or in terms of what is good for society ("collectivism"). Different ideologies are espoused by various groups within each country, but the author offers reasonable estimates of their distribution and relative weight and concludes that educational ideologies in the United States are moderately universalistic and individualistic—a combination labeled "meritocratic," while Germany, with greater internal variation, is assessed as most strongly particularistic of all eight countries classified and moderately collectivistic—a characterization labeled "paternalistic." This agrees well with our comments on the German educational system as well as with what was said above about dominant value orientations of the German middle and upper middle classes. See Earl I. Hopper, "A Typology for the Classification of Educational Systems," *Sociology*, 2:29-46 (January 1968).

92. Of the extended literature on legal education see Albert J. Harno, *Legal Education;* Lowell S. Nicholson, *The Law Schools in the United States* (Baltimore, Lord Baltimore Press, 1958); Alfred Z. Reed, *Training for the Public Profession of the Law* (New York, Carnegie Foundation, 1921); and A. Z. Reed, *Present Day Law Schools in the United States and Canada* (New York, Carnegie Foundation, 1928). Wagner Thielens, Jr., "The Socialization of Law Students," unpub. Ph.D. diss., Columbia University, 1965, gives a wealth of information and detailed analysis of the experience of professional socialization among law students at Columbia University.

93. See Blaustein and Porter, *American Lawyer,* pp. 176-179. The proportion of students at schools not approved by the American Bar Association is decreasing, while the standards for approval have been raised continuously since the 1920's; see ibid., p. 181-186. In 1928, only one-third of all law students attended approved law schools. By 1938 this proportion had passed the 50 percent mark; by 1951 it had reached 83 percent and it has grown further since. See Hurst, *American Law,* p. 273.

94. Data on shifts in career preferences similar to the statistics for all German students are not available, except for single schools. Thielens, Socialization, p. 392f., reports for Columbia students a slight decline in an originally rather high proportion of students who would like to become judges (from 20 percent to 16 percent), while the largest increase was found among those who aspire to become partners in medium or large firms: 13 percent of first year students versus 27 percent of third year students. For an insightful discussion of the new student activists and their criticism of legal education see Allan A. Stone, "Legal Education on the Couch," *Harvard Law Review,* 85:392-441 (December 1971). The impact of these new developments on the bar as a whole should not be overestimated, however, at least in the short run.

95. See Hurst, *American Law,* p. 284.

96. See Chapter 2 above for the internal stratification of the American bar, and the section on the political involvement of American lawyers in this chapter. Blaustein and Porter, *American Lawyer,* p. 198, report that the "percentage of judges among alumni graduating from unapproved schools is higher than the number from approved schools, and such institutions as Harvard and Columbia, which can boast of their many alumni in the United States Supreme Court, have a relatively small number of graduates in judicial posts generally." In part, this is probably the effect of a time lag, since judges are likely to be of higher average age, and both attendance of inadequate schools and the bypassing of law school altogether (18 percent of the judges in 1951 never attended law school in contrast to 5 percent of all lawyers, p.

223

197f.) were much more common in the late nineteenth and early twentieth century than in recent decades. For the education of members of the United States Supreme Court since 1789, see 'John Schmidhauser, "The Supreme Court: A Collective Portrait," *Midwest Journal of Political Science,* 3:23, 24 (1959).

97. See for similar conclusions Dan C. Lortie, "Laymen to Lawmen: Law School, Careers, and Professional Socialization," *Harvard Educational Review,* 4:353-369, esp. 367-369 (1959); see also Jack Ladinsky, "Careers of Lawyers, Law Practice, and Legal Institutions," *American Sociological Review,* 28:47-54 (1963).

98. Hurst, *American Law,* p. 357.

99. John H. Wigmore, introduction to Orrin N. Carter, *Ethics of the Legal Profession* (Chicago, Northwestern University Press, 1915), as quoted in Elliott E. Cheatham, *Cases and Materials on the Legal Profession* (Brooklyn, Foundation Press, 1955), p. 75.

100. The first quote is from Adolph A. Berle, Jr., "Modern Legal Profession," *Encyclopedia of the Social Sciences,* vol. 9, p. 344; the second is from argument of counsel in Barton v. the State Bar of California, 209 Cal. 677, 681, 289 P. 818, 1930, as quoted in Cheatham, *Legal Profession,* p. 74; and the third is from Harrison Hewitt's review of Codes of Ethics by Edgar L. Heermance, in *Yale Law Journal,* vol. 35, 1926, p. 393 as quoted in Cheatham, *Legal Profession,* p. 76.

101. Jerome E. Carlin found in New York that, in comparison to federal and state appellate judges, local and state trial judges are on the average "less experienced and less adequately trained," have shorter terms, "appear to be more dependent on political ties and more susceptible to political influences," are less likely to belong to elite bar associations and "have considerably more discretion in making decisions"; *Lawyers' Ethics,* p. 85f. Carlin has demonstrated convincingly that contact with lower-level courts and agencies is a major factor in raising rates of unprofessional conduct among attorneys (see his chaps. v and vii).

102. See Ford et al., *Government Lawyers,* p. 12, and the portrait of the values of higher civil servants in the federal government given by Warner et al., *American Federal Executive,* pp. 221-236.

103. See, for example, Carlin, *Lawyers on Their Own,* chaps. iv and v *passim*; Carlin, *Lawyers' Ethics,* chaps. iii and ix *passim*; Smigel, *Wall Street Lawyer,* chaps. i and x; and Handler, *Lawyer,* chaps. iv-viii.

104. Carlin found in New York City that lawyers with low-status clients are more frequently involved in the financial affairs of their clients ("on the look-out for investment opportunities, assisting them in obtaining financing"), while "control involvement (holding office or stock in the corporate client) . . . is more typical of the lawyer with high-status clients." *Lawyers Ethics,* p. 82.

105. Carlin found that opinions critical of the canons of the legal profession were significantly more frequent among lawyers with low-status clients and, independent of client status, among lawyers with an insecure practice defined by turnover of clients and experience of competition from other lawyers; *Lawyers' Ethics,* p. 69.

106. Seymour Warkov, *Lawyers in the Making,* p. 11.

107. See Hurst, *American Law,* pp. 322-375. More than half of the New York lawyers studied by Jerome E. Carlin did not disapprove of behavior contravening canons of professional ethics which "proscribe behavior not necessarily immoral or unethical in the wider community," *Lawyers' Ethics,* p. 51f.

108. Hurst, *American Law,* p. 332f.

109. Hurst, *American Law,* p. 371. The case of Justice Fortas, which developed as a public matter only after this chapter had been written, illustrates the same orientations, although from the opposite side. Fortas' difficulty in shifting from his role as counsel and advocate committed to his business clients and their values to that of a Supreme Court judge is analyzed by Fred P. Graham, "The Fortas Puzzle: What Was the Flaw?" *New York Times,* May 18, 1969, section 4, p. 1.

110. Eugene V. Rostow, to give one more example, states in his comments on the history of the prominent Cravath firm: "In Mr. Swaine's gallery of colorful and devoted men, there are very few—perhaps only Cotton—who were capable of real detachment toward the work they were doing." Review of Robert T. Swaine, "The Cravath Firm and its Predecessors,"

*Yale Law Journal,* vol. 58, p. 652, 1949, quoted in Cheatham, *Legal Profession,* p. 56.

111. Hurst, *American Law,* p. 375. See also Robert T. Swaine, "Impact of Big Business on the Profession. An answer to the Critics of the Modern Bar," *American Bar Association Journal,* 35:89-92, 168-171 (February 1949); Rostow, Review of Swaine, "Cravath Firm."

112. Cheatham, *Legal Profession,* p. 57, emphasis added.

113. The phrases are taken from the characterization of one Boston lawyer by another in the 1890's (Hurst, *American Law,* p. 346), but the reality which they describe is likely to be as common at present as it was seventy years ago. See Lortie, "Laymen to Lawmen," p. 368f., who emphasizes the limited number of lawyers who engage in what he calls "core law"; see also Carlin's description of the work of individual practitioners in Chicago in his *Lawyers on Their Own,* chap. ii; and Smigel's description of the work of partners in large law firms, *Wall Street Lawyer,* pp. 158-160 and 302-306.

114. Significantly, one of the sections of Hurst's discussion of the social functions of the bar is entitled "Master of Fact"; *American Law,* pp. 339-342. A sample of Harvard University Law School graduates was asked in the mid-1940's to rank six basic skills according to importance in their own work. "A 'sense of fact' is . . . given the highest position by a wide margin over any of the other skills." Committee on Legal Education of the Harvard Law School *Preliminary Statement* (MS), 1947, p. 26. Robert Fritz, a German judge, related in 1930 peculiarities of German legal thought and training to "an exaggerated caution and reserve in the development of the facts of a case at trial. This goes so far that one hears everywhere from American attorneys who cooperate professionally with German lawyers the insistent complaint that they would only rarely get from Germany sufficiently clear and concrete descriptions of fact . . . that letters of German lawyers would however contain a lot of legal argument." *Aus dem amerikanischen Rechtsleben* (Berlin, O. Liebmann, 1930), p. 44f.

115. These estimates cannot do more than indicate orders of magnitude, since no direct statistics are available. The term *freie Berufe,* liberal or free professions, referred originally to a kind of learning and work compatible with the dignity of a free man (*artes liberales*), disregarding employment status. During the nineteenth century the meaning of the term changed to self-employed professions, requiring university training. See D. Rueschemeyer, "Freie und akademische Berufe," W. Bernsdorf, ed., *Wörterbuch der Soziologie,* 2d ed. (Stuttgart, Enke, 1969), pp. 301-305.

116. Gabriel A. Almond, "The Politics of German Business," H. Speier and W. Ph. Davison, eds., *West German Leadership and Foreign Policy* (Evanston, Ill., Row, Peterson, 1957), p. 238. For the relationship of the more traditional cultural heritage to a modern profession like engineering see König, "Der Ingenieur."

117. Since the question asked for the prestige that these professions *should* have, the self-evaluations of lawyers may express the discontent of German lawyers with the prestige accorded them in German society. The same survey found that only a third of the *Rechtsanwälte* and as few as 13 percent of the judges and prosecuting attorneys believed without qualification that lawyers in Germany enjoy the prestige they deserve. The relationship between judges and *Rechtsanwälte* is complicated by income differences which are out of line with the relative evaluation of their positions in terms of "social importance." About half of the *Rechtsanwälte* earn a higher income than 90 percent of the judges and prosecuting attorneys. This descrepancy between perceived social importance and remuneration in the social status of the judiciary is likely to have affected negatively the latter's estimation of the prestige due to private practitioners.

There are important local variations in such evaluations. *Rechtsanwälte* in the southwestern German city previously referred to ranked, in answer to a slightly different question, the judge clearly behind the physician in "social usefulness," and even the entrepreneur had a slight edge over the judge. The rank distance between judge and *Rechtsanwalt* remained, however, similar to the rank order in Table 15. Wolfgang Kaupen, who supplied these data, made, in another context, the following comments on this local bar, its traditions and its situation: "Southwestern German liberalism; extremely large number of younger attorneys (conflict between generations); very dynamic economic development of the metropolitan area (construction prices are the highest in the Federal Republic.)."

118. Cohn, "German Attorney, I,", p. 589.

119. The first quote is from Burke Shartel and Hans Julius Wolff, "German Lawyers—Training and Functions," *Michigan Law Review*, 42:521-527 (1943); the second is found in Bader, *Die deutschen Juristen*, p. 22.

120. Wolfgang Kaupen has compared a number of opinions and attitudes held by *Rechtsanwälte* with lower and higher incomes and by judges and prosecuting attorneys. Income correlates with a dominance of business matters in one's practice. The sample of *Rechtsanwälte* includes an unspecified number of syndic-attorneys, often viewed as a separate group, not really a part of the *Anwaltschaft*.

| Opinions | *Rechtsanwälte* with annual income of more than DM 36,000 % | less than DM 36,000 % | Judges and prosecuting attorneys % | |
|---|---|---|---|---|
| According to their social importance, highest prestige (1 and 2 rank) is due to minister and priest | 26 | 36 | 37 | * |
| The lowest prestige (8 and 9 rank) is due to: | | | | |
| *Manager* | 49 | 62 | 65 | * |
| Artist | 36 | 26 | 28 | * |
| Characteristics someone in respondent's position should have (first rank): | | | | |
| Readiness to work hard, industry | 19 | 17 | 7 | |
| Responsibility for community | 8 | 6 | 11 | |
| Knowledge, technical ability | 48 | 44 | 45 | |
| Love of profession | 21 | 35 | 37 | * |
| Rewards someone in respondent's position should value more (first rank): | | | | |
| Gratitude, trust | 21 | 19 | 16 | |
| Prestige, income | 7 | 1 | 3 | * |
| Objective recognition of work | 39 | 41 | 42 | |
| Fulfillment, personal satisfaction | 32 | 38 | 38 | * |
| Lawyers are because of their commitment to law and order more inclined toward a conservative attitude | 29 | 32 | 37 | |
| Lawyers are because of their complex experience especially fit for positions of leadership | | | | |
| in society | 48 | 44 | 42 | |
| in business | 45 | 43 | 23 | |

| Lawyers, too, cannot succeed today without specialization in selected fields of law | 31 | 27 | 20 | |
|---|---|---|---|---|
| Lawyers enjoy in our society the prestige that is due them on the basis of their function | 34 | 26 | 13 | * |
| | (N=121) | (N=140) | (N=188) | |

Source: Kaupen, *Hüter.* . . , p. 194; supplemented by other information supplied by Mr. Kaupen. While a number of these items, especially those starred, point in the direction of some polarization with the attorneys who are less well off closer to the opinions of the judiciary, the overall homogeneity is perhaps more impressive.

121. Half the *Anwälte* in the southwestern German city referred to explained repeatedly that they entered the *Rechtsanwaltschaft* rather than another branch of the profession because of the independence a *freier Beruf* offers or because of their disinclination to become judges or generally servants of the state. On the other hand, while nearly one out of six never considered another career in the law, about a third did consider government employment, primarily a judicial career.

## NOTES TO CHAPTER 4

1. *The Canons of Professional Ethics* of the American Bar Association, adopted originally in 1908 and revised several times since, were replaced in 1969 by the *Code of Professional Responsibility*. (I refer to the Final Draft prepared by the American Bar Association Special Committee on Evaluation of Ethical Standards, July 1969). Essentially a restatement of the preceding canons and their accumulated interpretation, the code introduces a new format. It states nine general principles, the "canons," and develops for each a number of "Ethical Considerations" specifying what lawyers should aspire to as well as "Disciplinary Rules" laying down minimum standards. If the latter are not met, disciplinary action is suggested. Standards adopted by the American Bar Association do not have directly binding force. However, while authority over matters of professional discipline and regulations rests with the states, there has been a tendency toward uniformity which the new code is likely to reinforce.

The German "guidelines" are issued by the federal association of the *Rechtsanwaltskammern*. Together with a statute regulating the profession they constitute the body of standards ordering private legal practice. However, they differ in character from ordinary legal standards. They aim to represent the *communis opinio* of the *Rechtsanwaltschaft;* if it could be shown that actual opinion holds otherwise, they would not be binding. Further, they constitute a guide only; neither can the individual *Anwalt* invoke their letter if his behavior is in its particular context clearly against legal ethics nor is his behavior to be considered without exception unethical because it violates the letter of the guidelines. See Werner Kalsbach, *Standesrecht des Rechtsanwalts* (Cologne, O. Schmidt, 1956), pp. 13-19. Both statute and guidelines are reproduced and elaborately commented on in Werner Kalsbach, *Bundesrechtsanwaltsordnung und Richtlinien für die Ausübung des Rechtsanwaltsberufs. Kommentar* (Cologne, O. Schmidt, 1960), referred to in the following as *BRAO*.

2. J. R. Voûte and L. Hardenberg conclude in their report on the problems of an international code of ethics for lawyers that differences between national codes are generally outweighed by similarities; "Referat über einen Ehrenkodex des internationalen Standesrechts," report no. VII E at the meeting of the International Bar Association, Monaco 1953, reprinted in Kalsbach, *Standesrecht*, pp. 600-630.

3. One major basis for popular distrust and suspicion is precisely the combination of partisan loyalty to the client with responsibility for the administration of justice; see Chapter 1 above for a comparative discussion of the professional role of the lawyer.

4. Kalsbach, *Standesrecht*, p. 10.

5. Henry S. Drinker, *Legal Ethics*, (New York, Columbia University Press, 1953), p. 139. The new code stresses in Ethical Considerations 2-26 through 2-28 the moral obligation to accept unpopular cases and cases which involve the lawyer in conflicts with colleagues, public officials, and powerful members of the community. Neither the German guidelines nor the commentaries state such an obligation, but many German lawyers will feel similarly obliged.

6. Disciplinary Rule 2-109 does not permit employment if the purpose is obviously only to harrass or maliciously to injure another person or if it requires presenting a case in litigation which "is not warranted under existing law, unless it can be supported by good faith argument for an extension, modification, or reversal of existing law." See also Elliott E. Cheatham, *Cases and Materials on the Legal Profession*, 2d ed. (Brooklyn, N.Y.,Foundation Press, 1955), pp. 139-151. For Germany see Kalsbach, *Standesrecht*, pp. 225f and 227-229. Kalsbach, referring for justification to the required independence of counsel, even quotes approvingly the *Codigo de Etica Professional del Colegio de Abogados de Lima* which prohibits the advocate from arguing against his religious and political convictions. The difference is for most situations likely to be an academic problem. However, the tone of its discussion is quite different in the two bars. Thus, Drinker, *Legal Ethics*, p. 144, n. 30, quotes Kent: "[The lawyer] is not an expert as to moral as distinguished from legal rights. He may know less of these than his client. There is, too, such a difference of opinion as to mere moral rights that, generally, they do not constitute a basis for advice." Another quote from the same source (p. 144, n. 27) observes without moral admonishment: "Nature is very kind in allowing us to believe almost anything which it is for our interest to advocate."

7. See Max Hogrefe, "Referat zur Neugestaltung des Paragraphen 356 StGb," 1954, reprinted in Kalsbach, *Standesrecht*, pp. 350-364.

8. See Kalsbach, *Standesrecht*, pp. 347-421, and Kalsbach, BRAO, pp. 304 and 446-454. The exact relationship between the two rationales is a matter of some debate, though the consequences indicated are not; the above follows Kalsbach. The quotations are from Ethical Consideration 5-14 and Disciplinary Rule 5-105, respectively. Drinker, *Legal Ethics*, p. 105, also mentions the problem of ill appearances; but this is not included in the new code as a specific point.

9. See Kalsbach, *Standesrecht*, p. 405, and Drinker, *Legal Ethics*, p. 104.

10. See Voûte and Hardenberg, "Referat," p. 617. Jerome E. Carlin, *Lawyers' Ethics* (New York, Russell Sage Foundation, 1966), found that only 35 percent of the lawyers interviewed disapproved of the unethical action in a hypothetical case where a lawyer is asked to represent one of two business partners he has previously represented after a controversy develops between the partners. As to their own behavior, only 46 percent reported taking the ethical action, pp. 50 and 53. Joel F. Handler asked the same question in "Prairie City"; here, 49 percent disapproved of taking the case and 39 percent did or would violate the norm; see *The Lawyer and His Community* (Madison, University of Wisconsin Press, 1967), pp. 102, 137, and 141.

11. Disciplinary Rule 2-110. This and Ethical Considerations 2-32 and 7-8 contain the main norms.

12. Kalsbach, *BRAO*, p. 262; the guideline is given on p. 260.

13. Cheatham, *Legal Profession*, p. 151.

14. Kalsbach, *Standesrecht*, p. 46 and 47f. An anecdote, related by one of my older informants, indicates the flavor of professional independence that is an element in the heritage of the German profession. In one of his first letters, after joining his father's office, he acknowledged the mandate received from a client and inserted a conventional formula of thanking. His father had him rewrite the letter: "We don't owe thanks to any client."

15. Rome G. Brown, "Some Applications of the Rules of Legal Ethics," *Minnesota Law Review* 6 (1922), reprinted in Cheatham, *Legal Profession*, p. 182.

16. Cheatham, *Legal Profession*, p. 144.

17. Charles M. Hough, Review of Allen, "The Law as a Vocation," *Harvard Law Review*, 33 (1920), reprinted in Cheatham, *Legal Profession*, p. 134.

18. Kalsbach, *Standesrecht*, p. 46.

19. Cheatham, *Legal Profession*, p. 145f. However, Ethical Consideration 7-8 allows withdrawal if in a nonadjudicatory matter the client rejects the lawyer's judgment.

20. Opinion of the Strafrechtsausschuss der deutschen Rechtsanwaltskammern, quoted in Kalsbach, *BRAO*, p. 378. Even when taking the first course he has to be especially careful to avoid committing the crime of illegally favoring a criminal. The ways and means of this defense are not considered an appropriate subject for explicit rules because of the multiple overlapping of the different loyalties of the attorney. To choose the right course has to be left to his conscientious discretion in each individual case; ibid., p. 377f.

21. Thus the old Canon 5. See also Ethical Consideration 7-24 of the new code. It is interesting to note the difference in language. The German authorities speak of "knowing the guilt" while referring to a confession. The contrasting American phrase of "his personal opinion as to the guilt" was surely not chosen by accident.

22. Opinion No. 281, reprinted in Cheatham, *Legal Profession*, p. 142f.

23. The proportions disapproving of the unethical action ranged from less than half (advice to client that to bribe a revenue agent is "risky but your business") to 83 percent (lawyer makes or arranges for bribe to police official) in New York City and from 76 percent to 92 percent (with the same rank order of items) in Prairie City; see Carlin, *Lawyers' Ethics*, p. 50, and Handler, *The Lawyer*, p. 102. The rates of reported violation were lower though not insignificant in New York; see p. 53 and p. 197, respectively. The four hypothetical violations, ordered according to the number of lawyers in either bar disapproving, were:

"*Police Payoff*: Lawyer A makes or arranges for payment to police official to get a charge of homosexuality against a promising youth removed from the books."

"*Divorce*: Lawyer A decides to take divorce case in which both parties agree to a consent decree on grounds of adultery, (in Prairie City: physical cruelty), though adultery (physical cruelty) was not committed."

"*Client Payoff*: Client failed to report income on tax return, and is offered a deal by tax agent to overlook the matter for a sum of money. A tells client payment is his business, not to tell A anything about it; or that it would be risky to make payment, but if he wants to that's his business." Carlin, *Lawyers' Ethics*, p. 44f.

24. Roscoe Pound, *The Lawyer from Antiquity to Modern Times* (St. Paul, Minn., West Publishing Co., 1953), p. 5.

25. Kalsbach, *BRAO*, pp. 7 and 9; the emphasis is his.

26. Drinker, Legal Ethics, p. 174. Defining "clearly excessive fees," the new code invokes as a test the "definite and firm conviction" of "a lawyer of ordinary prudence," but it also quotes the ABA Opinion 320 (1968): "This Committee is not concerned with the amount of such fee unless so excessive as to constitute a misappropriation of the client's funds." *Code of Professional Responsibility. Final Draft*, p. 43, n. 137.

27. See Guideline 38 and the comments of Kalsbach, *BRAO*, p. 320.

28. See Kalsbach, *BRAO*, pp. 321-326 for the relevant rules. Benjamin Kaplan, Arthur T. von Mehren, and Rudolf Schaefer, "Phases of German Civil Procedure, II," *Harvard Law Review*, 71:1462 and 1466 (1957-1958), note that statutory fees are prevalent. One condition which contributes to this effect is the fact that the losing party has to reimburse the costs incurred by the winner, but only up to the amount fixed by the fee schedule.

29. See Kalsbach, *BRAO*, pp. 326-341, and Kalsbach, *Standesrecht*, pp. 432-437. The regulations always allowed for an exception from a strict interpretation of the prohibitive principle in collection cases where the lawyer may agree not to take the regular fees for his work if he is not successful. Here, too, the collective interests of the *Rechtsanwaltschaft* which competes with commercial institutions in this field are a guiding consideration; see Kalsbach, *BRAO*, pp. 322f. and 436-439. Kaplan et al., "German Civil Procedure," p. 1466, suggest that contingent fees of an attenuated sort are more widespread than the official standards allow: "We suspect that lawyers sometimes simply forego collecting all or part of their fees from their clients when they fail in the lawsuits, and this may be pursuant to a spoken or unspoken prior understanding."

30. See the "Report of the Advisory Bar Committee to Study the Problem of Contingent Fees," adopted in 1952 by the Association of the Bar of the City of New York, reprinted in Cheatham, *Legal Profession*, pp. 336-338. For a recent study of the problems of contingent fees see Frederick B. MacKinnon, *Contingent Fees for Legal Services* (Chicago, Aldine, 1964).

31. Quoted by Drinker, *Legal Ethics*, p. 177. Some ambivalence is evident in the language of Ethical Consideration 2-20: "Although a lawyer generally should decline to accept employment on a contingent fee basis by one who is able to pay a reasonable fixed fee, it is not necessarily improper for a lawyer, where justified by the particular circumstances of a case, to enter into a contingent fee contract in a civil case with any client who, after being fully informed of all relevant factors, desires that arrangement."

32. Max Radin, "Contingent Fees in California," *California Law Review*, 28:587 (1940), quoted in Cheatham, *Legal Profession*, p. 336.

33. See for the United States: Emery A. Brownell, *Legal Aid in the United States* (Rochester, Minn., Lawyers Co-operative Publishing Co., 1951); Jerome E. Carlin and Jan Howard, "Legal Representation and Class Justice," *U.C.L.A. Law Review*, 12:381-437, especially 408-423 (1965), and Jerome E. Carlin, Jan Howard, and Sheldon Messinger, "Civil Justice and the Poor: Issues for Sociological Research," *Law and Society Review*, 1:9-89 (1966). For Germany see the regulations of the statute and the guidelines in Kalsbach, *BRAO*, pp. 356-372 and 463f. Some evaluation of the actual functioning of legal aid in civil cases is given in Benjamin Kaplan et al., "German Civil Procedure," pp. 1467-1470; see also Fritz Ostler, *Der deutsche Rechtsanwalt* (Karlsruhe, C. F. Müller, 1963), pp. 16-18.

34. Carlin and Howard, "Class Justice," p. 417. There has been considerable progress since this study: "With the Association playing a large role, more progress has been made in the past five years in providing legal services to the poor than in the entire prior history of the country. Nevertheless, there is still a vast unfilled need for such legal services—a need that now is less than one fifth served." Bernard G. Segal, "President's Page," *American Bar Association Journal*, 56:611 (July 1970).

35. Kaplan et al., "German Civil Procedure," p. 1467.

36. Ostler, *Rechtsanwalt*, p. 18. The extent of legal aid in litigation is shown by the following estimates: "Legal aid is granted in perhaps twenty percent of all civil litigation (excluding dunning-process) in the regular courts: in divorce cases the figure is perhaps over fifty percent; in paternity cases nearly one-hundred per cent. Once financial inability of a party is certified, a considerable pressure is felt by the court not to deny him his chance in litigation." Kaplan et al., "German Civil Procedure," p. 1469. Commenting on regular small-scale work, E. J. Cohn, "The German Attorney-Experiences with a Unified Profession (II)," *International and Comparative Law Quarterly*, 10:113f. (1961), stresses the public spirit shown by the profession: "No German attorney is legally or otherwise compelled to accept instructions unless he wants to. He may agree to accept instructions only on condition that the client agrees to pay a special fee. It is, no doubt, remarkable that German attorneys only rarely refuse to act for the all too modest statutory fees in cases involving small amounts. There can be no doubt at all that the profession has over the years received far too little credit for the public spirit shown by it in this respect. It is the spirit shown by the profession, and not the statutory rule, which has enabled the small man to get his work done at what must be considered a more than reasonable price."

37. Kalsbach, *Standesrecht*, pp. 27-38.

38. Disciplinary Rules 9-101 and 9-102 are concerned with private employment in matters one has acted upon in a judicial or other official capacity, with improper claims of influence on government institutions or officials, and with preserving the identity of funds and property of a client. Even the relevant Ethical Considerations are more hesitant and hedged by qualifications than the general clause of the German guidelines and Kalsbach's commentary. See Kalsbach, *Standesrecht*, pp. 35-38, and *BRAO*, pp. 167-172.

39. Kalsbach, *Standesrecht*, p. 174; for the guideline and commentary see Kalsbach, *BRAO*, pp. 224-226. Before initiating civil litigation against a colleague, the *Rechtsanwalt* has to give the other an opportunity for a settlement out of court.

40. Harrison Hewitt, "A Letter to the Editor," *ABA Journal*, 15:116 (1929), quoted in Cheatham, *Legal Profession*, p. 525. Hewitt lists some of the other rationales discussed here, too. For the point that advertising would give a controlling influence to lay customers see William J. Goode, "Community within a Community: The Professions," *American Sociological Review*, 22:194-200 (1957).

41. Kalsbach, *Standesrecht*, p. 64, somewhat weaker in *BRAO*, p. 405; see also pp. 404-406.

42. Drinker, *Legal Ethics*, pp. 212 and 214.

43. See Disciplinary Rule 2-102. See also Quintin Johnstone and Dan Hopson, Jr., *Lawyers and Their Work* (Indianapolis, Bobbs-Merrill, 1967), p. 128f., who mention that fifty-eight law lists are currently approved by the committeee of the American Bar Association. A strong argument for the amendment of the old canons recognizing law lists was that lawyers should be given some relief against the advertising of collection agencies—another instance of the collective interests of the bar modifying the rules of professional ethics. It may be worth noting that the practice dated back to the 1870's, and the amendments were made in the 1940's.

44. Kalsbach, *BRAO*, pp. 412 and 415.

45. See for the United States, Disciplinary Rule 2-105, which also provides for other specialists if certified by appropriate state authorities. For Germany, see Kalsbach, *BRAO*, pp. 412-416; Guideline 68 is more flexible than the American rule in allowing the federal association of *Rechtsanwaltskammern* to decide which titles are permissible. Tax and public administration are the presently approved specialties.

Competitive interests of the profession as a whole in relation to tax consultants and accountants seem to be the major rationale in the case of tax law. Similar considerations appear to have been among the motivations of the private bar association, the *Deutscher Anwaltverein*, to favor specialty titles in all fields for which specialized courts exist; it happens that in most of these the *Anwalt* faces competition from other occupations with limited rights of representation, such as union officials; see Kalsbach, *Standesrecht*, p. 71, and *BRAO*, p. 414. See, for the general context of these regulations, the discussion of specialization in Chapter 2.

46. See Carlin, *Lawyers' Ethics*, p. 50, and the comparative table in Handler, *The Lawyer*, p. 112. Officially improper referral fees to colleagues were rejected by less than a third of the lawyers in either bar, gifts or free advice to clients in return for referrals by about half, and Christmas cards by 9 percent in New York and 25 percent in Prairie City. Ninety-four percent disapproved in both bars the money "kickback" to clients. According to a personal communication from Wolfgang Kaupen, in a southwestern German city, three-quarters of the *Anwälte* disapproved of Christmas and New Year's cards, if mostly only in a mild way.

47. See for the first quote Carlin, *Lawyers' Ethics*, p. 153, and for the second Kalsbach, *Standesrecht*, p. 82.

48. Johnstone and Hopson, *Lawyers*, pp. 122 and 126f. Handler, *The Lawyer*, and Carlin, *Legal Ethics*, give percentages of lawyers who reported they had or would violate different standards; these are generally lower in "Prairie City" than in New York, but they are, with the exception of referral fees to clients, considerable in both bars (15 to 58 percent in "Prairie City" and 17 to 75 percent in New York City); see Handler, *The Lawyer*, p. 112. H. S. Drinker writes: "The practice of 'ambulance chasing' is so well known and so obviously improper as to require no extensive comment. It is most prevalent in large communities, and comprehensive investigations and drives to stamp it out have been held, with more or less success, usually but temporary, in many such jurisdictions." *Legal Ethics*, p. 64.

49. *Taming of the Shrew*, Act I, end of scene ii; Drinker, *Legal Ethics*, p. 192.

50. Drinker, *Legal Ethics*, p. 196, and Kalsbach, *BRAO*, p. 227f.; see generally pp. 222-241.

51. Drinker, for example, after stating the general rule that an attorney has no right to sacrifice his client's substantial rights, adds: "Even in the honest belief that it is inequitable for the client to insist on such rights, he does the client a wrong for which he may be liable." *Legal Ethics*, p. 196. Kalsbach, though in basic agreement, emphasizes the opposite. The *Anwalt* has to use particular care in weighing whether in exceptional cases the interests of the client require him to neglect consideration for the colleague; *BRAO*, p. 228. If he has an alternative of pursuing his duty to the client without such neglect, he should generally not be able to claim the interests of the client as an excuse; *BRAO*, p. 227.

52. Disciplinary Rule 3-103; cf. Kalsbach, *BRAO*, pp. 241-250.

53. Drinker, *Legal Ethics*, p. 221. Detailed special problems can be neglected here.

54. Kalsbach, *BRAO*, pp. 23 and 44-48.

231

55. Kalsbach, *Standesrecht*, pp. 74 and 49; also *BRAO*, pp. 45 and 277f.

56. Sigbert Feuchtwanger, "Untersuchungen über Wesen und Wandlung des Standesrechts," *Festschrift für Albert Pinner*. (Berlin and Leipzig, 1932), p. 136.

57. Kalsbach, *BRAO*, pp. 432-436; see especially Kalsbach's criticism of the Guidelines on p. 434f.

58. Cheatham, *Legal Profession*, pp. 245-248, quotes at length judicial opinions on the adequate punishment for contempt of court in pursuit of the client's cause. The case, *In re Sacher*, concerned a defense counsel for leaders of the Communist Party. A dissenting circuit judge wrote: "So we have the result—surely anomalous and not duplicated anywhere in the precedents—of absolute disbarment of a lawyer whose conduct has no taint of 'venality or lack of fidelity to the interests of his clients,' but only an 'excess of zeal in representing his clients' or qualities 'unobjectionable in commercial fields' or making him in negotiations 'a trustworthy and highly effective representative.' There must be something topsy-turvy when in 'our contentious craft'—to use the Supreme Court's apt expression—a lawyer loses his profession permanently for displaying those very qualities most often associated with it. I do not believe that can be the law." The Supreme Court reversed the judgment.

59. See for example the "Report of the Committee on Law Reform" on "The Rules of Civil Practice and Procedure" (New York 1930), quoted in Cheatham, *Legal Profession*, p. 150f.: "Lip service is consistently paid to canons of ethics. Very little seems to be done in the way of translating these canons into effective practical standards." And Cheatham raises the following questions: "Are the suggested limitations on the full freedom of the advocate . . . so inconsistent with the adversary character of our system for the administration of justice that they cannot be enforced? At least, does not their enforcement call for additional support by the modification of our system of procedure, especially with respect to proceedings for disclosure and other interlocutory matters, or by wider judicial control or by the development of a stronger sense of professional responsibility, built up in part by more effective professional associations?" Ibid., p. 291. In spite of a critical attitude of German judges toward the *Rechtsanwaltschaft*, no comparable complaints and considerations are known in Germany.

60. Eustace Cullinan and Herbert W. Clark, *Preparation for Trial of Civil Actions* (1953), quoted in Cheatham, *Legal Profession*, p. 276.

61. Kaplan, et al., "German Civil Procedure," p. 1200. "A lawyer prepared to wink at the standard [of interviewing witnesses only for exceptional reasons] would have to take account of the further fact that German judges are given to marked and explicit doubts about the reliability of the testimony of witnesses who previously have discussed the case with counsel or have consorted unduly with a party." p. 1201. On the general Guideline 4 see Kalsbach, *BRAO*, pp. 186-194; on the problems in criminal cases, pp. 274, 377f. and 393-397. Kalsbach rejects the practice of some attorneys not to speak to witnesses even in criminal trials and even when the witnesses approach them, p. 394.

## NOTES TO CHAPTER 5

1. Joseph A. Schumpeter, *Capitalism, Socialism and Democracy*, 3d ed. (New York, Harper and Row, 1950), p. 12.

2. See Adolf Weissler, *Geschichte der Rechtsanwaltschaft* (Leipzig, C. E. M. Pfeffer, 1905), p. 287. Weissler's *Geschichte* proved very useful as a source of facts; however, in its interpretations it is rather nonanalytical and often reflects naively ideas of the time of its writing.

3. "Institutionally, organized Junker opposition to the absolute monarchy had its stronghold in the *Regierungen*, which were primarily supreme courts of law and had served, above all, the economic and social interests of the squirearchy." Hans Rosenberg, *Bureaucracy, Aristocracy and Autocracy. The Prussian Experience 1660-1815* (Cambridge, Mass., Harvard University Press, 1958), p. 55. See also Albrecht Wagner, *Der Kampf der Justiz gegen die Verwaltung in Preussen* (Hamburg, Hanseatische Verlagsanstalt, 1936).

4. Weissler, *Geschichte*, p. 296; "The position of an advocate was in a certain sense

bought . . . Applicants for salaried offices ordinarily paid a sum equivalent to a quarter of a year's salary; other positions were given to the highest bidder, though only if he met the requirements like education, examination, etc.'', p. 307. On occupational divisions and other aspects of the bar in "traditional and transitional societies" see Chapter 1, above.

5. Weissler, *Geschichte*, p. 307. In the 1860's, a decade before the liberalizing of admission to the bar, the ratio was 1:12,000; see Rudolf Gneist, *Freie Advokatur* (Berlin, 1867), pp. 22, 67f.

6. Weissler, *Geschichte*, p. 230. See also Erich Döhring, *Geschichte der deutschen Rechtspflege seit 1500* (Berlin, Duncker und Humbolt, 1953), chap. iii.

7. Weissler, *Geschichte*, p. 253. Weissler argues that delay was mainly the responsibility of the courts.

8. Through the better part of the eighteenth century the Prussian bar fought against royal orders that all advocates had to wear a certain kind of black coat. Dress regulations were common at the time, but this one was considered shameful and detrimental to the profession. Otto Hintze quotes the royal intention: "to make the crooks visible from afar so that you can avoid them"; *Acta Borussica,* vol. VI, 1:24. The spiteful intent is not to be doubted, but more important for our context are the implications about the king's and a broad public's opinion without which the regulation would not have caused any problems: The coat made visible the membership in a hated profession.

9 See Weissler, *Geschichte*, pp. 296-310.

10. Weissler, *Geschichte*, p. 338. For a more critical evaluation of Cocceji's work and a sober consideration of its impact on the balance of power, see Rosenberg, *Bureaucracy,* pp. 123-134.

11. Weissler, *Geschichte*, p. 375f.

12. Weissler, *Geschichte*, p. 548. In all German territories some elements of this civil service character of the bar were found, but "nowhere was (it) more distinctly developed than (in Prussia): by the letter of the law, the kind of professional education, the recruitment from the judiciary, and the connection with the Notariat." Ibid. On education and examination see pp. 361 and 427. Recruitment from the judiciary became significant since the middle of the eighteenth century; see Döhring, *Deutsche Rechtspflege,* p. 133.

13. "The original type of the *Advokat* that was the target of all the spiteful proverbs and bitter epigrams, expressions of popular dislike, nearly disappeared under the influence of economic conditions transformed into a larger scale and the growing power of ethical ideas." Edmund Benedikt, *Die Advokatur unserer Zeit,* 3d ed. (Vienna, Manz, 1909), p. 78. The interpretation in the text is supported by the fact that advocates had high standing in much earlier periods in centers of commerce like Frankfurt, Hamburg, Bremen, and Lübeck; on this see Weissler, *Geschichte*, p. 258f.

14. H. Rosenberg, *Bureaucracy,* p. 182. For a vivid expression of this spirit see the letters of Heinrich Christian Boie, a writer and jurist in the employment of the kingdom of Hannover and later a local judge in Danish services: Ilse Schreiber, ed., *Ich war wohl klug, dass ich dich fand. Heinrich Christian Boies Briefwechsel mit Luise Mejer, 1777-1785* (Munich, Biederstein, 1961). For an excellent analysis of the roots of this ideal of culture and personal cultivation see Hans Weil, *Die Entstehung des deutschen Bildungsprinzips* (Bonn, F. Cohen, 1930). The connection between such literary-humanistic traditions and the professions continued, if often in diluted form, throughout the nineteenth and into the twentieth century. It belongs to the ideal self-definition of the *Akademiker*.

15. "Before 1800, the doctrines of German idealism acquired political significance only in the Prussian bureaucracy . . . To the bureaucratic disciples of Kant, individual freedom to think was the gateway to professional happiness, to self-disciplined discretionary action, to their own political liberation, and to the replacement of erratic dynastic autocracy by a more magnanimous and more efficient form of despotic government, by humanized bureaucratic absolutism, 'which will find it advantageous to itself to treat man, who thenceforth is more than a machine, in accord with his dignity.' " Rosenberg, *Bureaucracy,* p. 189; the concluding quote is from Immanuel Kant's *Sämtliche Werke,* Grossherzog Wilhelm Ernst edition, vol. I, p. 171.

16. See H. Rosenberg, *Bureaucracy*, chap. ix; the quotes are from pp. 217 and 211. It may be noted that the German expression for a profession as a group is still *Stand*, as in *Rechtsanwaltsstand*.

17. See for the whole subject, in addition to Hans Rosenberg's excellent monograph, Reinhart Kosellek, "Staat und Gesellschaft in Preussen 1815-1848," W. Conze, ed., *Staat und Gesellschaft im deutschen Vormärz 1815-1848* (Stuttgart, Klett, 1962), pp. 79-112; and the brief discussion in Ernest Barker, *The Development of Public Services in Western Europe, 1660-1930,* 2d ed. (Hamden, Conn., Archon Books, 1966), pp. 18-28.

18. "The state as a guardian and servant of bourgeois society—this is the theoretical concept of the Prussian constitution of 1791/94." Kosellek, "Staat und Gesellschaft," p. 81.

19. Weissler, *Geschichte,* p. 548.

20. See Charles Warren, *A History of the American Bar* (Boston, Little, Brown, 1911), p. 5f. The continuities in the structure of the political system between Tudor England and America have recently been stressed by Samuel P. Huntington, "Political Modernization: America vs. Europe," *Political Order in Changing Societies* (New Haven, Conn., Yale University Press, 1968), pp. 93-139. Warren's *History* is basic to the following section; in addition see James Willard Hurst, *The Growth of American Law. The Law Makers* (Boston, Little, Brown, 1950); Roscoe Pound, *The Lawyer from Antiquity to Modern Times* (St. Paul, Minn., West Publishing Co., 1953); Francis R. Aumann, *The Changing American Legal System: Some Selected Phases* (Columbus, Ohio, Ohio State University Press, 1940); and Anton-Hermann Chroust, *The Rise of the Legal Profession in America,* 2 vols. (Norman, Okla., University of Oklahoma Press, 1965).

21. Warren, *History,* p. 4.

22. Warren, *History,* p. 4f. See also Aumann, *Changing American Legal System,* chap. ii, who, incidentally, discusses attempts in seventeenth-century Virginia to exclude attorneys from litigation reminiscent of the later Prussian episode.

23. This was particularly true for Maryland, Pennsylvania, Virginia, and South Carolina. From these colonies, 150 men were educated in the Inner and Middle Temple Inns during the twenty-five years from 1750 to 1775; Warren, *History,* p. 17. Jackson T. Main, *The Social Structure of Revolutionary America* (Princeton, N.J., Princeton University Press, 1965), p. 195, suggests that the law—like commerce, but unlike the landed "aristocracy"—may have been relatively open to men of lower background. The only quantitative data I know of are presented by Gary B. Nash, "The Philadelphia Bench and Bar, 1800-1861," *Comparative Studies in Society and History,* 7:219 (January 1965). With one out of four to five Philadelphia lawyers admitted in 1800-1805 coming from lower- (12 percent of the sample) and middle-class (16 percent) backgrounds, upward mobility into the profession was considerably lower than Main found among the top commercial groups in Philadelphia, Boston, and New York merchants even before the Revolution (pp. 185-195). In any case there is no doubt that the changing nature of legal practice and rising educational requirements raised the class level of recruitment considerably during the eighteenth century.

24. Hurst, *American Law,* p. 278. Alfred Z. Reed, *Training for the Public Profession of the Law* (New York, Carnegie Foundation, 1921), p. 67f., discusses the different regulations for admission. Chroust, *Rise of the Legal Profession,* emphasizes that a spirit of solidarity in the bar developed where "each court of general jurisdiction admitted persons to its own bar"; vol. I, p. 330.

25. Warren, *History,* p. 17f.

26. Pound, *The Lawyer from Antiquity to Modern Times,* p. 174. A study that failed to turn up evidence of the earlier patterns even in a frontier community is Elizabeth Gaspar Brown, "The Bar on a Frontier: Wayne County, 1796-1836," *American Journal of Legal History* 14:136-156 (April 1970).

27. Hurst, *American Law,* p. 253. "Lawyers . . . almost always belonged to the upper class. Their average income was probably £1,000 sterling if not more . . . and the law was regarded the most lucrative of all professions. Commerce might be as profitable, but the risks were greater, and many men in trade were small enterprisers." Jackson T. Main, "The Class Structure of Revolutionary America," R. Bendix and S. M. Lipset, *Class, Status and Power,*

2d ed. (New York, Free Press, 1966), p. 119. See also Main, *Social Structure of Revolutionary America,* esp. pp. 101-103 and 203-205. In politics, too, lawyers were eminent, although the proportion of lawyer-legislators—"about one eighth of the membership of the lower houses" (p. 205)—was significantly lower than in later American history.

28. Pound, *The Lawyer from Antiquity to Modern Times,* p. 185.

29. Warren, *History,* pp. 212f. and 214. The New York legislature suspended in 1779 all private practitioners who had been licensed before April 1777; see Aumann, *Changing American Legal System,* p. 82. Chroust estimates that one out of four lawyers left the bar because of the Revolution. He quotes L. Sabine: "The giants of the Law were nearly all loyalists," *American Loyalists,* vol. I, 1847, p. 52f.

30. Warren, *History,* pp. 295 and 301.

31. "As the Revolution took away the restraining hand of the British government, old colonial grievances of farmers, debtors, and squatters against merchants, investors, and large landholders had flared up anew; the lower orders took advantage of new democratic institutions in several states, and the possessing classes were frightened." Richard Hofstadter, *The American Political Tradition and the Men Who Made It* (New York, Knopf, 1948), p. 4.

The way anti-British sentiments and fears of the development of a domineering class were combined in attacks on the legal profession can be gleaned from the *Letters of an American Farmer,* written in 1787 by H. St. John Crevecoeur: "Lawyers are plants that will grow in any soil that is cultivated by the hands of others, and when once they have taken root they will extinguish every vegetable that grows around them . . . What a pity that our forefathers who happily extinguished so many fatal customs and expunged from their new government so many errors and abuses both religious and civil, did not also prevent the introduction of a set of men so dangerous . . . The value of our laws and the spirit of freedom which often tends to make us litigious must necessarily throw the greatest part of the property of the Colonies into the hands of these gentlemen. In another century, the law will possess in the North what now the church possesses in Peru and Mexico." Quoted in Warren, *History,* p. 217. For other documentations of this hostility against the bar see Nash, "Philadelphia Bench and Bar," pp. 209-214, and, less regionally confined, Main, *Social Structure of Revolutionary America,* pp. 200 and 203-205.

32. Hurst, *American Law,* p. 252.

33. So Benjamin Austin, an anti-Federalist Boston politician in his pamphlets published in 1786 under the name of Honestus; see Warren, *History,* p. 219.

34. "Our state rulers threaten to lop away that excrescence on civilization, the Bar; and Counsellor Ingersoll declares he'll go to New York. All the eminent lawyers have their eyes on one city or another, to remove to in case of extremes," wrote Charles Jared Ingersoll in a letter of December 1803 from Philadelphia, one of the largest urban centers of the time with a bar including the best lawyers in the country. See Warren, *History,* pp. 221 and 245. Some proposals, combined with devastating criticisms, were similar to the temporary Prussian attempt to "nationalize" the attorney's work. William Duane of Philadelphia, editor of the Republican newspaper *Aurora,* which vigorously and successfully campaigned for Jefferson's election, wrote a pamphlet the title of which is worth a full quote: "Samson Against the Philistines or the Reformation of Lawsuits and Justice made cheap, speedy and brought home to every man's door agreeably to the Principles of the Ancient Trial by Jury before the same was innovated by Judges and Lawyers." For the lower courts he proposed: "If a lawyer should be thought necessary, let him be appointed and paid by the government to assist to arrange and represent each party's cause to the jury." Warren, *History,* pp. 222 and 223.

35. Pound, *The Lawyer from Antiquity to Modern Times,* p. 182f. On the English solicitor of the eighteenth century see Robert Robson, *The Attorney in Eighteenth Century England* (Cambridge, University Press, 1959). On changes in admission requirements, inspired by egalitarian sentiments, see Hurst, *American Law,* pp. 276-285. On the changes in recruitment patterns see Nash, "Philadelphia Bench and Bar," pp. 214-219. Between 1800-1805 and 1860-61, the proportion of newly admitted lawyers from upper-class backgrounds declined from nearly three-quarters to less than half.

36. Differences in religious tradition are probably important in explaining such contrasting

attitudes toward civil authority. On varieties of Protestant traditions in this respect see Thomas G. Sanders, *Protestant Concepts of Church and State* (New York, Holt, Rinehart and Winston, 1964).

The shock of the Continental traveler at the behavior shown in America toward people in positions of authority and honor is well conveyed by the Duc de la Rochefoucauld: "One of my fellow passengers was Mr. Ellsworth of Connecticut, recently appointed Chief Justice of the United States. All the Americans who were with us, and they were almost all young people, showed him no more regard then if he had been one of the negroes, though he be, next after the president, the first person in the United States, or perhaps indeed, the very first. Disrespect to their seniors and to persons in public office, seems to be strongly affected among the Americans; such at least is the humour of the rude and ill-bred among them. This surely proceeds from mistaken notions of liberty . . . It is even astonishing to see how disrespectfully the people carry themselves in regards to the courts of justice. They appear at the bar with their hats on their heads, talk, make noise, smoke their pipes, and cry out against the sentences pronounced. This last piece of conduct is universal" *Travels through the United States of North America, the country of the Iroquois and Upper Canada, in the years 1795, 1796, and 1797, with an authentic account of Lower Canada* (1799), p. 533, quoted in Aumann, *Changing American Legal System*, p. 84f. On the high rate of mobility into the upper class even in Colonial and Revolutionary America see Main, *Social Structure of Revolutionary America*, chap. v.

37. Samuel P. Huntington makes this fact, together with the retention of political ideas and institutions from Tudor England, the basis for his contention: "In America, the ease of modernization within society precluded the modernization of the political system. The United States thus combines the world's most modern society with one of the world's more antique polities" (Political Modernization: America vs. Europe, p. 129). The conception of political modernization is here virtually narrowed down to bureaucratic rationalization of government. This conception as well as Huntington's view of Tudor continuities in America may not meet with agreement, but that would not invalidate the substance of the argument advanced in the text.

38. Germany "provides the best example of a national society with an advanced industrial economy still mainly under the political control of social forces of the Old Regime," says Eugene N. Anderson in a statement of central problems in "German Intellectual History" in the nineteenth and twentieth century, *Journal of World History*, 2:218 (1954-55). David S. Landes explores the differences and similarities of the Japanese and the Prussian/German patterns of development and stresses the parallels which derive from "politicized economic development"; see "Japan and Europe: Contrasts in Industrialization", W. W. Lockwood, ed., *The State and Economic Enterprise in Japan, Essays in the Political Economy of Growth* (Princeton, N.J., Princeton University Press, 1965), pp. 93-182. An important analysis of the social backgrounds as well as the changing style of life and outlook on politics and society of West German entrepreneurs is given by Friedrich Zunkel, *Der rheinisch-westfälische Unternehmer 1834-1879. Ein Beitrag zur Geschichte des deutschen Bürgertums im 19. Jahrhundert* (Opladen and Cologne, Westdeutscher Verlag, 1962).

39. Such comparisons are difficult to establish in detail, but the following judgment may be taken as representative of informed opinion: "To be sure, the German entrepreneurial scene does not present quite the same unrelieved panorama of rugged individualism as does America in the age of the 'great barbeque.' Germany had proportionately fewer Goulds, Vanderbilts, and Cooke's among its first generation of individual leaders, though the three years of frantic company promotion following the receipt of the French indemnity do offer a fairly choice assortment of the slick, sanguine, and unscrupulous type of individual freebooter. But the environment was generally unfavorable to the survival of this type. Germany lacked the vast expanse of unappropriated natural wealth which lay open to the American entrepreneur; German officials and especially judges had a long tradition of frugality and honesty which made it difficult to enlist their aid on converting the public domain into private preserves; and the law contained fewer wide open spaces for the bilking of investors, creditors, and customers." Ralph H. Bowen, "The Role of Government and Private Enterprise in German Industrial Growth 1870-1914," *Journal of Economic History,* Supplement 10:76 (1950).

40. For a comparative judgment on the role of cartels and pools in Germany and the United States see Thomas C. Cochran and William Miller, *The Age of Enterprise: A Social History of Industrial America*, rev. ed. (New York, Harper, 1961), p. 141. This concentration of private economic power did not, however, entail a social and political dominance of business leaders. See also David S. Landes, "Technological Change and Development in Western Europe," in J. J. Habakkuk and M. Postan, eds., *The Industrial Revolution and After*, Cambridge Economic History of Europe, vol. VI (Cambridge, 1965), p. 358.

41. Cochran and Miller, *Age of Enterprise*, p. 129.

42. Ibid., p. 119.

43. James Willard Hurst, *Law and the Conditions of Freedom in the Nineteenth Century United States* (Madison, University of Wisconsin Press, 1956), p. 820.

44. "While the common law of England and America was essentially shaped by judges, the civil law of the Continent of Europe was essentially built by university professors." Max Rheinstein, "Law Faculties and Law Schools: A Comparison of Legal Education in the United States and Germany," *Wisconsin Law Review*, 1938, p. 6.

45. The overall role of the courts in the development of law in nineteenth-century America is sketched by J. Willard Hurst: "Outside the realm of taxing, spending, and public lands disposal . . . the crudity of nineteenth century legislative processes was such as to leave to state appellate courts a big job of law making. From about 1810 to 1890 the courts defined a large part of the law needed to provide a framework of expectations and administration for operating the market, adjusting the play of private associations, validating personal status in marriage and the family, policing or redressing personal injury, and protecting social order." *Law and Social Process in United States History* (Ann Arbor, University of Michigan Law School, 1960), p. 47. Aumann observes: "the increasing use of judicial review in both national and state spheres makes the period between 1865 and 1900 an outstanding one in American legal history. Toward the latter part of the period, the American judiciary becomes an important, if not the controlling factor in the American governmental system." *Changing American Legal System*, p. 214. Benjamin R. Twiss, *Lawyers and the Constitution: How Laissez Faire Came to the Supreme Court* (Princeton, N.J., Princeton University Press, 1942), has shown that the thrust of this judicial law-making, shaped by argument of the bar's elite, tended to protect corporate business from public control.

46. "Conceptual jurisprudence" was "developed to its highest degree of perfection by the German Pandectists of the nineteenth century," states Max Rheinstein in his introduction to *Max Weber on Law in Economy and Society* (Cambridge, Mass., Harvard University Press, 1954), p. li. Rheinstein lists, following Weber, four postulates on which the legal thought of these scholars was based: "(1) that every decision of a concrete case consists in the 'application' of an abstract rule of law to a concrete fact situation; (2) that by means of legal logic the abstract rules of the positive law can be made to yield the decision for every concrete fact situation; (3) that, consequently, the positive law constitutes a 'gapless' system of rules, which are at least latently contained in it, or that the law is at least to be treated for purposes of legal practice as if it were such a gapless system; (4) that every instance of social conduct can and must be conceived as constituting either obedience to, or violation, or application, of rules of law." Ibid.

47. See, for instance, Joseph Katz, "The Legal Profession, 1890-1915. The Lawyer's Role in Society: A Study of Attitudes." Unpub. Master's thesis, Columbia University, 1953. Cf. also Robert T. Swaine, *The Cravath Firm and Its Predecessors*, vol. I (New York, Ad Press, 1946), p. 137.

48. "For a generation after the Civil War to be general counsel of a railroad was to hold the most widely esteemed sign of success." Hurst, *American Law*, p. 297. On the general shift toward counseling and business involvement see pp. 297f., 302-305, and 340-342.

49. Hurst, *American Law*, p. 336.

50. Landowners and nobles as well as civil servants had a large share of legislative positions in Germany throughout the century, the latter even in the revolutionary assembly of 1848. By contrast, attorneys in private practice and businessmen were relatively weakly represented, although the share of the latter increased in the imperial diet toward the end of the century; see L. Rosenbaum, *Beruf und Herkunft der Abgeordneten zu den deutschen und preussischen*

*Parlamenten 1847-1919* (Frankfurt, Societätsdruckerei, 1923), and the more detailed data for the *Reichstag* in Willy Kremer, *Der soziale Aufbau der Parteien des Deutschen Reichstags von 1871-1918* (Emsdetten, 1934). To take one example before 1848, the *Landtag* in Baden—one of the more liberal states in the early nineteenth century—had in 1834 more than 50 percent civil servants among its members while the share of attorneys was 5 percent; see Wolfram Fischer, "Staat und Gesellschaft in Baden," in Conze, ed., *Vormärz 1815-1848*, p. 149.

As noted previously, the proportion of lawyers in the American Senate was from 1800 to 1919 on the average two-thirds and in the House 60 percent; see Mapheus Smith and Marian L. Brockway, "Mobility of American Congressmen," *Sociology and Social Research,* 24:511-525 (1939/1940). Their tabulations also show an increase of the share of Congressmen classified as in "trade" after 1860, and—less clear-cut—a decline of lawyers.

51. See Weissler, *Geschichte,* pp. 530 and 532. See also Gneist, *Freie Advokatur.*

52. According to Gneist, *Freie Advokatur,* pp. 18, 22 and 67-70, the ratio between the number of attorneys and the population was in 1867 1:12,000 in the larger part of Prussia, which had not been under French administration. His statistics show similar figures for the years between 1838 and 1867. By contrast, England had in the 1860's a ratio of 1:1,250, France 1:1,970, Belgium 1:1,799. In German states where admission was free or handled in liberal fashion, similar ratios obtained, in Mecklenburg-Schwerin 1:1,700, in Sachsen 1:2,600.

The income of attorneys in those bars which had a *numerus clausus,* a limited size of the bar, was very high. One source indicates the income of Prussian *Justizkommissare* as between 2,000 and 15,000 Thaler in 1835; W. Kirchhoff, *Blumen und bunte Steinchen* (Greifswald, 1835), quoted in E. Döhring, *Deutsche Rechtspflege,* p. 153. This would have exceeded the income of judges in the lower courts by several hundred percent; see Döhring, *Deutsche Rechtspflege* p. 86f., where lower court judges in Prussia are reported to have earned 500 Thaler or less before 1848. In the 1860's, a county judge could improve his income from 600 to 3,000 Thaler by becoming an attorney, according to a well-informed anonymous article, "Die Advokatur in Preussen," *Preussische Jahrbücher,* 14:424-439 (1864); see p. 430f.

53. At the University of Halle, the proportion of law students whose fathers were in government service varied between 50 and 60 percent from 1770 to 1850; after 1870 it declined to about 40 percent, while the proportion of those from business backgrounds increased from 10 to nearly 20 percent; see Johannes Conrad, *Das Universitätsstudium in Deutschland während der letzten 50 Jahre* (Jena, 1884), p. 51f. Johannes Conrad, "Allgemeine Statistik der deutschen Universitäten," W. Lexis, ed., *Die deutschen Universitäten,* vol. 1 (Berlin, 1893), p. 140f., permits a detailed assessment of the backgrounds of students at Prussian universities in the years between 1887-88 and 1890. One striking piece of information is that of more than 12,000 students only twelve were sons of workers and nine came from families of lower white collar employees; none of these studied law. By contrast, in the Philadelphia bar—probably more exclusive than most local bars—there were 2 percent sons of workers among those newly admitted in 1800-1805 and 6 percent in 1860-1861; at both points in time, 12 percent of the new lawyers were classified as of lower-class background. See Nash, "Philadelphia Bench and Bar," p. 219f.

54. See Zunkel, *Unternehmer,* pp. 73-76 and 114.

55. Zunkel documents at various points that the cleavage was of some importance in politics and that differences of political opinion among bourgeois politicians were seen by the participants in these terms. To stand on legal principle, to neglect possibilities for pragmatic accommodation with conservative opponents and to underestimate factors that were crucial for the business world were frequent complaints about the politics of the *"Bildungsliberalismus."* See for example, *Unternehmer,* pp. 134, 195, 204f., 217f. and 224. These differences concerned important political decisions in 1848 as well as in the constitutional crisis in Prussia in the 1860's. In the 1830's, attempts to make public officials and jurists eligible for the provincial diet of the Rhineland failed in part because delegates of the "Third Estate" argued that for representing industry "practical businessmen were better suited than artists and scholars," p. 159f. The anonymous analysis of the Prussian bar quoted earlier complains that private practitioners participated little in politics. This may have been a withdrawal under cross-pressures. In addition, it indicates that the small number of attorneys was overemployed and yet curiously

removed from economic and other demands of social life. "Ask our great businessmen how few Rechtsanwälte there are who are able to draft the statutes of a business corporation, a bank or a loan association." "Advokatur in Preussen," p. 438.

56. Pound, *The Lawyer from Antiquity to Modern Times*, p. 353; see also chaps. vii-ix.

57. Ibid., p. 254. This book was prepared for the Survey of the Legal Profession. Its special assignment is stated in its subtitle, "The Development of Bar Associations in the United States." Another report for the Survey describes the history of the American Bar Association: Edson R. Sunderland, *History of the American Bar Association and Its work* (Boston, Lord Baltimore Press, 1953).

58. Pound, *The Lawyer from Antiquity to Modern Times*, p. 272. Hurst relates estimates about the numbers of city or county associations: "159 in 36 jurisdictions in 1890, . . . 623 in 41 jurisdictions in 1916, and . . . above 1,100 by 1930," *American Law*, p. 288; see generally pp. 285-294.

59. Pound, *The Lawyer from Antiquity to Modern Times*, p. 256; see p. 255 for the figures mentioned.

60. Cochran and Miller discuss the Tweed Ring and its decline in the context of what they call a "transition from political business to business politics," *Age of Enterprise*, pp. 157, 159, and 161. The preceding quote is from the association's constitution; see Albert F. Blaustein and Charles O. Porter, *The American Lawyer* (Chicago, University of Chicago Press, 1954), p. 311.

61. Edward S. Corwin, *Liberty against Government* (Baton Rouge, Louisiana State University Press, 1948), p. 237f. For the association's early history, see also Hurst, *American Law*, pp. 287-289, who notes "that there was almost no effective formulation or execution of policy in the name of the Association until in the years 1911-1919 the Association campaigned to rouse public opinion against the Progressive movement for adoption of the recall of judges and of judicial decision," p. 287.

62. Hurst, *American Law*, p. 286f.

63. The growing number of lawyers from ethnic minority backgrounds was often linked by bar leaders to problems of professional discipline, see Katz, *Legal Profession, 1890-1915*, p. 69; but discrimination and hostility were not based on authoritarian traditions as in Germany and did not reach the same dimensions as anti-Semitism in the German bar.

64. For an evaluation of the canons see Hurst, *American Law*, pp. 329-333. Katz, *Legal Profession, 1890-1915*, argues that most of those bar leaders who stressed broader public responsibilities of the lawyer were not corporate lawyers, while the latter dominated the American Bar Association and were strongly represented in the committee which framed the code; see pp. 51, 59, 66f. et passim.

65. Hurst, *American Law*, p. 260. For the history of legal education see also Reed, *Training for the Public Profession of the Law*, and Albert J. Harno, *Legal Education in the United States* (San Francisco, Bancroft-Whitney, 1952).

66. See, in addition to the sources cited in the previous note, Jerome E. Carlin, *Lawyers on Their Own* (New Brunswick, N.J., Rutgers University Press, 1962), pp. 21-23 and 28-30. The figures quoted are from his earlier "The Lawyer as Individual Practitioner," unpub. Ph.D. diss., University of Chicago, 1959, p. 52.

67. Hurst, *American Law*, p. 272.

68. Ibid., p. 274.

69. Carlin, *Lawyers on Their Own*, p. 36f., makes this argument. Whether law office study would have done substantially better under the new circumstances in large cities may be doubtful. That the level of competence actually declined is asserted by Reed, *Training for the Public Profession of the Law*, p. 59: "There can be little question but that, in spite of all recent efforts to raise bar examination standards, more incompetents are today admitted to the bar than when, under laxer formal requirements for admission and a smaller development of good law schools than we now possess, the generality of actual applicants nevertheless received a sound training in the office of an old fashioned practitioner."

70. Hurst, *American Law*, p. 280.

71. See ibid., p. 276.

72. Ibid., p. 375.

73. For this early history and for descriptive detail about the following developments see Weissler, *Geschichte,* pp. 502-522.

74. See Eckart Kehr, "Das soziale System der Reaktion in Preussen unter dem Ministerium Puttkamer," E. Kehr, *Der Primat der Innenpolitik* (Berlin, de Gruyter, 1965), pp. 64-86, esp. 75f. Aspirants were politically scrutinized and promotion was made dependent on presumed loyalty. In the judicial service, the ten oldest cohorts were removed from office, new judges had to serve for several years unpaid, and before their final installment they were thus subject to long observation on which political selection was based.

75. In 1864, it was predicted with amazing accuracy that open admission would increase the number of *Anwälte* in Berlin to 800; "Advokatur in Preussen," p. 432. On the actual development see Hermann Isay, "Die Anwaltschaft in Berlin," *Aus dem Berliner Rechtsleben. Festgabe zum 26. Deutschen Juristentage* (Berlin, 1902), p. 111. In Germany as a whole, the absolute numbers increased from 4,112 in 1880 to 12,324 in 1913, with the ratio per population climbing from 1:10,970 to 1:5,436; see "Bevölkerungszahlen und Anwaltszahlen," table appended to Julius Magnus, ed., *Die Rechtsanwaltschaft* (Leipzig, W. Moeser, 1929).

76. Sigbert Feuchtwanger, "Untersuchungen über Wesen und Wandlung des Standesrechts," *Festschrift für Albert Pinner* (Berlin, 1932), p. 126; Weissler, who was more critical of the new regulations, emphasizes the other side of the picture but does not contradict Feuchtwanger's judgment: "Opening the bar has given free reign to the able. However, it also destroyed numerous careers, overcrowded the big cities and aggravated the differences in legal practice." *Geschichte,* p. 614.

77. Max Jacobsohn, "Einzug der freien Advokatur in Berlin," *Festschrift zum Deutschen Anwaltstage* (Berlin, 1896), pp. 100-105.

78. Feuchtwanger, "Wesen und Wandlung des Standesrechts," p. 126.

79. E. J. Cohn, "The German Attorney—Experiences with a Unified Profession (II)," *International and Comparative Law Quarterly,* 10:115 (1961).

80. Article "Anwaltschaft," *Handwörterbuch der Staatswissenschaften,* 3. ed., vol. 1, (Jena, G. Fischer, 1909), p. 555. The extension of service to a broader range of clients is generally emphasized by Max Jacobsohn, "Freie Advokatur in Berlin," pp. 81-84, who contrasts the new situation in Berlin with that before 1879, when small cases of the "little man" had barely a chance to be taken care of and when one had to tip the office supervisor to get speedy service from *Justizkommissare* overloaded with work.

81. See Feuchtwanger, "Wesen und Wandlung des Standesrechts," p. 126f. See also Rudolf Friedländer, *Der Arbeitspreis bei den freien Berufen, unter besonderer Berücksichtigung der deutschen Rechtsanwaltschaft* (Munich and Leipzig, 1933), p. 119f.

82. Benedikt, *Advokatur unserer Zeit,* p. 137f.

83. See Edmund Benedikt, "Die Zukunft der deuschen und oesterreichischen Anwaltschaft," *Festgabe der Deutschen Juristen-Zeitung zum 31. Deutschen Juristentage in Wien* (Berlin, 1912), p. 41. Benedikt, who is more realistic than most writers of the time, compares German and Austrian patterns explicitly with conditions in the American bar. See also Paul Jessen, *Anwaltschaft und Treuhandgesellschaften* (Leipzig, W. Moeser, 1925), pp. 9-11, and Herbert Strauss, *Rechtsanwaltschaft und Steuerberatung* (Leipzig, W. Moeser, 1931), esp. p. 5; both state even for later years that there has been no success in extending the bar's work into such matters.

84. See Ernest Hamburger, "Jews in Public Service under the German Monarchy," *Leo Baeck Institute, Yearbook,* 9:206-238 (1964); and Adolf Weissler, *Geschichte,* pp. 436-438. In 1907, the proportion of Jewish lawyers in the whole German bar was 14.7 percent; see Hans Martin Klinkenberg, "Zwischen Liberalismus und Nationalismus," Konrad Schilling, ed, *Monumenta Judaica. Handbuch* (Cologne, 1963), p. 380. The aspirations of an underprivileged group and the discrimination in many other upper middle- and middle-class occupations are reflected in the contrast of these proportions with the percentage of Jews in the total population, which was in 1910 one percent in Prussia and somewhat less in Germany; ibid., pp. 366 and 367.

85. See the glaring contradictions in the writings of Friedrich Paulsen, professor of education at the University of Berlin around the turn of the century, or the attitudes of Bismarck as

discussed by Hamburger, "Jews in Public Service," pp. 220f. and 230f. The widely read novel *Soll und Haben* by Gustav Freytag, a prominent liberal, is another example.

86. Sigbert Feuchtwanger, *Die freien Berufe. Im Besonderen: Die Anwaltschaft. Versuch einer allgemeinen Kulturlehre* (Munich and Leipzig, Duncker und Humblot, 1922), p. 165f. Max Jacobsohn says of the 1880's, "the anti-Semitic movement then had not yet taken hold in the Anwaltschaft," For a general analysis of anti-Semitism in Imperial Germany see Paul W. Massing, *Rehearsal for Destruction. A Study of Political Anti-Semitism in Imperial Germany* (New York, Harper, 1949). George L. Mosse, "Die deutsche Rechte und die Juden," Werner E. Mosse, ed., *Entscheidungsjahr 1932. Zur Judenfrage in der Endphase der Weimarer Republik* (Tübingen, Mohr, 1965), p. 198, relates an incident of 1907 when law students expressed disapproval at the mentioning of a commentary co-authored by a man named Levy. When the professor remarked that Levy had been murdered, the students applauded. Mosse comments that the episode was extreme, but indicative of the atmosphere in the student body.

87. Cf. Eckart Kehr, "Zur Genesis des Königlich Preussischen Reserveoffiziers," *Der Primat der Innenpolitik*, pp. 53-63. By allowing and inducing large numbers of bourgeois people—the "feudalizable part of the bourgeoisie"—to become reserve officers, Prussia at the same time solved personnel problems of the army and invented a powerful instrument of insuring loyalty to conservative orientations among the middle classes.

88. Feuchtwanger, "Wesen und Wandlung des Standesrechts," p. 123.

89. See, for instance, Weissler's remarks at the end of his history of the *Rechtsanwaltschaft*: "If today the quest is again for a *Weltanschauung*, if louder than ever the question is raised: What should I do to gain salvation? it is for us our calling, deeply and purely conceived, which gives a large part of the answer. To serve the law means also to work for the kingdom of god. And the service of the law is for us a hard service, a never ending hard struggle with sin." *Geschichte*, p. 616.

90. Hans Fritz Abraham, "Vom Beruf des Juristen als Ausdruck seiner Persönlichkeit," *Festschrift für Albert Pinner*, p. 16f. Different facets of this composite picture are vividly portrayed in the autobiography of Max Hachenburg, who was a leading expert in commercial law, *Lebenserinnerungen eines Rechtsanwalts* (Düsseldorf, 1927), or in the moving "A Memoir of My Father" by Reinhard Bendix, *Canadian Review of Sociology and Anthropology*, 2:1-18 (1965).

91. An address by Karl Oestreich, delivered at the convention of the *Rechtsanwaltschaft* in 1929, makes the same points more or less explicitly; see Justizrat Dr. Oestreich, *Anwalt, Volk und Staat*, supplement of the *Juristische Wochenschrift*, 1929, no. 45, esp. pp. 4f. and 22f. Toward the end of his speech Oestreich discusses ideological objections against a legal order based on Roman law which supposedly violated the popular sense of justice. These resulted in virulent agitation which populist and conservative anticapitalist groups launched against the existing legal system and its agents. In retrospect, we recognize here currents of opinion which merged with and contributed to the rise of National Socialism. It is noteworthy that Oestreich's remarks leave the issue, which he considers the deepest cause of the "anti-lawyer neurosis which prevails in our country," essentially open: the *Anwaltschaft* either must fight these sentiments or must demand a new legal system. In truth the bar itself was divided in its basic attitudes toward the legal system.

92. See the three articles on "Rechtsanwälte im Nebenberuf" by Willy Althertum, von Kassler, and Carl Siehr, in *Anwaltsblatt*, 12:40-42, 42-45 and 66f. (1925). Althertum estimates the proportion of syndic-attorneys in cities over 100,000 population one-seventh to one-eighth of the *Anwaltschaft*. The quoted phrase is from the discussion at the nineteenth convention of the Deutscher Anwaltverein, see supplement to *Anwaltsblatt*, vol. 13, 1926, p. 84. Problems of professional ethics in relation to the growth of business law are commonly discussed in the literature of the period; for the discussions about a possible formal division of the bar see Willy Althertum, *Vom Rechte das mit uns geboren* (Berlin, 1929), Oestreich, *Anwalt, Volk und Staat*, p. 12f., and Feuchtwanger, "Wesen und Wandlung des Standesrechts," p. 128.

93. Feuchtwanger, "Wesen und Wandlung des Standesrechts," p. 128f.

94. See George L. Mosse, "Die deutsche Rechte," pp. 193-200. After a clash in 1927

between the Prussian ministry of education and the *Deutsche Studentenschaft,* the largest student association, over anti-Semitic elements in the latter's constitution, a National Socialist was elected president of the association in 1931. In 1929, the convention of German students demanded a quota limitation for the admission of Jews to university studies, which were otherwise open to everybody who had passed the final high school examinations (p 194f.). In the last year of the pre-Nazi period, conservative student representatives gained in student elections at the expense of the Nazis, but their anti-Semitism differed only in nuances, and republican and socialist student organizations remained the least influential (p. 197f.). See also Karl Dietrich Bracher, *Die Auflösung der Weimarer Republik* (Villingen, Ring-Verlag, 1960), pp. 146-149.

95. By social origin, they were closer to the business world. In 1933, nearly half of all Jewish members of the labor force were self-employed and the statistical category of "commerce and transportation" comprised more than 60 percent; see Kurt Düwell, "Das Schicksal der Juden am Rhein im nationalsozialistischen Einheitsstaat," *Monumenta Judaica,* p. 608.

96. Founded in 1928, the *Bund Nationalsozialistischer Deutscher Juristen* had 233 members at the end of 1930 and 1,347 at the end of 1932 as compared to 80,000 at the end of 1933; see Karl Dietrich Bracher, Wolfgang Sauer and Gerhard Schulz, *Die nationalsozialistische Machtergreifung* (Cologne and Opladen, 1962), p. 518. In 1936, 22.6 percent of all members of the *Bund* were also members of the party; see Siegfried Lachenicht, "Sekundäranalyse der Rechtsanwälte 1936," seminar paper, Sociology Seminar, University of Cologne, 1966. On the later waves of joining the party, see Hermann Weinkauff, "Die deutsche Justiz und der Nationalsozialismus. Ein Uberblick," *Die deutsche Justiz und der Nationalsozialismus,* vol. I (Stuttgart, 1968), p. 109f.

97. Legislation of April 1933 empowered the ministries of justice to revoke the admission of all Jewish attorneys except those who had been admitted before 1914, those who had served in battle during World War I, and those who had lost a father or son in the war. About one out of three of all attorneys not considered "Aryan" lost their profession during the first year, others emigrated, and in 1938 all "non-Aryan" lawyers were excluded from the bar; see Düwell, "Schicksal der Juden," p. 613; see also Bracher, Sauer, and Schulz, *Machtergreifung,* pp. 284 and 519f.; and Horst Göppinger, *Die Verfolgung der Juristen jüdischer Abstammung durch den Nationalsozialismus* (Villingen, Ring-Verlag, 1963), pp. 34-38.

The board of the *Anwaltverein* met in March 1933 and voted, its Jewish members abstaining, to resist discrimination against Jewish colleagues. A resolution was published, however, which did not mention this point. It acclaimed the "strengthening of national thinking and commitment in the German people" and proceeded to insist in the principles of law and justice which should be observed even if "great changes are usually brought about by way of power"; it called upon the bar to remain united in "this service of the national idea," *Juristische Wochenschrift,* 62:937 (1933). Two weeks later when the anti-Semitic legislation was promulgated, the president asked the Jewish members of the board to resign, and within the same month he encouraged all lawyers to join the organization supporting the new government. In September, the *Anwaltverein,* now under new leadership, excluded all Jewish members. See Göppinger, *Verfolgung,* pp. 35 and 44-48. It is also noteworthy that the first article in the *Juristische Wochenschrift* on the anti-Semitic legislation concerning the bar only described the statutory regulations and withheld comment because of the principle of the journal to abstain from political discussions and because a judgment might be "premature"; see Rechtsanwalt Professor Dr. W. Fischer, "Neuestes deutsches Anwaltsrecht," *Juristische Wochenschrift,* 62:1049-1051 (1933).

98. See Albrecht Wagner, "Die Umgestaltung der Gerichtsverfassung und des Verfahrens- und Richterrechts im nationalsozialistischen Staat," *Die deutsche Justiz und der Nationalsozialismus,* vol. I, pp. 323-325.

99. "Encountering active antagonism only on a reduced scale, the National Socialist government succeeded in wiping out real or imaginary foci of resistance without recourse to a radical reorganization of the legal system; it applied purely administrative coercion or, exploiting whatever remained of the erstwhile authority of the courts, assigned the law-perverting court chores to known Hitlerites or opportunists willing to do a special stint for promotion or better pay."

Thus the summary analysis of Otto Kirchheimer, *Political Justice: The Use of Legal Procedure for Political Ends,* (Princeton, N.J., Princeton University Press, 1961), p. 302. See also Karl Dietrich Bracher, *Die deutsche Diktatur* (Cologne and Berlin, Kiepenheuer und Witsch, 1969), pp. 381-393, 396, and 496f.; and the monograph on the administration of justice in Hamburg by Werner Johe, *Die gleichgeschaltete Justiz* (Frankfort, Europäische Verlagsanstalt, 1967), esp. chap. iii on special courts.

100. In courts with jurisdiction over civil disputes involving more than 500 marks, the number of cases declined from 319,000 in 1929 to 112,000 in 1937; see Otto Kirchheimer, "The Legal Order of National Socialism," Kirchheimer, *Politics, Law, and Social Change* (New York, Columbia University Press, 1969), p. 101.

101. See Bracher, Sauer, and Schulz, *Machtergreifung,* p. 520, for a number of qualitative judgments to this effect made at the time. In stable marks, it was not before the early 1960's that the bar came close to the relative affluence it had enjoyed in 1929; see the analysis of income statistics by Wolfgang Kaupen, *Die Hüter von Recht und Ordnung* (Neuwied and Berlin, Luchterhand, 1969), p. 116.

102. See Cohn, "German Attorney, II," p. 104. The judgment was also confirmed by several of my German informants.

103. On integration as a basic functional problem of all social systems and its relation to differentiation see Talcott Parsons and Neil J. Smelser, *Economy and Society* (Glencoe, Ill., Free Press, 1956), esp. chap. v; Talcott Parsons, "Some Considerations on the Theory of Social Change," *Rural Sociology,* 26:219-239 (1961); and Neil J. Smelser, "Mechanisms of Change and Adjustment of Changes," W. E. Moore and B. F. Hoselitz, eds., *Industrialization and Society* (Paris and The Hague, Unesco and Mouton, 1963), pp. 32-48. See also Chapter 1 above.

## NOTES TO CHAPTER 6

1. Talcott Parsons, "A Sociologist Looks at the Legal Profession," *Essays in Sociological Theory,* 2d ed. (Glencoe, Ill., Free Press, 1954), p. 371. For the development of law to the point where a distinct occupational group with all the essential features of modern private counsel becomes necessary see Chapter 1. The emergence of a system of "generalized universalistic norms" in the overall process of social evolution is discussed by Talcott Parsons in his "Evolutionary Universals in Society," *American Sociological Review,* 29:350 (1964).

2. See for instance the special issue of the *Yale Law Journal,* vol. 79, May 1970, devoted to these developments.

# INDEX

Abolishment of private legal counsel, 149-150, 158, 236n22

Absorption of lawyers into bureaucracies, 8, 182

Acceptance of a case, norms about, 125-126, 129

Achievement as value, 87-90

Administration of justice: autonomy of, 21, 69-71, 80; centralization of, 7; under National Socialism, 182; and obligations of counsel, 20, 21, 124, 142-143; in pre-industrial societies, 10-11; in Prussia, 147-148, 149-150; *see also* Judiciary; Litigation

Admission to the bar: in America, 40-41, 107, 158, 166, 172; in Germany, 40-41, 103, 141-142, 174, 181; in Prussia, 147, 149

Adversary system of trial, 20, 29, 36, 130, 134

Advertising: professional norms about, 15, 137-140, 141; and specialization, 44, 47, 138-139

*Akademiker*: background group of lawyers, 96-98, 108; development of self-image, 101-102, 103; reference group of lawyers, 67, 92, 94, 117-118, 121-122, 165-166; values of, 117-118; *see also Bildung*; Professions

American Bar Association, 61, 138, 168-173 *passim*

Anomie in professional-client relations, 17, 18

Anti-Semitism, 177-178, 180, 181

*Anwaltverein, Deutscher*, 60, 174, 181

Appearances, ill, in legal ethics, 126, 129, 136

Apprenticeship: in American bar, 106, 154, 157, 170-171; in German bar, 104; *see also* Preparatory service of German lawyers

Areas of legal practice, *see* Work of lawyers

Ascription of status, 18, 65-67, 88-89, 200n8, 224n91

Associates in law firms, 45, 75, 206n47

Associations: business, 79; professional,

245